T0305059

Seasons of a Scholar

Seasons of a Scholar

Some Personal Reflections of an
International Business Economist

John H. Dunning, OBE

Emeritus Professor of International Investment and Business Studies, University of Reading, UK and Emeritus State of New Jersey Professor of International Business, Rutgers, The State University of New Jersey, Newark, USA

Edward Elgar
Cheltenham, UK • Northampton, MA, USA

Published by
Edward Elgar Publishing Limited
The Lypiatts
15 Lansdown Road
Cheltenham
Glos GL50 2JA
UK

Edward Elgar Publishing, Inc.
William Pratt House
9 Dewey Court
Northampton
Massachusetts 01060
USA

A catalogue record for this book
is available from the British Library

Library of Congress Control Number: 2008935928

PEFC
PEFC/16-33-111
CATG-PEFC-052
www.pefc.org

ISBN 978 1 84844 181 1 (cased)
ISBN 978 1 84844 188 0 (paperback)

Printed and bound in Great Britain by MPG Books Ltd, Bodmin, Cornwall

Contents

(With acknowledgement to William Shakespeare, Act II, scene 7 of *As You Like It*)

Preface

Over the past two decades, there have been several publications describing my professional career as an international business (IB) scholar. These include two Festschrifts – one edited by Peter Buckley and Mark Casson in 1992,[1] and the other by H. Peter Gray in 2003[2] – and a book of essays on the eclectic paradigm edited by John Cantwell and Rajneesh Narula in 2003.[3] In several of my own books[4] and in my short autobiography published in the *Journal of International Business Studies* in 2002[5] I have also sought to relate the evolution of my own thinking on the role and activities of multinational enterprises (MNEs) in the global economy to that of other IB researchers.

In this volume, I try and set out a more personal perspective on my life's journey. What indeed have been the driving forces behind the contents and outcomes of that journey? Although most of the volume is focused on my career as a university teacher and researcher, I share with the reader some aspects of my family life, my hobbies, my likes and dislikes and my beliefs; and I hope these will be of particular interest to those friends, colleagues and others who have expressed interest in knowing more about the 'man beyond the face – or the pen!'

As with everything else I have written over the last 40 years, the first draft of this book was written by hand. Over the years I have been fortunate to benefit from the services of several most excellent secretaries. In the case of this volume I am greatly indebted to my good friend and part-time personal assistant Jill Turner, for so cheerfully and efficiently transferring my pencil scrawl into a manageable typescript.

I dedicate this volume to all those who have been part of the seasons of my life, but above all to Christine, my loving wife and best friend. Thank you, my family, friends, colleagues and students for sharing your knowledge, experiences, companionship and love with me. I am sure my life has been the richer for your involvement with it.

NOTES

1. *Multinational Enterprises in the World Economy*, Aldershot, UK and Brookfield, US, Edward Elgar, 1992.

2. *Extending the Eclectic Paradigm in International Business*, Cheltenham UK and Northampton, MA, USA, Edward Elgar, 2003.
3. *International Business and the Eclectic Paradigm*, London and New York, Routledge.
4. For example *Alliance Capitalism and Global Business*, London and New York, Routledge, 1997, and *Global Capitalism at Bay*, London and New York, Routledge, 2001.
5. 'Perspectives on international business research: a professional autobiography. Fifty years researching and teaching international business', *Journal of International Business Studies*, **33** (4), 817–35.

Part I: 1927–1952

Spring

1. 'At first the infant':[1] early childhood

As I retrace my life over the past eight decades, I feel as if I am drawing apart a veil over my past feelings, experiences and relationships. Yet time plays strange tricks with one's memory. Some of the distant happenings of my life are crystal clear; others, only a few hours old, are already blurred. Most of my recollections are pleasant to recount; but there are a few I would prefer to forget. Yet my memories are the record of a personal journey through the seasons of my earthly life.[2] Others, including the readers of this volume, may have shared a fragment of these memories, but, at the end of the day, they are uniquely mine; and, for good or bad, come what may, no one can take them away from me.

****

What, I wonder, were my parents' expectations of their first child? After ten years of marriage I can imagine their joy and excited anticipation, knowing of my impending birth in the summer of 1927. But who was this baby? Who was me? They were not to know if the child my mother was carrying was to be a boy or a girl. I understand from one of my aunts that my father wanted a daughter and my mother a son! Looking at early photographs of me (p. 52), I might be forgiven for thinking that my father wanted to pretend I *was* a girl – at least for the first few months of my life. But once he had become reconciled that I was unlikely to change my sex, he began to like me and make plans for me. When I was about ten, I began to understand that he would have liked me to follow in his own footsteps into the Baptist ministry, or to enter Parliament as a Liberal MP. If these were his goals for me I will have disappointed him, although I have long since cherished many of his liberal ideas and ideals. Moreover, throughout my life, I have always maintained a strong interest in politics and religion.

****

I was born under the Zodiac sign of Cancer, and those who know me well think I have many of the attributes of the crab – not least my tendency to crawl sideways in debating contentious issues! (I like to think of it as a

3

balanced view!). The day of 26 June 1927 was like many other days. As usual, the news was mixed. The *Sunday Times* reported that Charles Lindbergh had just flown solo across the Atlantic; that Canberra had been chosen as the capital city of Australia; that television was first demonstrated to the citizens of New York; and that the British Broadcasting Corporation (BBC) as we know it today was born.

The world into which I was born was a very different one from that of today. A look at a world atlas in 1927 showed large swathes of pink-coloured territory – depicting the far reaching boundaries of the British Empire. Excluding China, more than 60 per cent of the world's population were directly or indirectly under the jurisdiction of Great Britain. However, in the international economic arena, the United Kingdom was now surrendering some of its pole position to the US and Germany, and only two years prior to my birth, the UK government had been forced to abandon the gold standard which had served it so well in the nineteenth and early twentieth centuries. Domestic politics was dominated by two parties, the Liberals and Conservatives. At the time of my birth, Stanley Baldwin – a Conservative – was Prime Minister. John Maynard Keynes had yet to write his seminal treatise which revolutionized economic thinking in the 1930s, but the experience of the 1920s, which culminated in the widespread collapse of capital and financial exchange markets throughout the world, sowed the seeds of a very real dissatisfaction with the way economic affairs were managed in the Western world.

The lives of most people in Britain in 1927 were much simpler than they are today in the early 2000s. The average home was a two-bedroom, two-reception room terraced or semi-detached house, which cost about £400 to buy. It was likely to be lit by gas and heated by solid fuel. Many homes – particularly in the north of England – did not have inside toilets. The radio – or wireless, as it was then called – and the gramophone (with 78 rpm records) were the main sources of family entertainment, along with the piano, which was far more ubiquitous than it is today. The talking pictures had just come to the UK cinemas. Only 1 in 50 homes owned a motor car; 1 in 40 a telephone, and 1 in 100 a refrigerator. The American company Hoover first opened a factory in West London in 1936 to supply the British housewife with a vacuum cleaner, but all dishwashing and most laundering had to be done by hand.

In 1927, the minimum school leaving age was 14, and the average life expectancy of a newly born baby boy was 62. Illnesses or diseases like diphtheria, polio, tuberculosis and whooping cough were often fatal; penicillin and antibiotics had not yet been invented; Hernia, appendicitis and prostectomy operations involved major surgery; and one in 10 women died in childbirth. Capital punishment was still part of the British criminal code; and corporal punishment was widely practiced in most homes in the land.

Most people worked five and a half or six days a week, and had one week's holiday a year. The average wage of a factory worker was £4 a week. Travel was mainly by steam train. It was another 20 years before the first motorway was built; and the 400-mile road journey to Edinburgh from London took 12–14 hours, three times that of today. Only a minority of Britishers took their holidays abroad, and less than 1 in 500 had ever travelled in an aeroplane.

In the shops, most household electrical goods we now take for granted were not yet commonly available. The computer had not yet been invented. Neither had man-made textiles or plastic goods. Most fresh produce, particularly fruits and vegetables, were only on sale during the English season. Chicken was a luxury, and turkey even more so: by contrast beef and pork and most kinds of fish were relatively inexpensive. Eating out in restaurants – so common in contemporary Britain – was a rare treat for the majority of people outside London; there were few ethnic, and virtually no fast food restaurants. McDonald's and Kentucky Fried Chicken were unknown names, while one of today's largest food chains – Sainsburys – was just entering the market as a small-scale grocer's shop. There were, however, a few foreign-owned retailing outlets. Woolworths, a US-owned company which claimed it sold no item in its British store for more than 6d (2.5 new pence) was one of the first and most frequented multiple retail stores.

Finally, in the early twenty-first century, Britain is a much more multi-cultural and multi-religious society than it was 80 years ago. The 1930 Census of Population showed only 10 per cent of the inhabitants of the UK were born outside the UK. By 1960 this had risen to 15 per cent, by 1980 to 25 per cent and by 2000 to 33 per cent. Issues to do with national security, the environment and climate change were nowhere on the political agenda. In the 1930s, it was the exception rather than the rule for couples to live together outside marriage; homosexuality and lesbianism were still regarded as criminal offences; and only one in eight marriages ended in divorce.

At the same time, a twenty-first-century visitor returning to 1927 would find much with which he (or she) could readily identify. In many respects, our contemporary social and institutional fabric is as it was then: and, of course, much of Britain's economic and political heritage dates back several centuries. The Monarchy, Parliament and the Church of England, though bowing slightly to the social mores of the twenty-first century, and now under increasing scrutiny, have remained largely unscathed; and, in spite of the incursion of many hundreds of miles of new motorways, urban development, widespread electrification of the railways, and the building of several new towns and cities, the British landscape is as green and beautiful as it has ever been. Indeed, thanks to the excellent efforts of such organizations as the Countryside Commission and the National Trust, Britain's natural assets – and especially the magnificence and wild life of its 6000-mile coastline – have been most lovingly and carefully preserved. Anyone taking an air flight from London to Glasgow, or from Newquay in Cornwall to Stansted Airport in Essex, might be forgiven for disbelieving the fact that England is one of the most densely populated countries in the world.

And of course, some things, like British fish and chips, the Blackpool Illuminations, the tourist attractions of Westminster Abbey, the Tower of London, Windsor Castle, Stonehenge, the Lake District, the Brecon Beacons in Wales, the Scottish Highlands, and the weather – not to mention the character and temperament of the British people – never change!

****

My birthplace was Sandy in Bedfordshire, a small market town, 100 miles north-west of London. Today Sandy is perhaps best known as the head-quarters of the Royal Society for the Protection of Birds (RSPB). It was there on an exceptionally cold Sunday morning in June while my father, who was the pastor of the local Baptist church, was preaching, that my life began in the nearby family home. On his return there from conducting morning worship, my father was so excited that, after greeting my arrival and congratulating my mother, he proceeded to throw me up and down a half a dozen times! I understand that psychologists believe that one's very early experiences in life often help shape one's future personality and attitudes. Perhaps these early moments of trauma help explain my lifelong queasiness about heights, and my dislike of roller-coasters at fairgrounds. But I do enjoy air travel!

****

Nature or nurture? Experience or inherited genes? What most determines the direction and character of the life of an individual, of his or her belief systems, behaviour and values? To me, at any rate, it seems self-evident that, at the time of birth, the content and pattern of one's inherited genes are of paramount importance; but that as one goes through life, one's own personal and social environment, and one's beliefs and experiences, increasingly shape one's mindset and actions. We are what we are because of the lives which we have led, and the people with whom we have had dealings and relationships. Each decision we take may cause us to modify our life's content and trajectory, and sometimes dramatically so. Yet even this is a

simplistic viewpoint. Why do children from loving and caring homes sometimes turn against their parents or behave in a way so alien to them? Could
it be that a particular combination of inherited genes placed in a particular economic and social milieu, and nurtured in a particular way, tends to
fashion one's thinking and behaviour; and that one's ancestors might have
conducted themselves differently had the environment in which they lived
been different? Certainly it is difficult to deny that we are all creatures of
our past, or, indeed, that the expression 'The sins of the fathers shall be
visited on the children' has more than a grain of truth in it.

Yet, I am also persuaded that we do have some freedom to make choices
and take responsibility for the our actions; and for the attitudes, values and
behaviour we affirm. Of course, each of us may react differently to circumstances and experiences, and to the relationships which we form. But at the
end of the day, I believe the critical issue is whether we regulate and control
our inherited thought processes, emotions and acquired knowledge, or
whether they regulate or control us! At the same time, if we are honest, I
think that as we get older all of us come to recognize the traits of our
parents in ourselves. I certainly do – and I am grateful for it! Why is it, I
wonder, that many of us increasingly think to times past? Are we like
homing pigeons? And why do we often yearn to return to the haven of our
family roots; and so, perhaps, escape from the trials and tribulations of the
world? Or is there something more fundamental underlying our feelings?

****

Both my father and mother came from country stock, although, for most
of their adult life, they lived in or near London. For most of the nineteenth
century, my immediate forefathers lived in Eastleigh, Hampshire; and my
paternal grandfather and great-grandfather on the Dunning side were
train guards on the old Southern & South West Railway. Indeed, my great-
grandfather was proud to be one of the guards on the first steam trains. A
love of anything and everything to do with railways and travel runs strongly
through the Dunning family. My great-grandfather on my paternal grand-
mother's side worked at Waterers, a leading plant nursery in Bagshot
(Surrey), and he even had a rhododendron named after him.

My mother's family originally lived in Somerset, but her father moved to
Battersea in South London to start a greengrocer's shop in the late 1890s.
Named Anne Florence, she was the eldest of 12 children, and it was while
serving behind the counter that she first met her future husband. One of the
most endearing traits of my father was his puckish sense of humour. The
story goes – how far it is apocryphal I am not sure! – that his first words to
my mother were 'Have you any gooseberries without hairs on?'

My mother and father made an attractive couple but their family backgrounds were very different. My father – John Murray Dunning – had been brought up in a loving, but strict Victorian Christian home. By contrast, members of the Baker household were altogether more down-to-earth, and were of the entrepreneurial working class. Up at five o'clock every morning to buy fruit and vegetables at Covent Garden Market in Central London, my grandfather was a man who believed in experiencing life to the full. He was a rumbustious and gregarious character with strong views on Queen (Victoria) and country. This background showed itself in my mother's good business sense, and in her pragmatic attitude to problem-solving. My father, although appreciating the good things of life and being socially active was, I think, at heart a very private man. He was happiest in a one-to-one encounter, a trait I have inherited from him. I rarely saw him lose his temper, and he always tried to see the best in others. I believe that, for most of their lives, he and my mother enjoyed a warm and loving relationship with each other.

****

Six months after I was born, my parents moved to Walthamstow in East London. If invited to do so, Baptist ministers are free to move between pastorates, and at that time most did so every five to seven years. In the 1930s, Walthamstow was at the edge of Epping Forest in Essex. It was then home to some of the leading UK furniture manufacturers, although many of its residents daily commuted to the capital by way of a steam train that spewed all the smoke it had accumulated on its 30-mile journey into a long tunnel approaching Liverpool Street Station. Though things are different today – Walthamstow is connected to central London by an underground railway – I can still breathe in the smoke of a galaxy of locomotives berthed at the London terminus.

We lived in a late nineteenth-century three-storey end-of-terrace house at the bottom of a small hill, at the top of which was housed a kindergarten school run by a Mrs Whitehouse at her own home. It was there I received my earliest education at the age of 4½. Apart from copying the letters of the alphabet in copperplate and reciting my arithmetic tables without looking at the back of my blue exercise book (which set out a lot of weird measurements to do with rods, poles and perches), my most vivid earliest past memories are the making of small woollen and raffia purses for my mother. (What became of these, I wonder?) I also recollect a Christmas pantomime when I was to play the role of 'a rabbit'. (What on earth was the pantomime, you may ask?) And also some pretty hair-raising firework parties at which shrieks of children's excitement were inevitably mixed with howls of pain.

I can name many of my playmates. These included my best friend Kenneth, who lived next door to the school, Geoffrey, Graham, Jean, and Margaret who lived further up Prospect Hill, and Diana who lived opposite to us. Diana I remember particularly well. Diana was our doctor's daughter, who at the age of six initiated me (at the age of seven) into the difference between boys and girls! Being an only child, I had to pick up such knowledge as best I could, from where I could!

Outside school, I suppose, like any other child, my early memories are made up of the unusual rather than the humdrum events of life, I remember, for example, one particular Christmas when my father made me a lovely engine shed for my model railway. I recall spending several itchy days in bed with measles, and also with occasional bouts of whooping cough. As I shall describe later, I especially treasured the times I spent with my father, who was normally heavily involved in his preaching or pastoral duties. But most of all, I remember my early holidays. Most years my mother, and sometimes my father, spent two weeks in Folkestone, a coastal resort near the White Cliffs of Dover in Kent. We stayed at a guest-house run by a lady called May Hardy. May had been a member of my father's church in Walthamstow, but had moved to Folkestone after a nasty accident coming down a helter-skelter at a fair and getting a huge splinter in her thigh! I loved these holidays, from the moment we left on the 12.55 p.m. train to Folkestone from Charing Cross Station in London to the following Saturday when we returned.

In my week at the seaside, I indulged in two of my youthful passions. The first was to spend long afternoons at Folkestone Station at the front of the platform on the London side. Almost all express trains stopped on the way from Dover Priory, including the boat trains that originated from Calais or Boulogne. I even got to know some of the drivers; and they frequently chatted to me as they filled their steam engines with water.

My second great pleasure was to watch Kent play cricket at the county ground next to the station. In particular I remember the Australian tour of 1938. Kent were thoroughly beaten by the bowling of O'Reilly and Fleetwood Smith. But, for me, Kent's defeat was more than compensated for a week or so later. I well recall one day in August returning with my mother from a journey on Britain's only regularly timetabled miniature passenger railway that trundled its way from Dungeness to Hythe. The paper placards outside Hythe Station were proclaiming the record-breaking innings of 364 runs by Len Hutton in the final test match between England and Australia. By the end of the week, England had easily won the match. That summer I was also introduced to the amazing batting performance of a cricketer who was to become my childhood hero – Denis Compton of Middlesex. The contrast between the style of Hutton and Compton – the former a master craftsman, dedicated and serious, the other a self-taught and free-spirited individual who played for fun – always epitomized to me two different approaches to life's challenges and opportunities. While I fully acknowledged – and still do – the merits of the Huttons of this world, I have always been attracted to the carefree, yet no less dedicated attitudes of the Comptons. Regrettably, however, in my attempts to emulate Compton, my own cricketing efforts often came to nought as, more often than not, I failed at the crease. The lesson I learnt then was that for most of us to succeed in life, the hard work, dedication and perseverance – not to mention the technical expertise – of a Hutton is obligatory.

As it happened, our annual holiday in September 1939 was not at Folkestone, but at a resort called Little Holland just outside Clacton-on-Sea in Essex. At the time, the war clouds were fast gathering in Europe, and German troops had invaded Czechoslovakia and Poland. We returned home on 2nd September. By this time, we had moved to North Harrow, and my father's church was at Wealdstone just a mile or so away. On the following day, the Church Secretary passed a message to my father in the pulpit, which informed him that the Prime Minister had just announced we had declared war on Germany. No sooner had my father finished speaking than an air-raid siren disturbed the quietness of the sanctuary. After a short break, in which those of the congregation who wanted to leave did so, the service continued. The 'all-clear' came 15 minutes later; the warning had been a false alarm.[3]

For most of the first decade of my life, I took little interest in the events of the outside world. I was, for example, completely oblivious to Adolf Hitler's accession to the chancellorship of Germany in 1933, the design and implementation of Franklin Roosevelt's New Deal in the US, the outbreak of Spanish Civil War in 1936, and to the Olympic Games held in Berlin in 1934. We had a liberal newspaper – the *News Chronicle* – delivered to our house each day, but I was much more interested in my weekly children's comic *Tiny Tim* which appeared on our doormat each Thursday. I do, however, vividly remember the death of our King George V in 1935, and the black draping over my father's pulpit in his church at Walthamstow. I also recall the following Christmas when the news about the romance between the new King, Edward VIII, and Mrs Simpson dominated the headlines, and of how carollers parodied the well-known carol by chanting, 'Hark the Herald Angels Sing, Mrs Simpson's Pinched Our King'. Edward VIII, King George's eldest son, was never crowned King. In 1936, he abdicated from the British monarchy, and for the rest of his life lived as the Duke of Windsor, mainly in France. He married Mrs Simpson shortly after abdicating, and she then became the Duchess of Windsor.

Much of the news I absorbed came from a weekly visit to the local cinema. My mother loved the 'moving pictures', and Wednesdays were half-day at school. So come what may – rain or shine – we took a No. 38 bus to the Savoy Cinema in Leytonstone (about three miles from Walthamstow). In those days you could enjoy a good seat in the stalls for 6d (2.5p); and this bought you a programme consisting of two full-length feature films, a news-reel and one or two cartoons. And, if you so wished, you could see the whole programme through again, as the performances were continuous. By the time I was ten, I had become an ardent film buff, and an avid reader of the weekly comic *Film Fun. Film Fun* was in fact the most widely read comic of the day. It featured such kings and queens of comedy as Jack Hulbert, Cicely Courtneidge, Jack Buchanan, George Formby and, of course, Laurel and Hardy. But I never did care for Harold Lloyd, as, when I was very small, his large horn-rimmed glasses frightened me! I have kept my interest in and liking for the cinema and its offshoot, television, throughout my life; and, even today, find watching the small screen a very relaxing pastime at the end of the day. Notwithstanding a lot of (what I think is) trash on TV, some of the natural life, historical and current affairs pro-grammes (particularly on UK TV) are most informative and enjoyable.

I loved both of my parents dearly, but it was a real treat when my father and I could spend a full day together. He adored the sea, and every so often travelled around the coast of Britain on a tramp steamer or mail boat. He also enjoyed the rivers and canals of the UK. On one Saturday at Staines, Middlesex, we boarded a Salters boat plying the Thames, had lunch at Windsor, and in the afternoon meandered our way to Henley where the boat moored for the night. Little did I realize at the time, but 30 years later I was to make my home in the town which, in the 1930s, had more churches and pubs per head of population than anywhere else in the UK. On other occasions, we took a day trip on the paddle steamer – the *Royal Sovereign* – and sailed downstream on the Thames from Tower Bridge in the centre of London to Margate (in Kent) and Southend (in Essex) near the mouth of the river. We usually went ashore at Margate where we spent the afternoon at Dreamland, then one of the largest amusement parks in England. Among its main features, it had one of the largest miniature railways in the country. In the early evening, we re-embarked on the steamer, arriving back at our starting point at about 10 p.m. We did this trip three times, and once – I think it was on my ninth birthday – we had an evening meal on board. Sheer luxury and complete magic. We passed under Tower Bridge with the lights of London twinkling all around us. And, of course, the weather was perfect – as it always seems to be in one's childhood memories!

****

My parents were desperately keen that I should have the best education possible. As I have already written, even in my earliest days my father had
visions of my either following him into the Baptist ministry or becoming a
Liberal Member of Parliament. Why liberal? Partly because at the time, the
Liberal Party best reflected my father's own ideals and values; and partly
because he was a great admirer of one of its past prime ministers, David
Lloyd George.

My father, and an acceptable academic record at my primary school,
helped me, at the age of ten, to gain a place at one of the best grammar
schools near to our home in Walthamstow – the Forest School at the edge
of Epping Forest. It was here that I first started to study Latin. When he
could manage it, my father would walk with me the 2 miles or so to the
school from our home; on these occasions I vividly remember reciting our
Latin verbs together. Conjugating the verb 'to love', we chanted *Amo,
amas, amat, amamus, amatis, amant* – I love, you (singular) love, he or she
loves, we love, you (plural) love, they love. When requested, and when he
was at home, he would also give what help he could with my homework,
and particularly with my English assignments. My father was particularly
fond of the writing and poetry of several nineteenth-century authors –
notably Charles Dickens, Thomas Hardy, Alfred Lord Tennyson, William
Wordsworth and John Ruskin; but, no less, he valued the power of rea-
soned thought, particularly when reconciling the message of the Christian
gospel with new discoveries of science and technology, and with the more
relaxed attitude to Victorian virtues and belief systems then beginning to
surface.

If I learnt the value of knowledge and disciplined thinking – not to
mention the tenets of the Christian faith – from my father, then my mother
helped instil in me more practical virtues. She was a woman replete of life,
love and compassion. True to her Baker genes, she was quite a spirited and
independent lady. Though I didn't know it at the time, I think she led my
father a merry dance – but she absolutely worshipped him. My mother, too,
had an irrepressible sense of humour, which did not always go down so well
as it might with some of the staider Baptists. I do not think my mother
found it as easy as my father did to embrace fully the richness of the
Christian faith. She was a more questioning soul, but her heart was in the
right place, and she was no mean speaker if she had to be. She was a wonderful support to my father in his ministry, daring anyone – including me
in later years – to direct criticism against him or his views. To me, she provided the loving security which should be every child's heritage. She always
seemed to be there when I came home from school; indeed, whenever I
needed her. When she was not at home to greet me from school I not only
missed the warmth of her presence, but had to put up with my Dad's thickly

sliced bread and dripping sandwiches, and occasionally, as a treat, a plate of winkles which he so adored.

Both my father and I were completely spoilt by my mother's household talents and devotion, and sometimes I believe my father – who was a typical product of his generation – took advantage of her selfless nature. I don't think he ever washed up a cup, saucer or plate in his life – not at least when she was alive. The mysteries of cooking, laundering and cleaning were unknown to him; and the coal scuttle seemed to be in her hand more than in his. But, of course, those were the years when there was a strict division of labour in most UK households. My father's job, like that of most other men of the 1930s, was perceived to be providing his family with their material needs, managing the financial affairs and tending the garden. My mother's was to look after the house, and the children. Although my mother had a lady to help her clean the house, her life, nevertheless, was a tough one – which I believe contributed to her various bouts of illness in later years.

Fortunately for my father and myself, my mother was a home-loving person. She was certainly queen of her kitchen. She loved cooking and entertaining. Her Sunday lunches – and especially her desserts – were acknowledged as the best around; but it was her Sunday suppers for which she was the most renowned. On most Sundays, our house was full of people being entertained after the evening service. But while other hostesses would make do with coffee and sandwiches, my mother turned out the most delightful hot savoury dishes and desserts. I was completely spoiled, and all those who have cooked for me since then have had a hard time living up to (what I thought to be) my reasonable expectations.

But only in later years did I come to appreciate my mother's culinary expertise properly. Like many boys of my age, I preferred the sickly looking cakes displayed by the local bakeries. They looked more interesting than home-made fruit or chocolate cake. But there was one speciality of my mother's that I could never have enough of. And neither could one of my father's colleagues. Every two months or so, there was a meeting of the local Baptist ministers at our house to share experiences, and discuss matters relating to their local parishes. Then there was the tea, to which mother and I were invited. My mother took these occasions as a culinary challenge. On one occasion, she baked a three-layered sponge cake, which had fillings of marzipan and strawberry jam between the layers, and icing, cherries and walnuts on the top. I remember watching, with keen interest and some concern, the popularity of the cake among the ministers. The reason for this was that I was only allowed to have a piece after the others had been served. There was one gentleman by the name of Phelps who was obviously besotted by the cake. He had already partaken of two slices, and there were only two left. 'Do have another slice Mr Phelps,' invited my mother. My hopes that he would say 'No' were to be dashed. 'Thank you Mrs Dunning, this is the nicest cake I have every tasted,' said he, taking his third slice. Ever after these words this particular sponge was labelled 'Phelps's Paradise'.

****

Growing up as an only child brings both its advantages and its disadvantages. I must own that, at the time, I was unaware of any of the disadvantages. I never seemed to have any difficulty in keeping myself occupied and amused. At no time can I remember being lonely or bored, though on reflection I think I would have quite liked to have had a younger sister. I was extremely good at make-believe, and had lots of imaginary friends. I was also lucky to have most of the toys I ever wanted (often given to me by my father's parishioners); modern consumerism among the young had not yet come about. At our house in Prospect Hill, I was fortunate enough to have a playroom (or rather an attic) to myself. When I was very young, I modelled myself completely on my father. Every Sunday, I used to conduct religious services in the attic with my teddies and other stuffed animals. Later, I can recall wanting to get back from morning church to play with my trains; how very lucky I was to have a whole room for my 0-gauge Hornby railway and its accessories. Regrettably, when we moved to North Harrow in 1937, I no longer enjoyed this particular luxury.

In my later years, I have often thought about setting up and running a model railway. But I never got round to doing so, and in February 2008 I disposed of several train sets, a large amount of track and many accessories. Yet, I still find the hobby a most fascinating one – although as my wife Christine sometimes reminds me it is a rather unsociable hobby. I am afraid that may be an illustration of the disadvantage for at least some of being only children. Their self-sufficiency can sometimes lead them to shun social intercourse. However, with Christine, I continue to enjoy train journeys both in the UK and abroad, and to explore new 'off main line' routes – particularly of the small gauge steam railways – as and when we can.

And so on to my second decade – Shakespeare's second age of man – over one-half of which was lived at a time of war with Germany, with all the lifestyle changes that brought about.

NOTES

1. William Shakespeare's first age of man, *As you Like It*, Act II, scene 7.
2. The title of this book is taken from the last verse of a well-known hymn 'Just as I am Without One Plea'. See No. 316 of *The Book of Common Prayer* of the Church of England.
3. For an excellent account of the war years in the UK as it affected the lives of ordinary men and women see Juliet Gardiner's *Wartime Britain 1939–45*, London, Headline Books, 2004.

2. 'The whining schoolboy':[1] towards adolescence

Moving house can be an unsettling experience, particularly when it is not your choice, and you do not want to move. I was just in the process of settling down to life at Forest School in Snaresbrook when, in September 1937, my father accepted the ministry of Wealdstone Baptist Church in Harrow, about 20 miles across London from Walthamstow. I remember crying when I learnt I had to leave my friends and the only home which I had known for all but six months of the past ten years! But then I tried to look on the bright side of things. We were to take possession of a brand new and larger house in a quiet residential road. It was ideally located five minutes walk from a park, part of which I had already marked out as a place to play cricket with any newly found friends. And the nearest railway station, just two miles away, was on the London Midland and Scottish (LMS) main line to Glasgow.[2] From a footbridge near Wealdstone Station I could happily watch the *Coronation Scot* and other express trains hurtling their way north and south. And the promise of a brand new bicycle and another engine for my beloved train set considerably sweetened the bitter pill of the relocation, the actual process of which I have now completely forgotten.

****

For the next five years I attended John Lyon School, North Harrow. The school was established in the nineteenth century by the educationalist of that name to teach day boys who, had they been boarders,[3] would have gone to the better-known Harrow School – which was about a mile up Harrow Hill from my own school. After an unpromising beginning – at the end of my second end of term report the Headmaster wrote (in red ink!) 'He has done little to deserve his admission' – I made satisfactory, though unspectacular, progress and at the age of 15 sat for, and passed, my General Certificate of Education (GCE). But more of this later!

****

My memories of school are inseparable from those of the Second World War. As I recalled in the previous chapter, it was on 3rd September 1939 that my father announced from his pulpit at 11.15 a.m. that Britain had declared war on Germany. Yet only a year or so earlier, most of my schoolmates – no doubt expressing their parents' views – thought that Neville Chamberlin had helped negotiate a lasting peace treaty with the German Chancellor, Adolf Hitler. I also recall the short-lived euphoria following his famous 'peace for our time' declaration on the tarmac of London Airport after his return from Berlin. Nevertheless, when I returned to school for the autumn term two weeks after the Prime Minister's statement, everything was completely normal – except that, for the first few months at least, my gas mask joined my satchel as my constant companion. This was a period of time that came to be known as the 'Phoney War'; which came to an abrupt end in the summer of 1940.

As I have said, one of the 'bribes' to assuage my unhappiness at moving from Walthamstow to Harrow was a brand new Raleigh bicycle – with the latest three-speed gear! It cost my father just under £6, about two-thirds of his weekly stipend of £9. I treasured that bike and used it constantly. Every day for nearly four years in every sort of weather I cycled the 4 miles or so from our home in North Harrow to Harrow on the Hill. As far as I can recall, the only concession the school made to Hitler's daytime bombers in the second half of 1940 was to shorten the school day to run from 9.15 a.m. to 3 p.m. This it did by altering the lunch break to 45 minutes. So added to my gas mask and my satchel, my saddle bag contained my lunch box as well. As it happened, no daytime bombs were dropped near the school, and I can only recollect moving to the school dugout (air-raid shelter) below the school gym on two or three occasions.

For the most part, my school days at John Lyons were very happy. I liked most of the teachers, particularly one by the name of Worrell who was also the school's cricketing coach, and played for Surrey Second Division. My favourite subjects were geography and history. I quite liked maths, but was rather put off by one of the teachers who enjoyed throwing the chalk at, and tweaking the ears of, most of his class.

As to sport, I was never very keen on football – possibly because I don't think my feet were designed to kick a ball about! Why, I do not know, but my school never took up rugby. My great love was cricket, which I played as often as possible.

However, like several of my contemporaries I suffered at the hands of bullies, but the only time I was beaten (with a cricket stump) was by a prefect who, at the time, seemed to have taken a particular dislike to me. I well remember that on one school break returning from the tuck shop down the hill, he and two of his cronies frogmarched me to the prefects' room where the unwelcome act took place. I was told the reason for the beating was that I had been cheeky to the prefect earlier in the term, but I later discovered it was quite normal for boys of 12 or 13 (as I was then) to be picked on by this particular trio of sadists who revelled in inflicting pain. Naturally, I kept as much out of their way as possible. Whether this experience fashioned my thinking or not, I do not know, but I have always thoroughly disapproved of larger boys beating up smaller boys, and indeed of corporal punishment in general; although I am not averse to the fagging[4] system as such as, at its best, it can teach the idea of service to the younger boy, and a sense of responsibility to the older boy.

I can never remember being frightened by the war. But I do recall that, when the City of London College playing fields at the back of our house in Mottingham (near Eltham) were taken over by the Army as an anti-aircraft station, our windows were constantly being replaced. The period of 1940–41 was a time of intense continuous bombing of London by the Luftwaffe, but many provincial cities such as Southampton, Exeter, Coventry, Swansea and Plymouth were also targeted. In 1941 a German bomb found its target just four houses away from ours. We heard the explosion in the concrete air-raid shelter which was immediately outside our own house in Priory Road, but I did not realize it was so near. When we emerged after the all-clear, there was just a gaping hole where someone's home had been. Mercifully, no one was hurt as the occupiers were not in residence at the time. Indeed, all our neighbours had been in one or other of the shelters in the road. When we returned to our own home, about half of our windows had been blown out.

Yet it is an ill wind that does not blow someone some good. During the war, the glaziers, along with the other building trades, flourished – that is, when they could obtain the necessary supplies of materials! But sometimes we had to wait for weeks, or even months, before the damage was dealt with. 'Don't you know there's a war on?' was sometimes a genuine reason for a lengthy wait for a repair; all too frequently, however, it was an excuse for inefficiency. In this case, it took three weeks to get our windows fixed. In the meantime, we had to make do with cardboard, cellophane, newspapers and sticky tape – no plastic in those days!

This is about the nearest encounter I had with the enemy until the time of the pilotless planes – also named doodlebugs – in 1944.[5] Although my father's church was damaged by the fallout from a Molotov cocktail (a string of incendiary bombs named after the Russian foreign minister). And a landmine – perhaps the most powerful and frightening of all the bombs dropped in the Second World War – landed in a recreational ground about 400 yards from our house. But fortunately for us it was probably assembled by some unfortunate Pole or Czech worker in a German armaments factory. This was by no means an isolated case. Only about one-half of all the landmines which parachuted their way to British soil from Hermann Goering's bombers ever detonated. Most of the rest were sabotaged in their assembly by continental European workers opposed to Hitler's regime.

****

It was not long before I settled down to a new life in Harrow. At school I made two close friends, Geoff Ellis and Alan McCartney, who were in the same form as myself at John Lyon, and who lived nearby to me. I was particularly friendly with Geoff, who was in the same cricket team as myself. I suppose we were fairly typical of boys of that age in our early teens. I cannot remember much of what we did except that we did like putting on plays (sketches would be a better word) in the garage of my house, which parents, willingly or otherwise, came to watch! I continued to enjoy my model railway. By that time, I had graduated from an 0-gauge Hornby railway to Twin Twix (Bassett Lowkes) 00 gauge, and continued to drive my mother mad by trying to spread the track to as many of the downstairs rooms of the house as possible! In what seemed to be endless summer days the track even found its way into the garden. The fishpond which my father had so lovingly built with his own hands served as an excellent terminus, which was supposed to represent the beginning of the English Channel at Folkestone Harbour!

****

I was less enthusiastic about my father's hobby as an apiarist, which became all too serious for my liking when we moved to North Harrow. In his book *The Key to the Hive* which was published in 1945, my father tells of how he was first introduced to bee-keeping by a member of his church at Sandy, and how it became one of his life's passions. I could never understand why, as whenever I got anywhere near one of the dear little creatures it seemed to have an irresistible desire to commit suicide by stinging me.[6] For his part, my father seemed to be immune from stings. For her part, my mother had to tolerate patiently her kitchen being taken over by her husband at harvest time, when for days on end – or so it seemed – he extracted and refined the honey from the honeycombs he had purloined from the bees.[7]

I think, for different reasons, both my mother and I thought the honey collected from the beehives small compensation for the trouble my father's hobby caused us both. For my part, from a very early age I was weaned on 'God's nectar', and by the age of 12 I was heartily sick of the syrup. But I did enjoy the copious harvest we had from our small orchard of cherry, greengage, apple and pear trees; and which my father assured me was entirely due to the efforts of the thousands of his furry friends which occupied the six hives, each of which were strategically placed in our garden to minimize the flying time of the worker bees from hive to tree!

****

I was 14 when I first fell in love – and it was with my Sunday School teacher. Her name was Betty Hann, and she was herself only in her early twenties at the time. It was very much a case of puppy love, and the only occasion when I think I displayed my feelings was on an annual Sunday School summer outing to Southend in 1941. I shamelessly tried to monopolize her attention as we savoured the delights of the longest pier of the world; and, whenever possible, I sought to hold her hand! On the train returning to London, we were all very jolly and friendly, and I managed to steal a kiss! I also believed that Betty was fond of me too. She may have been – I don't really know – but later events showed she was attracted to my father rather more! Only at the time of my father's death in 1966 did I discover why, when I told my mother of my boyish infatuation back in 1941, I sensed a distinct coolness in her reaction. I never mentioned how I felt about Betty again. In any case, it quickly died a natural death, when six months after that memorable railway journey we moved from north-west to south-east London.

****

For my last year at John Lyon, I travelled every school day across London from our new home at Mottingham to school at Harrow. The trip took me 70 minutes – 90 on a bad day – and involved a ten-minute walk from my home to the local train station, three separate train journeys and a bus ride! I did not mind having to get up early, or getting home late, even in the depths of winter, or when Hitler's Heinkel bombers launched their last all-out attack on the English capital. Looking back, I can understand how my parents must have been extremely worried about my long daily journey; and how good they were to bow to my wishes not to resettle me at Eltham College, an extremely good grammar school just half a mile from where we lived. For myself, loving trains and timetables as I did, every day was a new adventure. My main concern centred around questions like, 'Would the 8.06 from Grove Park be on time at Charing Cross? Would I be able to catch the 8.35 express from Baker Street to Harrow? Would indeed I get a seat on these trains or would I have to stand all the way?'

I got a lot of homework done on these journeys – a behavioural pattern which perhaps helps explain my later proclivity for working on books or articles at 30 000 feet on long aeroplane journeys. Over the last 30 years, I must have travelled across the Atlantic or the Pacific more than 100 times, yet it is only when I have a pencil in my hand and a drink in the other that I can fully enjoy the flights. Every part of the early drafts of this volume was written on several long-distance trips on British Airways, Virgin Atlantic or United Airlines. Whether it is the height, or the motion of the plane, or the fact there is no one to disturb me – except (hopefully) charming flight attendants (who cater to my every need!) – I don't know, but my colleagues (although not my secretaries!) have often talked about hiring a plane to fly me round the world to increase my output. At least I think that is the main reason!

Every Wednesday in the summer of 1942 was different from the other school days. That was the afternoon I played cricket. I only once made the school first eleven, but I did enjoy a couple of years as captain of the Under-14s – which included the season during which I celebrated my fifteenth birthday.

I remember one occasion in early July 1942 when I was waiting on Wembley Station for my train back from Harrow seeing a huge red glow in the sky towards London. I discovered later that over 100 German bombers had strafed the London docks that afternoon. Much damage was done, a host of fires were started and many people were killed. The railway system was also badly disrupted, and this was one of the few occasions when I got home late and my parents really began to have second thoughts about my continuing school at Harrow. But then the summer holidays came, and by the autumn, the Luftwaffe's daytime attacks on London had all but ceased.

****

I do not know if my parents were disappointed or not, but shortly after I was born, my mother was told it would be unwise for her to bear more children. To this day, I have mixed feelings about being an only child. On the one hand, I am grateful for my strong sense of independence and being comfortable with my own company. On the other, I think single children can be self-centred and introverted, and are not always good team players or able to form close personal relationships. Throughout my life, I have always preferred being one-to-one with another person; and I am least at ease at cocktail parties and similar gatherings when one is expected to engage in polite and trivial conversation.

The other feature of being an only child – and particularly if one is surrounded by a large number of maiden aunts – is that he or she can be very spoilt. Fortunately, my parents could never afford to buy me all the toys I might have liked, or take me on treats (although I believe I had more than my fair share of each)[8] but they did lavish a lot of love and attention on me. And this was compounded by three of mother's sisters – aunts Doll, Cissie and Mabel; and two of my father's sisters – aunts Winnie and Louise. It seemed that every time any of the aunts paid a visit to our Harrow home they bought some little gift for me. Naturally, I greatly looked forward to these occasions.

My father had one brother, Tom, who also entered the Baptist Ministry and in 1958 became President of the Baptist Union. His son, also called Tom, was seven years older than myself, but despite the age difference we got on well with each other – mainly, I think, because of our mutual interest in model railways. The 1930s were still the days of 0-gauge steam powered locomotives which did absolutely no good for the floor-covering on which the track was laid. On my mother's side, Aunt Cissie who was nearest to my mother in age had two children – Pamela and Barry – and I saw a good deal of them during most of my childhood, and particularly during the war when they were evacuated to Whitchurch, near Aylesbury in Buckinghamshire. Occasionally on these visits, one of my other Baker cousins, Marley, was also present. She was a lovely girl of about my age. But in adult life we drifted apart, and it was not until 40 years later that we met up again. In the meantime, among her many other accomplishments, Marley had become the British Women's Champion golfer!

Possibly because my parents were so involved in church life, we did not go family visiting a great deal. Perhaps the main social event of the year was at Christmas as our house was full with Baker aunts and uncles and their children. Yet, I can never remember any of the Dunning family being present on these occasions. My paternal grandparents, who lived close to their elder son Tom, usually spent Christmas with him and his family – as did their two daughters (neither of whom married until quite late in life).

On my mother's side, I learnt when I was 12 that Grandfather – who by the age of 50 had fathered 16 children – had retired to his bed at the age of 65. Although, so I was told, there was nothing wrong with him, he stayed there until he died of bronchial pneumonia at the age of 90. My mother took me to visit him once, but I think she was a little worried lest some of his less intemperate (but by no means unattractive) traits – including drinking a bottle of whisky a day – might rub off on me! Later, I always wondered how my grandfather's second wife Lily, who was the same age as my mother, managed to put up with his eccentric ways. But to his credit, Ben Baker always had a great fund of conviviality and humour, which stood him in good stead with his family and friends.

It was on such festive occasions as Christmas that my mother came into her own, and could demonstrate her culinary skills to the full. As the war proceeded, this became increasingly challenging. Most meat, butter, cheese and preserves were rationed from 1940 onwards. Many other provisions, such as chicken, eggs, milk and several kinds of vegetables, were continually in short supply; and any imported fruits such as citrus fruits, bananas and pineapples were completely unavailable. By contrast, beer, bread and potatoes were never rationed. In December 1941, a points system supplemented rationing. This system allowed the consumer to choose how to allocate his or her expenditure between such items as tinned fruits, fish and confectionary.

****

My life entered a new phase at the end of 1942. Although I could have stayed on at John Lyon school in the sixth form, I was getting tired of my cross-London journeys. At the same time, I did not particularly relish starting a new school nearer home. I thought instead that I wanted to work in the City of London and, on the off-chance in November 1942, applied for a junior clerical position in an insurance broker's office in Lombard Street – S.E. Higgins & Co. I got the job and began work on 1st January 1943 at the age of 15½; and was paid a princely weekly salary of 32s 6d (£1.62).

I enjoyed my first job, and within six months became a 'junior substitute' for my firm. The term 'substitute' refers to an employee of an insurance broker whose task is to get the tangible or intangible assets of individuals or organizations insured by underwriters at Lloyds of London. Each day I would visit The Room at Lloyds of London, in which about 200 underwriters and their clerks sat in little booths ready to receive proposals from brokers on behalf of their clients. More often than not, I was given straightforward policy renewals to handle. I remember, for example, having to renew an annual motor insurance policy for a road haulage firm called E.R. Fifoot. This particular risk, involving a fleet of lorries and costing several thousand pounds to cover, was considered too much for a single underwriter to handle. So I had to visit about eight underwriters, each of whom signed their name on a slip of paper for a certain proportion of the assets to be insured. Sometimes, there were long queues of substitutes at the booths – but, rather than wait, I would go for a break at one of the coffee houses in an adjacent market, where some of the marine insurance business was originally done in the eighteenth century. I would have to know which particular underwriting companies concentrated on different kinds of insurance, for example household property, fire and theft, commercial properties, motor vehicle insurance, and so on; and so, when eventually I was allowed to act on behalf of a completely new client, I knew which of the underwriters I should approach.

The principle of underwriting insurance has remained largely unchanged over the last 40 years, although e-Commerce and the digital revolution have dramatically affected the way of doing business. Yet the Lutine Bell, which was originally rung when a ship was lost or damaged at sea, is still located at the centre of The Room which is housed in a larger and more modern glass-fronted modern building. Likewise, the time-honoured tradition of getting in touch with a colleague working in The Room remains the same. The procedure is for the person wishing to make contact to inform a red-coated 'porter' who sits in a booth below the bell to call out the name of the wanted individual and his (or her) firm; and for that person to come to the centre of The Room where his colleague would be waiting.

Back in the office of S.E. Higgins, I was less content as I was the junior office boy, and every morning I had to open the mail for the Senior Secretary – a charming lady by the name of Miss Geary (I never did know her Christian name) – and in the evening seal and stamp tens of envelopes, and then take them for posting at the Post Office just around the corner. I think it was this aspect of the job – and to my regret there was no one else junior to myself recruited in the two years I worked there – that led me to seek other employment in the City; and when the opportunity came to join a Spanish-owned bank – the Banco de Bilbao – in Old Broad Street, for a salary twice what I was then getting, I took it with alacrity.

As it happened, this move proved critical to my future career, as to make progress in the banking world it was necessary for me to take and pass the Institute of Bankers professional examinations. So it was back to school! In the autumn of 1944 I began attending evening classes at the City of London College in Moorgate – which, unbeknown to me at the time, I should be returning to as an undergraduate student four years later. Over the next few months, I took courses in English; The Elements of Banking; Accounting; and Foreign Exchange, and in April 1945 sat and passed my first set of examinations.

In many ways, my work at the bank was less interesting than that of my previous job. I certainly missed my visits to the coffee houses around Lloyds! But I did get some excitement out of receiving messages on the tele-phone from Spain and other European countries. I had the opportunity of learning about the principles and practice of banking, and also something about managing a subsidiary of a foreign-owned company. I was also for-tunate to have a very conscientious and kindly training manager, who greatly stimulated my interest in commercial banking and finance. We also developed a close friendship, but I fear I may have been a disappointment to him as he failed completely to convert me to his views as a member of the Plymouth Brethren.

****

In June 1941, Germany invaded Russia. One consequence of this act, which was eventually to prove Hitler's downfall, was that the Luftwaffe diverted its bomber attacks from the UK to supporting the German ground forces as they drove eastwards towards Moscow. But to keep our ack-ack defences on the alert, the German airforce continued isolated bombing raids on London. And it was in one of these raids that the home of the Treasurer of my father's church at Eltham was virtually destroyed. The Bellamy family, which consisted of father and mother and their two daughters – Melva aged 21 and Ida aged 14[9] – had to find temporary accommodation. In discussion with my parents, it was decided that rehousing of the family should be split up between two middle-aged spinsters, who lived opposite to us in Grove Park Road,[10] and ourselves. I remember trying to persuade my parents to invite the two daughters, the younger of whom I was already quite friendly with, as we attended the same youth activities at my father's church, and often played tennis together.

Whether or not I had anything to do with their decision I do not know, but Melva and Ida came to live with us, and until they moved to a new house in Petts Wood (about ten minutes away) in 1945, it was as if I had suddenly acquired two very pretty and lively sisters. During that time I not only entered adolescence, but passed through it in a most enjoyable, but totally unexpected way. Unlike some of my contemporaries I was quite shy in dating girls and, apart from my very early encounter with Diana, mentioned in Chapter 1, and the stolen kiss with Betty Hann, I had had absolutely no physical contact with the opposite sex. I do not think I read my first sex education book (bought, I well remember, in a bookshop in Cheapside in London) until I was 15. Certainly neither of my parents had advanced my education in this sphere of life, and the only knowledge I had picked up was the result of conversations with some of my workmates in the bank in London.

My mother and father obviously believed in my complete innocence, although, in retrospect, I think they were either very trusting or very naive in allowing Ida and I to sleep alongside each other (admittedly with all our clothes on) in the space under the stairs of our house during the German air raids for much of 1944. Night after night the Dunning household and its guests had to abandon their beds, and sleep in what my father deemed in his wisdom to be a safer place in the house.[11] Melva and my mother also camped down in another hall cupboard opposite to us, while my father took up his position as chief aircraft watcher close to the upstairs landing window. The aircraft in question was, in fact, a doodlebug – or to give it its proper name a pilotless plane, with a bomb attached to it – and was the first of Hitler's secret weapons which he deployed in a desperate attempt both to inflict further damage and to reduce the morale of the British people towards the end of the war. Between March 1944 and January 1945 some 5000 V1s (as they were also known) were launched from various sites in France and the Low Countries, and directed almost exclusively at London. The flight path was fixed, but the precise moment when their 'phut-phut' motor might cut out and they dived to earth – 40 seconds or so later – was quite uncertain. It was during these 40 seconds that my father frequently abandoned his lookout position to charge down the stairs. About a third of all V1s were destroyed by our own Air Force, or by our anti-aircraft guns. Of the rest about one-half got through to London, but many fell short of their target.

Our local village, Mottingham – which was 15 miles from central London – was on one of the flight paths of the doodlebugs, and was the unwelcome recipient of more than 100 of them, including one which fell in a field opposite our house. It was not so much that doodlebugs did an enormous amount of physical damage or killed a large number of people,[12] but that the psychological harm could be (and was frequently) very considerable.

By the time the flying bombs came to an end – helped by the precision bombing by the Allies, and some sabotaging by the French and Belgian factory workers – the nerve ends of most Londoners were pretty raw. But scarcely had that particular vehicle of destruction ended than another started. This was the V2, a huge explosive and frighteningly damaging rocket which Hitler showered down on the south-east of England between September 1944 and March 1945.[13] These rockets gave virtually no warning to their victims. Had the Führer managed to despatch them a year or so earlier, the outcome of the war might well have been different. Certainly it would have been devastating for the morale of already tired and jaded Londoners. As it happened, however, most of the continental rocket sites were quickly destroyed by the Allied forces, who by this time had already advanced well into continental Europe.[14] These were the last bombs to fall on England in Hitler's War.

****

As well as my blossoming friendship – later developed into a full-blown courtship – with Ida, I was becoming increasingly interested in the Christian religion. I even started to listen and try and understand my father's sermons! I should, however, emphasize that in no way did my father seek to influence my own beliefs. He left all his preaching to the pulpit, but his and my mother's example of Christian attitudes and standards of behaviour could not fail to rub off on me. When Ida was baptized by total immersion[15] in May 1944 it made a very deep impression on me, and I followed her through the waters a month later.

I do not think I could articulate my religious beliefs as a 17-year-old, although I must have made some attempt to do so to two church members who interviewed me prior to my being accepted into church membership. But although I had no sudden conversion or 'Road to Damascus' experience, I was increasingly coming to the realization that not only did the teachings of Jesus Christ make sense, but that if I was to claim these teachings for myself, I needed the gift of His spirit within me. It was this awareness, coupled with the experience and counselling of older and wiser Christians, which helped me to take the leap of faith in accepting – albeit very tentatively – the main tenets of the Christian gospel. And if life has taught me one thing, it is that my own resources are insufficient to allow me to be the kind of person I would like to be; and it is only by drawing upon the love of a transcendent God, and the teachings of Jesus Christ and his disciples, that I even get to first base. While I admire people who are blessed with being 'naturally nice', I think they lose a lot if they cannot acknowledge the source of that niceness and draw comfort from it. Today, as I write, I fully recognize that the Christian religion is not the only source of such spiritual enlightenment and guidance; and that to many people, Islam, Judaism, Buddhism and Hinduism – to mention just a few of the many religions throughout the world – are no less meaningful and helpful in influencing their belief systems and day-to-day social mores. But again, more of this in chapter 6 of this volume.

****

The year following my baptism was one of the happiest of my life – although I do not claim there to be any causal relationship! I enjoyed my work and the evening classes at the City of London College which I attended twice a week. I was growing very fond of Ida and we spent much of our free time together. We both enjoyed cycling, tennis and playing Monopoly (the board game which was all the rage at the time), and we were both active in a wide range of church activities. These included my taking a Sunday School class of 10–11-year-old boys. Try as I could, I could never keep discipline, and my class quickly achieved the unenviable reputation for being the noisiest in the whole Sunday School! I remember that, at the time, our Sunday School superintendent, a Mr Marvin by name, was *not* amused; neither were Ida and a group of senior girls who were unfortunately participating in a class in a room next to the corner of the church to which I was assigned. Yet amazingly enough, most of the boys I taught stayed the course – including the worst-behaved lad of them all, who was eventually to become one of the leading lights of the Eltham Baptist Church.

On most Saturdays, Ida and I went to one of the local cinemas. On one of these occasions, we spent four and a half hours watching *Gone with the Wind*. This, however, was not because of the length of the film itself, but because its showing was constantly interrupted by air-raid alarms. Following each of these alarms, the film was stopped – even though most the audience remained in their seats!

****

By the spring of 1945, the Second World War in Europe was coming to an end. Most of the German-occupied territories had been liberated,[16] and the German army was being squeezed in its own fatherland between the advancing forces of the British and US armies coming from the west, and those of the Russians pummelling their way from the east to Berlin. On 30th April Hitler killed himself and his mistress Eva Braun; and only two days earlier Mussolini (the Italian dictator) and his mistress were shot by Italian partisans. On 2nd May, Berlin was captured by the Russians, and on 8th May, the war against Germany was officially declared as being over.[17]

As a 17½-year-old, I was greatly interested, and not a little excited, by these events, particularly as in January 1945, and much to the concern of my parents, I had volunteered to serve in the Royal Navy. Why the Navy? Partly because of my love of the sea; and partly because I did not wish to be conscripted into either the Army or the Air Force![18]

NOTES

1. William Shakespeare's description of the second age of man, *As You Like It*, Act II, scene 7.
2. In the 1930s there were four main privately owned railways. Each radiated from a London station. The London Midland and Scottish line (LMS) ran from Euston up the west side of England and Scotland to Glasgow and Inverness. The route of the London North East Railway (LNER) to Scotland from King's Cross took in eastern cities such as York and Durham before terminating at Edinburgh and Aberdeen. The Great Western Railway (GWR) served the south west of England and parts of Wales from Paddington; and the Southern Railway (SR) covered all the southern counties of England from the London termini of Waterloo, Charing Cross and Victoria.
3. The term 'boarder' refers to pupils in residence during the term time. By contrast day pupils were those who lived in their own homes.
4. Fagging means that younger boys undertake various tasks, for example preparing meals, making beds, cleaning shoes, and so on, for older boys – usually prefects.
5. These were automatically guided rocket-like planes with a bomb attached. They were launched from German occupied territory, mostly in France and Belgium, and targeted principally at London.
6. Once a honeybee ejects its sting it dies.
7. It may come as a surprise to some readers, but bees do not intentionally produce honey for human consumption! So, in return for stealing the bees' food, we humans have to

supply the bees with copious amounts of sugar. I remember that the sugar my father obtained from the Ministry of Agriculture and Fisheries during the war to feed his bees was about 20 times our own weekly ration.

8. Including quite frequent visits to one of the Lyons Corner Houses in London where I could indulge in a variety of ice cream sundaes.
9. Their son Derek was serving in the Army.
10. Just a mile away from the Bellamy's home.
11. Although I occasionally refused to move from my bed. Instead I put on my tin hat and hoped for the best!
12. Although more than 6000 people were killed by V1s the greater majority were resident in London, Kent, Sussex, Hampshire and Essex.
13. The V2 was 46 feet long, 5 feet in diameter and it carried a ton of explosive, which could cause a crater 50 feet wide and 10 feet deep.
14. The invasion of continental Europe having taken place on 6th June 1944.
15. In the Baptist denomination babies or young children are dedicated not christened, so when they become committed Christians they are baptized and not confirmed.
16. Paris was freed by the Allied Forces on 25th August 1944 and Antwerp, Brussels and Amsterdam in September of that year.
17. That between the Allies and Japan continued until 14th August 1945 – eight days after the first atomic bomb was detonated in Hiroshima.
18. In early 1945 youngsters at the age of 18 were being conscripted into one or other of the three armed forces.

3. 'And then the lover' (I):[1] a naval interlude

Early in 1945, I began to think about my future! Though the Allies were advancing across Europe, the European War was still very much alive, and I had already received a notice from the Ministry of Defence that, on my eighteenth birthday, I would be eligible for conscription. At the time, although a conscript could express a preference for serving in one or other of the armed forces, there was no guarantee that his preference would be respected. So I decided to volunteer for the Royal Navy, which I strongly preferred to either the Army or Air Force. I tried, but failed, to get admitted to King Alfred College in Brighton for officer training in the seamanship branch. Instead, with my own particular background in mind, it was suggested I tried later for a commission in the Supply and Secretariat Branch of the Navy. My call-up papers arrived in April and I was instructed to present myself at Skegness Naval Training Establishment on 3rd May 1945.

I remember my Uncle Tom bidding me farewell at King's Cross Station on the morning of my departure to the Lincolnshire coastal resort; although he seemed more interested in the locomotive drawing my train than in my departure! It was my first time away from home for more than a few days. Neither my parents nor I had wanted me to go, and 24 hours later I wondered if I had made the right decision!

****

It only took the German army five days to surrender once I had joined the Navy! VE Day on 8th May saw me on leave in Skegness – a seaside town in Lincolnshire – in the afternoon, after scrubbing the floor of the Wrens' dining room (or 'mess') in the morning! The first thing I recall about my new home – which before the war was one of the earliest Butlins holiday camps – was the tea we had on my arrival. I remember it for the thickest piece of bread I had ever seen in my life, and some turnip jam to go with it; but mostly for the peculiar taste of the tea. Only later was I told that the tea was liberally dosed with bromide, an additive intended to calm any unhealthy (!) sexual proclivities which might otherwise tempt the new rookies!

HMS *Arthur* at Skegness (all naval land bases are given the names of ships) was essentially a transit camp or sorting office for new naval recruits, and where it was decided what branch of the Navy they should spend the rest of their service life in. The choice was wide. One could be a seaman, a signaller, an electrician, a stoker, a writer, a cook, an electrician, a supply assistant or a medical orderly. My experience as a clerk in an insurance office and bank, and my total uselessness in anything to do with mechanical or electrical implements (a deficiency which I have to this day!) made the choice of my superiors – including a naval psychiatrist who put me through a fascinating series of tests – quite straightforward. Unless I had any serious objections (and I do mean serious!) I was to be assigned to the Supply and Secretariat Branch as a Writer – the naval name for a clerk or secretary, responsible to an officer (or officers) of that branch.

In the meantime, over the next two weeks, I had to be inoculated and vaccinated against all manner of potential ailments, and lectured on a variety of medical matters. I remember that these lectures were generally poorly attended, apart from the one on sexually transmitted diseases! Because there was a lot of time left over after these briefing sessions, and the naval authorities believed that idle hands would only get up to mischief, we new recruits (about 60 of us), were assigned different (physical) chores at the beginning of each day. These varied from cleaning out the latrines (toilets to the layman!), peeling potatoes, washing dishes in the kitchen (no mechanical aids!), sweeping driveways and scrubbing floors, to gardening and general household duties.

As to our living accommodation, six or so recruits were assigned to a chalet originally designed to accommodate two holidaymakers. This was an experience which quite put me off going near a Butlins holiday camp for the rest of my life! I had previously led a rather sheltered and cosseted life, and was quite unprepared for the personal behaviour and social habits, not to mention the language, of my room-mates. I do not think I got a decent night's sleep in the whole time I was at Skegness!

****

After just three weeks at the transit camp I was transported to another naval establishment, HMS *Duke* at Malvern in Worcestershire, where for six weeks I and other ratings took our basic training in naval drill (square-bashing as we called it) and the elements of seamanship and gunnery. Among other things, I learnt how to use a rifle and to bayonet a stuffed dummy, to slope arms, read a compass, walk several miles across the hills around Malvern with full kit, distinguish a battleship from a destroyer, identify a range of aircraft – both British and foreign – tie knots (I never got the hang of the difference between a granny and a sheepshank knot), and to row a small boat (why did my boat always seem to go round in circles when everyone else's went straight?). After this sort of initiation, I was sure that if I was not recruited into the Supply and Secretariat Branch of the Navy – or at least an activity well removed from anything to do with actually running a ship – I would be forced to leave the Navy there and then!

There are three other memories I have of Malvern. The first is knowing how to ration out a casserole of stew or a jam roly-poly to 15 hungry sailors – and to save some for yourself, the last to be served! Once every two weeks my turn came round to collect the breakfast or dinner (naval ratings had dinner – officers had lunch!) from the kitchen on a large tray, and then serve it to those ratings seated at 'my table' in the mess (dining area). Drawing on my mother's expertise in this direction, I think I did quite well even if I did usually finish up with the smallest portion! My second memory is my eighteenth birthday when I was put on No. 16s! 'What on earth is that?' you might ask. Well, No. 16 is one of the minor punishments in the Naval Code of Disciplines otherwise known as *King's Regulations*. (Why 16, I do not know, for No. 1 is not decapitation or hanging!) A dose of No. 16s is awarded for very minor altercations – in my case for refusing to obey an order by a Chief Petty Officer[2] to stop talking to another rating as we queued for our weekly pay of 21 shillings. The punishment consisted of two hours physical labour – in my case, weeding the gardens around the single-storeyed wooden huts in which we lived. As the weather at the time was fine I really did not mind the punishment at all, but I was a little concerned that it would be recorded for ever on my naval career certificate, which followed me around to wherever I was posted.

The third memory was – or I should say could have been – more dramatic. All ratings were required to donate a pint of their blood, at least once during their time at Malvern. The time came for my great sacrifice, and I settled myself comfortably on the bed, looking forward to my cup of tea and biscuit afterwards. After about ten minutes once the drip for the blood transfusion had been fixed up, I noticed that the bottle by the bed, into which the blood was supposed to go, was not getting any fuller. Another five minutes went by and I began to feel distinctively queasy and light-headed. I bent over the bed, and saw a huge pool of blood – *my* blood. Somehow or another the tube had come out of the bottle, and my life was literally draining away! Nobody seemed particularly concerned about the crisis that might have been; but I did, at least, get two biscuits with my cup of tea! For their part, the Navy never did get my blood!

****

After Malvern my real training began – this time at Wetherby, a small Yorkshire town just off the A1 between York and Leeds. Before that came my first leave, when I proudly displayed my 'probationer' Writer's uniform to Ida and my parents. This was not traditionally the jack-tar uniform worn by most ratings, but an ordinary serge dark blue suit with black buttons. This I wore with a white shirt and black tie and a red star with a 'W' (badge) which was attached to the right sleeve of my jacket. The uniform was topped up with a peaked cap, which I wore at a suitably rakish angle!

****

My four months at Wetherby at HMS *Demetrius* was broken into two halves of 17 weeks each, with a long weekend of leave in between. The first half consisted of a set of instruction courses about organizing an office in a naval establishment or on board ship; and of ordering and ensuring an adequate provision of everything from food and drink, clothing and hammocks, to boilers, typewriters and propellers. In this part of the course, ratings intending a clerical or secretarial career were taught alongside those (with an 'S' badge on their sleeves) more interested in the supply of foodstuffs and equipment.

The second part of the course focused on the training of the kind of office skills necessary to support the efficient running of a secretariat or personnel office. This included typing, bookkeeping, letter writing, and composition of reports and statements, as well as everything to do with personnel matters – namely, pay, promotion, discipline and the elements of naval law. I learnt that as with any other large organization there was a particular form to complete for almost everything, whether it be applying for a free railway pass (which all naval personnel were allowed for two leaves each year) to logging all latecomer ratings returning from an evening ashore. Once again, I was introduced to *King's Regulations*, the naval bible which set down everything expected of an officer or rating and, no less important, what he (or she) was *not* allowed to do. I learned how to distinguish between male naval officers according to the branch they were in. Between the gold rings at the bottom of their sleeves, those in the engineering branch had maroon coloured rings, electrical officers had green rings, education officers had blue rings, supply and secretariat officers had white rings, doctors had red rings and dentists had orange rings.

At the end of the course, there were a number of written and practical examinations. As it happened, I did very well, coming second out of my class of 30. But much more important, I managed to gain a sufficiently high set of marks to allow me to claim automatic promotion to Leading Writer within six months of completing the course. I thought it might also mean I might be assigned to one of the more interesting office assignments in the Navy. I was wrong!

Life at Wetherby did not only consist of course work. Everyone had to do a stint of kitchen and guard duty. Indeed on VJ Day[3] on 15th August I had the dubious distinction of being one of two ratings guarding the entrance to HMS *Demetrius*, with most of its 600 inhabitants celebrating the end of the Japanese war! I remember some brave soul sneaking us both a drink late in the night – surely a capital offence had we been found out! We had regular drill, gymnastics and sport. I was introduced to hockey, which later stood me in good stead when I was in a men's team playing a group of Wrens, each of whom seemed to have the single aim of incapacitating every member of the opposite sex! We had frequent debating groups; I remember especially one of these in which I had to defend my views against capital punishment – an opinion which I continue to hold to this day. Every Sunday morning there was a church parade, during which officers and ratings who were Roman Catholics (RCs), Anglicans or 'others' (including Baptists) were marched to the sanctuaries of their preference. As far as I can recall, no provision was made for non-Christian faiths, notably Judaism and Islam. I am sure things would be very different today.

There was still time for me to pursue my leisure interests. On most Saturdays I took a bus either to the Yorkshire Dales, and walked to villages like Ilkley for tea; or to Leeds to take in a film or a live show at the famous Palace of Varieties. Usually I went by myself, as most of my friends seemed to be more interested in female company than mine – there was a large 'Wrennery' at a nearby naval base. On one occasion, I was persuaded to join two of my friends on a blind date. I cannot say I enjoyed the experience, particularly as my companion wanted to be a little more friendly than I did. At the end of the evening, I did escape with a brief kiss – and a promise of a further date. To my shame, this was never kept, but in my innocence I thought going out with another girl would have been disloyal to Ida!

****

After HMS *Demetrius*, I had a week's leave, during which I was told I would be informed of my first posting. By now it was September 1945. The European and Japanese wars were over, and early conscripts to the armed forces were already being demobbed. We latecomers were informed that, unless there were compassionate or other persuasive grounds, it would take about three years before it was to be our turn. In any event, it took some time for warships to be decommissioned and shore bases to be run down. And even if the Second World War was over, there were many regional or civil wars and disturbances going on at the time, for example, in Java, Malaysia, and especially in India which was approaching the turmoil of independence. And where there was the possibility of wars or civil unrest, the Navy was needed to keep the sea lines open for British shipping.

In the event, my posting was delayed and I was required to report to the officer in charge of a small naval transit camp (HMS *Pembroke*) just outside Chatham in Kent. Here, my duties were very light, and I was able to spend long weekends at my home in Mottingham. But my good fortune did not last. In October, I was told that I had seven days embarkation leave prior to being assigned to a post in the Far East. Exactly where in the Far East was not made known to me at the time. Apparently a troop ship HMS *Patroller* – a US escort carrier[4] leased to the Royal Navy – was to transport 500 naval officers and ratings out to Ceylon (now Sri Lanka) and then on to Australia. But it was not until after I had completed my embarkation leave, and had reported to my home base at Chatham,[5] that I learned – somewhat to my disappointment – that my own destination was HMS *Mayina*, a land-based naval station in Colombo, rather than – as I had hoped – HMS *Golden Hind*, a similar establishment in Sydney.

So, late on one cold November afternoon in 1945, a number of us were marched from our barracks to Chatham Station, from where we boarded a train to Victoria. From there we were taken by naval buses to Paddington. We were transported by the overnight express, which thrust its way through the English countryside to arrive at Plymouth at 5.30 the following morning. Further buses took us to Devonport dockyard, where we were given breakfast. Around 10 a.m. on the same day we embarked on HMS *Patroller*, and were reunited with our kitbags and other luggage that somehow had miraculously – and as it turned out safely – followed us on our 250-mile journey from Chatham.

At 12 noon on an unusually lovely Sunday we sailed out of Plymouth Sound and away from England. At 18½, this was the first time I had travelled outside my home country. I had no passport – only my naval identity card. I was quite looking forward to the adventure. Unlike thousands of personnel from the three armed services who had sailed from Plymouth over the previous six years, I did not feel I was in any danger; and although His Majesty's accommodation and food left much to be desired, I was excited at the prospect of visiting parts of the world I only knew about in geography books – and to do so at His Majesty's expense!

Our first port of call was Malta, a British-owned island in the Mediterranean. Up to that point in the voyage, the sea had been remarkably calm for the time of year, even across the Bay of Biscay. As I was a transportee on board, most of my time was free; except that about once every other day I was assigned certain watch-keeping duties. On board ship, the naval day is divided into a number of four-hour watches, each of which is overseen by an officer of the watch. Immediately responsible to the Captain of the ship is a No. 1 – usually, in the case of an aircraft or escort carrier, with the rank of Commander. His responsibilities include the overall safety of the ship, and matters of supply management and personnel discipline. The time of my watches varied. On two or three occasions they were in the middle of the night, from midnight to 4 a.m. My task during these watches was to walk the length and breadth of the ship every hour or so, checking that, in accordance with fire and other safety regulations, all the passage and other designated doors were either shut and bolted, shut and not bolted, or left open – depending on whether the door was labelled A, B or C.

The duties could hardly be called demanding. More difficult was keeping awake in the small hours of the morning in a cramped watch-keeper's office which was towards the bow of the ship. I read a lot during these times and also wrote some letters. All went well until the second night out from Malta, when the sea – the Mediterranean Sea which I had always assumed to be as calm as a boating lake – started to become extremely rough. The 19 000-ton vessel heaved and groaned, pitched and rolled – and so did my stomach. Not only did I start to feel extremely seasick, but the claustrophobia of the tiny cabin was making me feel quite faint. Yet I could not leave my post – so I had to deposit most of my previous evening's supper on the floor of the watch-keeper's room! Although I eventually disposed of the mess, I did not get rid of the smell, which the succeeding watch-keeper on the 4 a.m. shift was not slow to point out.

Apart from the change in climate, my first impression of setting foot on foreign soil was one of culture shock. Everything seemed so different to that at home – and especially the people. For unlike the 2000s, and certainly in my own walk of life in the 1940s, one did not meet foreigners very often, let alone experience their customs and social mores. Practically my first encounter on shore in Valetta was with a lad about 12 years of age, who not only wanted to show me a snapshot of his older sister, but suggested I might like to come to his home to meet her! This was something which our instructors had earlier warned us about. Though I politely refused the invitation, I sometimes wonder what would have happened had I accepted it. But that fairly innocent encounter was nothing to the one I had in Port Said. On the ship, the quarters of some 500 of the transportees were in the giant aircraft hanger of the ship. I was allocated a top bunk in one of the two-tiered beds; all our personal belongings were housed in a kit cupboard positioned nearby. One early morning while in dock I was woken by an Arab youth of about 16 wanting to climb into my bunk. Believe it or not, at that time I had no idea what he was up to! I only knew that my response at the time was anything but the Christian one of 'turning the other cheek!' (No pun intended.)

****

After passing through the Suez Canal – an experience in itself – and a week crossing the Indian Ocean, HMS *Patroller* docked at Colombo early one warm and sunny December morning. Those of us (about 150 ratings) selected to disembark were driven in covered trucks through the busy port to a naval camp, HMS *Mayina*, just 3 miles away. At that time, Colombo was a dignified city with an imposing main thoroughfare, some grand colonial buildings, and one of the finest coastal promenades on which was situated the famous Galle Hotel. The naval base was less impressive. The buildings mainly consisted of a large number of Nissen huts and an enormous open-sided thatched-roof dining-room where we had most of our meals. I well recall my first Christmas Day away from home when I sat down to a lunch of roast turkey with all the trimmings, with the drips from a tropical rainstorm joining forces with the gravy on my plate! Afterwards, in the evening of a sweltering hot day, I listened to a recording of carols from King's College, Cambridge on the radio while watching a floodlit soccer match.

It rained almost continuously in the three weeks I was in Colombo; and I experienced, at first hand, the devastation of a full-blown monsoon which I had been taught about in my geography class at school. Thirty miles north of Colombo and 500 feet higher at HMS *Ukussa*, a Royal Naval Air Station (RNAS) at Karakarunda, where I was to be based for the next four months, the weather was both cooler and dryer; although, to enjoy the best scenery and climate in Ceylon, one had to go further inland and 3000 feet into the hills to the beautiful city of Kandy. This was, in fact, where many British servicemen chose to spend their leave.

****

The Rear Admiral commanding the naval air station was responsible for the South Asian theatre of naval air operations. His office dealt with all supply and personnel matters. The personnel section to which I was assigned was commanded by a Lieutenant(S), but my immediate supervisor was a pert and feisty Petty Officer Wren Writer, who took herself and her work very seriously! My specific task was to keep the 'pay and rations' ledger, which recorded everything to do with the wages and allowances of the 300 ratings accommodated at the air station, up to date. This was not quite as simple as it sounds, as every day someone was promoted, got married, had another child, had his or her pay stopped or deducted because of some minor offence, or wanted to change the allowance he or she sent back home to his or her dependents. Occasionally, I was also required to do some typing, or duplication on an extremely old and temperamental Roneo machine which sucked up more bottles of duplication spirit than glasses of water I drank in a day! And I did drink regularly and copiously, as the temperature in the office was well beyond anything that His Majesty's Inspector of Factories would ever have allowed in the UK.

HMS *Ukussa* was divided into two separate areas which were bisected by the main road to Colombo. The first comprised a score of dormitories where the ratings were housed, officers' accommodation, a very large canteen, a couple of shops, a theatre where nightly films or shows were put on, a medical centre, and various sporting facilities. The second consisted of the air strip and surrounding buildings, and the offices of the Rear Admiral. It was the Fleet Air Arm's responsibility to patrol the Arabian Sea and Indian Ocean, and particularly to service and protect the main naval port at Trincomalee on the north coast of Ceylon.

I spent most Saturdays and Sundays either at the beach at Mount Lavinia, a beautiful sandy cove just outside Colombo, or in the city itself. It was at the Grand Hotel at Mount Lavinia that Lord Mountbatten had one of his many GHQs (General Headquarters) at the time of the Burma Campaign, but I remember it mostly because one day I was nearly decapitated by a *kayak* (a long rowing boat) ploughing its way towards the beach. I was floating in the water with my back to it when someone yelled out a warning. It was only by ducking below the surface and pushing myself sideways that I managed to avoid a very nasty accident.

Apart from this incident, my memories of Colombo are very pleasant. I spent many happy hours wandering around the docks, and exploring some of the older parts of the city. I remember well a restaurant in the city which served the best Spanish omelette I have ever eaten in my life. I recall some of the most scrumptious afternoon teas, provided free of charge by a group of ladies that ran a 'home from home' for servicemen in a large rambling house opposite the Galle Hotel; I recollect worshipping on many Sundays in an imposing and very English-looking Anglican church which was just five minutes walk from where I had tea. On most Saturday afternoons I relaxed at the poolside at the Galle Hotel, and later played billiards and snooker at a very congenial and efficiently run nearby YMCA.[6] I also did my fair share of browsing around the many interesting stalls and shops in Colombo for souvenirs. However, at the time, my weekly pay packet of 32s 6d did not allow me to buy some of the beautiful silks and precious stones which no doubt would have made not only very acceptable presents, but also excellent investments.

Unlike today, Colombo in 1946 was a perfectly safe place to wander around at night, though I never did so by myself. There were always two or three of us who spent the day together, before being picked up by the open-sided naval truck at 10 p.m. for our hour's trip back to camp. If the outward journey had its hazards of being driven at a breakneck speed, trying to avoid bullock carts and any unfortunate pedestrian going about his daily business, the return journey – at a seemingly even faster speed – was memorable for the frequent screeching of brakes without which some unfortunate nocturnal creature, including the occasional bullock or elephant, would have met an untimely end.

I cannot say that I paid much attention to world affairs during the months I was out of the UK. I do, however, remember reading about the death of David Lloyd George; and the Nuremburg Trials of the Nazi leaders. I also recollect many heated discussions about the partitioning of India and Pakistan, the launching of the United Nations, and the ceding of several Central and Eastern European countries to Russia. At home, the most consequential event of the time was the election of the Labour government in 1945, and the replacement of Winston Churchill by Clement Attlee. The programme of the new government was both unique and far-reaching. It included the nationalization of the Bank of England, the coal mining and several basic industries, and of the railways; a restructuring of the education system and the raising of the school leaving age to 15; and the introduction, for the first time in Britain, of a National Health Service, which *inter alia* promised free medical and hospital treatment for all citizens. However, it was not until 1954 that food and points rationing finally came to an end.[7]

****

In March 1946, I had completed my first six months as a Writer, and was duly promoted to Leading Writer. I proudly displayed the badge of my new office – a red anchor on my left arm (wired gold on my best uniform). My feat in achieving this newly exalted status in the quickest possible time also impressed the young Lieutenant(S) in charge of the personnel office at Katakarunda. On one of the few occasions we actually spoke to each other, he suggested that, if I would like to apply for entry into an officer's training course (in the Supply and Secretariat Branch) he would do his best to persuade the Rear Admiral to recommend me. Since the location of this course was back in England – at HMS *Demetrius* at Wetherby no less – I reckoned that by the time my application was approved (if it was), I would have sampled most of the delights Ceylon had to offer; so I let my name go forward. As it happened, the application was processed and approved in double-quick time, and before I could enjoy my first long weekend leave in

Kandy, I was posted to a destroyer, HMS *Carysfort*, shortly to leave from Colombo for Portsmouth.

****

I joined my new ship late on a Sunday afternoon in April 1946. The 1700-ton destroyer had been in dry dock for several days having a thorough overhaul, after being involved in some minor action off the coasts of Java and Sumatra. This was the time of the Indonesian people's struggle for independence against the Dutch, and several British ships, including some which carried contingents of Royal Marines, were sent to the region to help protect British interests, and if necessary evacuate British citizens. The Indonesians were not slow to fire on any foreign ship in the region, and HMS *Carysfort* was targeted on several occasions, though no serious damage or casualties were caused.

Apart from one night at Chatham, I had never slept in a hammock before. It is incredibly comfortable – but, to me at any rate, no amount of comfort could make up for the tedious (and, to me, difficult) job of roping it up each morning. I never did get the complete hang of it, and compared with the neatness of those of my fellow seamen and stokers[8] whose quarters I shared, mine bulged out all over the place and looked a complete shambles. In the end, by mutual consent, it was agreed I could sleep on one of the benches which stored the hammocks, and which lined the mess.[9]

Although again I was a passenger on board, I assisted the only writer who acted as the secretary to the Lieutenant in charge of supply and personnel matters. But other than taking my turn with normal mess duties which included cleaning, collecting the food from the galley and making the tea, my time was my own, and I spent a lot of time on deck catching up with my reading. Before I left England I had received news that I had passed most of the subjects in Part I of my Institute of Bankers examinations; and once I had settled down at HMS *Ukussa* in Ceylon, I had asked the Education Officer if he could arrange for a couple of the recommended books in advanced banking to be sent out to me. However, it was only when we were crossing the Indian Ocean on the way home that I found the time and interest to take up studying again.

The voyage back to England, via the Suez Canal and through the Mediterranean, took two and a half weeks. We stopped for refuelling at Port Said and Gibraltar. On both occasions, I went ashore with my fellow Writer and a couple of seamen with whom I had struck up a friendship. One of these – I remember him well as when we were in port he acted as ship's postman – was Jimmy Dickinson who, in later years was to become captain of Portsmouth Football Club. The Captain, a handsome and rugged

Commander in the RNR (Royal Navy Reserve) also had some claim to fame – not just for his own wartime exploits in the Atlantic and the Mediterranean, but for being married to one of the most attractive film stars of the day, Greta Gynt. We spent just long enough on Gibraltar for me to explore the famous Rock. This, *inter alia*, housed a huge armoury of weapons which, if necessary, could be used to defend one of Britain's oldest and most vital possessions. I also experienced, at first hand, the mischievous and sometimes quite malevolent habits of the large colony of Gibraltan apes.

The journey across the Bay of Biscay was as rough as I imagined it would be, and I and most of the rest of the crew were heartily seasick! Why, I wonder, did I eat such a hearty breakfast of bacon, egg, sausage, baked beans and lashings of fried bread? At least, however, I could suffer in the open air, as the weather, although overcast, was pleasantly warm. By the time we sailed into Portsmouth Harbour, our decommissioning pennant flying and with all hands on deck, the skies had cleared and it was a beautiful June day. I was delighted to see my father among the welcoming group of relatives and friends on the quayside, and we spent one of the most pleasant days I can remember walking around the docks at the naval base, before I had to return to my ship. About one-half of the ship's complement of 150 were immediately granted two weeks leave; the rest – including myself – had to remain on board until their return. In the meantime, HMS *Carysfort* sailed a little way upstream to berth alongside one of her sister destroyers, HMS *Carthage*, in company with literally dozens of warships that had been 'retired' from active service! It was a sad sight, even though the 'mothballing' of the proud vessels meant the end of six years of death and destruction.

****

I began my three-month officer's training at HMS *Demetrius* (shortly to be renamed HMS *Ceres*) in August 1946. There were 12 of us on the course, and we were distinguished from the other naval ratings by displaying white bands around our caps. We were also treated with a good deal more respect, by both commissioned and non-commissioned offers; and instead of sharing a dormitory, there were just two of us in each bedroom. My roommate was a handsome young Scot, David Renton, and we immediately struck up a close friendship; as I did too with another cadet, Jim Forbes – who was one of the most relaxed and carefree spirits I have ever known!

If I thought I had finished with naval drill, I was mistaken. It was Malvern all over again, but tougher! There was also plenty of physical exercise, route marches, cross-country running, and gymnastics. The course was an upgraded version of what I had been taught before; but this time,

the instructors were experienced officers, and the emphasis was on personnel and procurement management; and on the different kinds of duties and
responsibilities a junior Supply and Secretariat officer might be expected to
shoulder. Since I, and another five cadets, intended to specialize in personnel management, we attended a different set of lectures than did those interested in the supply, storage and distribution of the physical needs of the
Navy (which, as I have already indicated, might include everything from a
turbine engine to a side of beef, or from a naval staff car to a Wren's
uniform). I found all aspects relating to employment, pay, working conditions and other aspects of office organization extremely interesting, and
although many decisions one might be called upon to make were laid down
in *King's Regulations*, there was sufficient number of issues – particularly
on those related to allowances, discipline, postings and compassionate
leave – which allowed some room for judgement.

The three months passed exceedingly quickly and ended with a series of
written and oral examinations – which, I am pleased to say, each of us
passed. Prior to that, as budding officers, we had been measured for our new
uniforms by Gieves, the naval tailors, which had a retail outlet in Leeds. All
but two cadets were to have the insignia of a Sub-Lieutenant in the
RNVR[10] – a wavy single gold ring at the bottom of their jacket sleeves. The
other two – of whom I was one – had not reached the critical age of 19½
and had to be content with the title of 'Midshipman' or 'Snotty', the lowest
rank of officer in the Royal Navy. Not for us a golden braided band topped
with another one of white felt, which informed everyone (or everyone who
knew about such things) what branch of the Navy we were in. Instead, two
white epaulets on the lapels of our jackets, that made us look like a combination of a head waiter and a lift attendant! But no one was prouder than
I when I first donned my new uniform and officer's cap, and received my
commissioning certificate from the Commanding Officer of HMS *Ceres*. In
marching up and saluting to receive the title deed of my new status, I think
I overdid it, so surprised was I to pass out first for my drilling capabilities!
Even now, I think my instructors got me mixed up with someone else;
although I hope that being ranked third out of the 12 cadets for my overall
performance was genuine enough.

One of the great privileges of being an officer was that one could travel
first class on public transport at His Majesty's expense! I really felt that I
had arrived at my proper station in life as I boarded the night express from
York to King's Cross, and made my way to a first class compartment! I was
so excited I could hardly sleep that night. This is the only way to travel, I
thought, and in my early eighties, I still think so today!

****

My parents met me at King's Cross Station at 4.30 a.m., both proud to share my change of status, and to show me their brand new car – a Morris Minor (8 hp). In November 1946, new cars were like gold dust in the UK, and usually took a year or more from ordering to be delivered. Because of his occupation, my father managed to get one a little quicker. Had he wanted to, he could have immediately sold it for more than twice what he had paid for it (£350). As it was, he (or more accurately my mother) sold his 1935 Austin 8, which he had bought three years earlier, and which seemed to be as much in the garage as out of it, for £150. I do not think my father ever had a possession he treasured more in his life than that car. I took it as a great favour that he allowed me to drive it. Earlier I had been taught how to drive in Ceylon. Admittedly my vehicle had been a 10-ton truck, but at least I knew how to double declutch! When on leave, I found my father's vehicle very useful, particularly as Ida had moved back to live with her parents in a new house in Petts Wood, about 15 minutes away from us by private car, but much longer by public transport. It also provided a useful courting medium when we wanted to be alone.

But I am afraid my father's trust in my driving capabilities was misplaced, for on a treacherously icy day in December 1946, driving down a hill near Swanley in Kent about 10 miles from our home, I lost control of the vehicle. It skidded across the road and up a small bank, and then turned itself over, leaving both Ida, who was with me at the time, and myself upside down in our seats. Miraculously, neither of us was seriously hurt, but the car was badly damaged. Much to his credit, my father did not explode at me as he might have done. Instead he made the best of a bad job by arranging for the car to be resprayed in a silver grey, a colour which he had wanted in the first place but was not allowed to have!

The accident rather put a damper on my Christmas leave, which was a prelude to my taking up a new appointment at the HMS Royal Naval Air Station (RNAS) at Arbroath on the north-east coast of Scotland. However, one bright spot was that on 26th December I was promoted to Acting Sub-Lieutenant, and at last felt I was a real naval officer! Early in January I took the overnight sleeper – the *Aberdonian* – from King's Cross in London to Aberdeen. As the train sped north, the weather steadily deteriorated, and by the time it arrived at Arbroath (two hours late!) a raging blizzard had set in. This appalling weather signalled the start of the coldest winter and spring in the UK in living memory. It lasted well into April, and nearly put paid to my first weekend leave in March. Although the leave was only 72 hours, I wanted to be home for Ida's birthday. The only way I could arrange this was to hitch a lift on one of the aeroplanes – a Dakota – that often plied between Arbroath and Lee-on-Solent, the headquarters (HQ) of the Fleet Air Arm. The first part of the journey on Friday morning went fine, and I rather enjoyed the experience of sitting in the rear gunner's seat – with a parachute strapped to my back! We got as far as Nottingham, at which point bad weather forced us to land at a nearby RAF airfield. I made arrangements with the pilot to pick up his return flight at Lee on Monday morning. (I assumed that, later in the day or sometime over the weekend, he could make his way further south.) I took a bus to a local station at Staveley, and then travelled by train for the rest of the journey arriving back at Mottingham quite exhausted at 7 p.m.

After a pleasant weekend, I woke on Monday morning feeling a little under the weather. My father drove me to Lee-on-Solent, and I boarded my flight back to Scotland. By the time I returned to Arbroath a couple of hours later I felt distinctly unwell, and decided to rest in bed. As I undressed, I noticed I was covered with large spots and I then discovered I had contracted German measles![11]

****

HMS *Condor*, the RNAS at Arbroath, was located just 2 miles from the town which is situated between Dundee and Aberdeen. Arbroath is an ancient royal borough, and home to 25 000 residents. It is one of Scotland's primary fishing ports, best known perhaps for its smokies (a particular kind of smoked haddock), and also as the site of one of the oldest abbeys in Great Britain, where, at one time, the Stone of Scone was housed on which Scottish monarchs were crowned.[12] At the time I was stationed in Scotland, it also boasted one of the finest Scottish football teams, and was just becoming one of the east coast's leading tourist attractions.

As well as being responsible for all naval air activities throughout the east coast of Scotland in 1946, the naval air station at Arbroath also housed the headquarters of an engineering Rear Admiral who had responsibility for the overall management of 12 naval air establishments in the UK. The Admiral's office was located in a large Victorian house just off the main campus. His staff consisted of 50 officers from various branches in the Navy – electrical, engineering, educational and supply – whose job it was to oversee and coordinate the operations of their opposite numbers in each of the 12 air stations in England and Scotland. HMS *Condor* was, in fact, the head office of an integrated group of naval air stations. The supply and secretariat functions were overseen by a Commander(S), but the section in which I worked, which dealt exclusively with personnel matters, was the responsibility of a young Lieutenant(S) aided and abetted by two Wren officers and myself. We all shared a large office with a delightful view across the garden, and a huge fireplace which in the winter housed a blazing fire. Each morning we and the Wren officers were picked up from our respective quarters by bus and driven to the office. Betty, a Second Officer[13] was always quick off the bus and even quicker to claim her place in front of the fire where she stood for several minutes warming her backside, and smoking a cigarette perched on the end of a long cigarette holder. This was much to the annoyance of Violet, a most attractive Third Officer, who hated smoking and did not care too much for work either, though she was quite efficient in her own way. Her interests, I remember, were rather more concentrated on a naval pilot who paid more visits to our office than he really needed to!

I was designated as P1 (Personnel Officer No. 1). This was a junior position to that of the two Wren officers Betty and Violet, who were respectively known as P2 and P3, and whose own work entailed making recommendations about personnel matters to the Commander (or his immediate deputy), which had been referred to us by the air stations under our jurisdiction. These were usually to do with appeals against action taken by local Secretariat officers on pay and discipline, requests for extended leave, transfers of appointment, early demobilization on compassionate or other grounds, serious breaches of discipline (for example grievous bodily harm, overdue leave, theft) and last (but not least) paternity suits! Sometimes, these latter offences led to naval court martials. Though I rarely got involved directly with these matters, I often had to assemble or prepare documents about the background and career of those accused.

For the most part, I enjoyed the work. Sometimes my immediate superiors approved my proposed recommendations; sometimes they did not! Frequently, if there were technical issues influencing the conduct or request of a particular rating or junior officer,[14] I had to get the advice of the Engineering Commander or the Electrical Lieutenant Commander. Sometimes, the four of us in our office would have a mini conference. Sometimes, the Lieutenant – Michael Slattery, a regular officer who eventually achieved the rank of Captain before he retired – and I would deal with the problem. Sometimes, and especially on allowance matters where a senior NCO (non-commissioned officer) or junior officer was involved, the matter would be referred to the Commander himself for a decision.

I found life as a naval officer both pleasant and privileged. At a time when most foodstuffs and clothing were still rationed in Britain, we lived like lords. In addition to enjoying all the meat and dairy products we needed, the RNAS in Arbroath ran its own farm, and we were never short of fresh vegetables and fruit. The food in the officers' mess was outstandingly good, and we were waited on hand and foot by Wren ratings. I had a good-sized bedroom in a long prefabricated building which, for most of the 15 months I was at HMS *Condor*, I had to myself, but which for a short period I shared with a young electrical officer whose passion seemed to be church organs rather than anything to do with his trade! Along with a dozen other officers (mostly naval flyers who regularly played football or cricket along the corridor outside my room), I shared a Wren 'servant' who was responsible for cleaning our room, and seeing that our laundry was looked after. To some of the other officers, I seem to recall, our Wren (Gwen by name) provided other services as well!

I made more friends at Arbroath than at any other time in the Navy. I got on particularly well with the Junior Medical Officer and the Dental Officer of the station; and scarcely a lunchtime passed that we did not have a round of billiards together. I always preferred billiards to snooker as there was a great chance of earning a score; and I got the greatest satisfaction from ricocheting my white ball off the red into one of the pockets. Arbroath, being a training station for young naval airmen, also housed several 'schoolies' (education officers), four of whom lived in an adjacent building to mine. I quickly struck up a close friendship with two of the schoolies, Ron Horner and Vivian Price. As a pair of friends they were very different from each other. Ron was a dark-haired, serious young man – though with a good sense of humour – and dedicated to school teaching. Vivian, who like Jim Forbes had come from the top drawer of English families, was inclined to take life much more lethargically. Ron was engaged to a girl who taught in a local school in Arbroath and, in due course, they got married and I was the best man at their wedding. Later, Vivian performed the same duty at my own wedding! After he left the Navy, Ron taught at a school in Bembridge in the Isle of Wight before migrating to become Headmaster at a school in Adelaide. Vivian took up the law and eventually became a Recorder (a regional judge) in the South of England. To the best of my knowledge – and we exchanged correspondence in 2002 – he is retired and living in Kent.

Perhaps, more than anything else, it was my friendship with the schoolies which prompted me to think carefully about my own future. What did I want from my post-naval life? I decided to use my spare time at HMS *Condor* to complete Part I and start on Part II of the Institute of Bankers examinations, in the belief that I was likely to return to a banking career. And so I was introduced to Economics. I decided to take a correspondence course, organised by the Institute for Members of H.M. Forces, and for six months I diligently ploughed through the elements of supply and demand, and money and banking, as propounded by Benham, Cairncross, Silverman and Crowther. I took to the subject immediately, and wondered why even the name had put me off studying it before. It was some years later that I discovered it was taught at my old school – John Lyon. Together with advanced English, I took two examination papers under the eagle eye of one of the schoolies in July 1947, and in the following October passed with credit in both subjects.

****

During my time north of the English border, a number of events of national or international importance occurred. In London, the Attlee government completed its programme of nationalization, and the National Health Service was well established. In June 1947 Marshall Aid was inaugurated, from which six years later I was to receive a modest benefit. On 15th August of the same year India and Pakistan assumed dominion status. As I have already recorded, the partitioning of the two countries caused much bloodshed; and over 2 million people migrated between them. On 20th November 1947, I was one of tens of millions of people who listened on their radios to the broadcast of the wedding of Princess Elizabeth and the Duke of Edinburgh. Then in January 1948 Mahatma Gandhi was assassinated.

These events, however, had little affect on our daily lives at Arbroath, where most of the time was directed to training pilots in the Fleet Air Arm, and helping to place the air stations in Scotland and England for which we were responsible, on an efficient and peaceful footing.[15]

****

By early 1948, I began to look forward to returning to civilian life. Yet somehow a banking career did not seem as appealing as it once had. For one thing, the Navy had given me a good deal of confidence in myself; for another, I had developed – rather belatedly – a taste for learning and I certainly did not fancy the routine of a 9 a.m. to 5.30 p.m. occupation. In the Arbroath Library one day, I read about some special arrangements for ex-servicemen to enter university, and have all their tuition and expenses paid by the government. I sent for the details, and found that to be eligible for the scheme I had to take a Special Entrance Examination of the University of London. This was because I had not done sufficiently well in my GCE exams which I had taken five years earlier. I was informed that if I sat and passed two three-hour exams in economics and geography this, together with my GCE results, would give me the necessary qualifications for university entrance. And so, in December 1947, I travelled south to take the examinations at the University of London. Late in the afternoon of the same day, after I had written my two papers, I was called in by the examiners who asked me a few questions, and then told me that I had passed both examinations – and done so with some distinction!

Much enthused, I returned to Arbroath at the beginning of 1948 and began to apply for a place at London University. I decided I wanted to read economics as that was the subject which interested me most; and that meant I was restricted in my choice of college to the London School of Economics (LSE) and University College London (UCL). Both turned me down flat, not because I was unqualified, but because, with the flood of ex-service men then seeking places in universities, there were many with better GCEs, or even Higher Certificates of Education (HCEs),[16] than I possessed. It was suggested that I should either apply to another university, or take an external London degree by attending one of the university or technical colleges which prepared students for such a qualification. In the end, I chose the latter course of action, and was eventually accepted as a BSc (Econ) student at the City of London College, which was located in Moorgate, just a short walk from the City's financial district.

****

In the meantime, my fondness for Ida had blossomed, and on leave in July 1947 we became engaged. Later in the year, when I heard I was to be demobbed in the following March, we set the date of our wedding for 3rd April 1948. Even in those days, I believed that if you could combine romance with some financial perks you should do so! Not only did marrying Ida in the last day of the tax year give me a tax allowance for the whole of that tax year just ending, but the proposed timing of the nuptials enabled me to pick up nearly eight weeks of my discharge pay as a married man.

I had been entirely faithful to Ida for the time I had been in the Navy, although I did permit myself the mildest flirtation on a couple of occasions. The first when my schoolie pals dared me to take out the Wren servant (Gwen) who looked after my room and often served me at table in the officers' mess, who they knew I found rather attractive. I was reluctant to do so until Ron suggested we make up a foursome to go to Dundee one Saturday and take in a theatre in the evening. So I agreed, and very hesitantly asked Gwen who accepted (I don't think very enthusiastically).

As it happened the outing was not a great success. Gwen and I seemed to have very little in common, and she did not like the performance at the theatre – one of J.B. Priestley's classics, I seem to recall. We missed the bus back to Arbroath which we needed to catch for her to be in at curfew time (11 p.m., I think), so I had to telephone the Wren officer on duty at the air station to apologize that Gwen would be late, and that I was to blame for this. The officer on duty turned out to be Betty (the P2 in my office) who was none too pleased! Indeed, later, she told me off for taking advantage of my position as an officer. Gwen was none too amused either. I think she had found the whole day rather boring, and being late back at the station did not help either. Thereafter, our relationship became distinctly cooler; and about a couple of months later she was reassigned to other duties at the air station.

The second occasion was when I was virtually ordered to accompany a young lady to a Scottish ball. Apparently, it was quite usual on such occasions for the Commander of the Air Station to be asked to provide suitable male escorts for young and suitable (!) unattached ladies, and three other officers and myself were deputed to do the right and honourable thing. Decked in our evening dress (namely our best uniforms and bow ties) we were picked up by a limousine at 6 p.m. on the Saturday evening of the ball, and driven about 30 miles through the Angus countryside to a magnificent Scottish mansion which was beautifully lit up. After being stylishly entertained to a rather sparse meal of poached white fish (not the luxury of a naval wardroom for that family!) and home-made gooseberry tart, we were then introduced to our respective partners for the evening. Mine was an attractive well-built Scottish lass of about 19, who was almost as shy as I was. She was beautifully dressed in a long blue gown.

The ball was held in the Town Hall of Forfar, and was attended by about 200 of the local gentry. The evening programme consisted of a score or so of Scottish dances, about one-half of which I could cope with, as I had earlier been to Scottish dancing classes with Ron and his girlfriend.[17] We were also entertained by a Scottish pipe band and a local brass band. A sumptuous buffet served about midnight more than made up for my earlier disappointment (it then occurred to me that my hostess knew what we might be eating later in the evening!); and altogether I greatly enjoyed my evening – and night. The party broke up at 4 a.m., and after a polite kiss on the cheek of my escort, the other three officers and myself were driven back to Arbroath. I crawled into bed at 5.30 a.m. just as daylight was about to break. That was one of the few Sundays that I failed to appear for breakfast in the wardroom!

****

My farewell departure from HMS *Condor* was something I – and I suspect every officer at the air station – will well remember. On one evening each month and on special occasions, such as the celebration of Nelson's victory at Trafalgar on 21st October 1805, a formal dinner was held in the wardroom. All officers were expected to attend, and to be dressed appropriately. Such an occasion also provided an opportunity for the Captain to welcome new officers, and to say farewell to those leaving for other postings. In March 1948, the Captain of the air station and myself – one of his most junior officers – were both leaving the air station. Naturally the

Captain was guest of honour, and placed at the centre of the top table. I was at the end of one of the arms spanning out from that table. My schoolie friends, the doctor and the dentist surrounded me. Vivian was at his most mischievous. First he made sure I was getting my fair share of alcohol, which flowed freely throughout the evening. Secondly he engaged in one of his favourite pranks in crawling under the table and taking off shoes of young officers who he either did not like, or thought took life too seriously. Then another officer started to take my shoes off, and before long our part of the mess was in complete disarray. The Captain's second in command decided that things were getting a little out of hand and announced (as was the custom when an officer's behaviour had become socially unacceptable) that two of the offenders on my table, including Vivian, were to pay the customary fine of paying for a round of drinks for the assembled company.

The time came for all those present to toast the departing officers. The Captain replied graciously for both of us, and afterwards I went up to him, slapped him on the back and wished him well in his retirement. I had never spoken to, or been spoken to, by the man before. Ron and my doctor friend gently dragged me away and put me to bed. To this day, I do not think I have ever been so inebriated. I later apologized to the Captain for behaving out of turn, but he said he had already forgotten the incident, and hoped that I would enjoy civilian life. A short while afterwards, my three years in the Navy came to a close.

****

NOTES

1.   William Shakespeare's description of the third age of man, *As You Like It*, Act II, scene 7.
2.   A Petty Officer in the Navy is the most senior non-commissioned naval officer.
3.   The day the surrender of Japan to the Allies was celebrated.
4.   An escort carrier is a small aircraft carrier.
5.   Depending on their home towns, naval ratings were assigned to three naval bases – Chatham, Portsmouth and Devonport (near Plymouth).
6.   Young Men's Christian Association.
7.   For an excellent survey of the post-war history of Britain, see Andrew Marr, *A History of Modern Britain*, Basingstoke: Macmillan, 2007.
8.   A stoker is a rating who works in the engine room.
9.   The naval term for the living quarters of seamen.
10. Royal Navy Volunteer Reserve. Those in the regular Navy – the RN – had a plain gold ring; and those in the Royal Navy Reserve a crinkly ring.
11. A relatively mild reoccurrence of the disease which those who had earlier been affected by measles – as I had, when I was nine – were liable to catch.
12. Much to the chagrin of the Scots it is now located in Westminster Abbey. In December 1950, it was in fact stolen from the abbey but was returned the following April.

13. In those days Wren officers were differently ranked to their male equivalents. A Third Officer, with one blue ring on her arm, corresponded to a Sub-lieutenant, a Second Officer (with two rings) a Lieutenant, and a First Officer (with three rings) a Lieutenant Commander.
14. I was allowed only to see documents relating to officers of rank of Lieutenant or below.
15. Most of which have been since shut down, but some, for example the RNAS at Yeovilton (Somerset) and Culdrose (Cornwall) remain active.
16. The equivalent of A level certificates in the early 2000s.
17. While I have never been able to get my feet properly placed for ballroom dancing, I have always been able to manage the sequence of a Scottish or country dance!

With my parents
1927

Aged one
1928

HMS *Carysfort*
May 1946

With naval friend
Arbroath 1947

Receiving Southampton PhD Degree
from Duke of Wellington
1957

My mother, Philip and Ida
1958

UN Group of Eminent Persons
New York 1972

Participants at Seminar on Economic Analysis
and the Multinational Enterprise
Bellagio 1973

With Governor Park
Nr Seoul 1977

With King of Lesotho
1989

4. 'And then the lover' (II): to university

In March 1948 I left the Navy in style, taking with me a ceremonial sword borrowed from a regular officer, which I was to wear on my wedding day. I boarded an early morning London train from Arbroath, and disembarked about midday at York to go through a demobilizing procedure at a local army barracks at York. There, I was kitted out with a new suit, a raincoat, a trilby hat, two shirts, two vests and pairs of pants, a tie, two pairs of socks and a pair of shoes – all of which I could choose from a fairly wide range of items on display. With my new belongings neatly wrapped in a cardboard box, I resumed my journey to London, and then to my home in Mottingham. I had returned home after just two years and ten months of being in His Majesty's service!

****

For the most part, I had enjoyed and appreciated my naval interlude; and I believe it helped me to become a more confident, resourceful and understanding human being. I am sure I learned from the roughness and discipline of my early experiences, just as I gained in maturity from the management skills and authority I exercised as an officer. I was rubbing shoulders with a wide variety of people from all walks and stations in life, and came to realize that, if you try and place yourself in their shoes, it is not difficult to get on well with most individuals. I made several new friends, and gained new insights into my own capabilities and limitations. I visited places in the world I would otherwise not have done. And although, for most of the time, my travelling conditions were far from ideal, my experiences abroad gave me a taste for international travel which became stronger over the following half-century.

But now, it was time to get on with the rest of my life! Helped by a generous loan from Ida's father and a 90 per cent mortgage, I was able to buy a small end-of-terrace fully furnished house in a district near my parents' home for £1800. The owners were emigrating to Australia. No matter if the roof of the conservatory – an extension to the house which had been made into a kitchen – frequently leaked; or the garden (which was about 40ft x

15ft) was completely overlooked from all sides; or that one of our neighbours spent most of her time screeching at her three small children; or that there was no heating in the bedroom; or that the solid fuel boiler frequently failed to function – it was our first home and we loved it!

My father married Ida and myself at his church in April 1948. It was a full naval wedding. Vivian Price was my best man, and he, Ron Horner, Mike Slattery and the 'Doc' formed a guard of honour with raised swords forming an archway under which we passed. We had a wedding reception in an adjacent school hall. There were no alcoholic beverages – after all we were on Baptist premises – but the trifle was liberally laced with sherry! Whether my Uncle Tom, who was a strict teetotaller, recognized this or not I don't know, but he pronounced it as the most delicious trifle he had ever eaten!

Our honeymoon was spent in Bude in Cornwall after a first night at the Cumberland Hotel in London. We left the following day on the 11 a.m. Plymouth express train from Waterloo. My father's cousin (on his mother's side) who was stationmaster at the London terminus personally escorted us to our first class compartment (I was still a naval officer even though I was on demobilization leave!). We enjoyed lunch as the train sped westwards through the English countryside. At Okehampton in Devon, we changed trains, and after a delightful ride through the undulating hills and valleys of north Devon, arrived in Cornwall as the sun was setting.

We spent two contented weeks exploring the majestic coastline and charming villages of north Cornwall. We visited Tintagel Castle, reputed to be the birthplace of King Arthur in the ninth century, Padstow, a fishing village, now the home of Rick Stein's well-renowned fish restaurants, and St Ives – an artists' paradise with its glorious beaches.

On our return home, I took a temporary teaching job at a nearby school, and once again discovered I was absolutely no good at keeping discipline. Ida started a new secretarial job at the local (Sidcup) factory of Kolster-Brandes, a US-owned subsidiary, which manufactured radio and communications equipment. As part of my contribution to the household chores, I did most of the main shopping of the week on Saturday morning. After the plentiful supplies of food in the Navy, I soon learned the harsh reality of living in post-war Britain. In 1948, each person was entitled to a weekly egg, 1s 6d (7.5 new pence) of meat, ½ lb of butter, ½ lb sugar, and 2 oz of cheese. Our weekly diet was supplemented by such off-the-ration goods as rabbit, whale meat and chicken, and duck eggs; and, in season, fresh vegetables and fruits. If we dined out, we could expect to pay about 1s 6d (7.5 new pence) per head for an evening meal; and indeed, to protect the consumer against profiteering, no restaurant in 1948 was allowed to charge more than 5 shillings (25 new pence) per head.

In September 1948, I walked into the lofty portals of the City of London College. During the following nine months I took courses for the Intermediate BSc(Econ) examination in Economics, Economic History, Geography, Logic and Scientific Method, and British Constitution. I especially enjoyed the latter two subjects, neither of which I had studied before. There were about 30 students in my class, and apart from six of us who were ex-servicemen, the rest – about one-half of whom were girls – were aged 17 or 18.

I found it particularly fascinating to compare the different styles of teaching. Our Economic History lecturer remained seated, and virtually read from a textbook. Our Economic Geography instructor paced slowly around the room between the desks distilling all relevant knowledge at dictation speed. In both these teachers' classes I felt very much as if I was back in school again. By contrast, our Economics tutor – who both looked and acted the part of a university don – preferred to teach his own particular brand of economics! Whether or not you liked this style of teaching, Mr Aaranson kept us on our toes by challenging us to relate what he said to our recommended textbook, Frederick Benham's *Economics*. Our British Constitution lecturer could best be described as an elderly sage. He brought what otherwise might have been a dull subject to life, by drawing upon his own very considerable experiences in living through some tumultuous years of parliamentary history. Those included the full enfranchisement of women in 1928, the Abdication Crisis in 1936, the Coalition government of the war years, and the institution of a comprehensive social reform programme by the post-1945 Labour government.

I had no real difficulty in coping with any of these subjects, and the good grades I achieved for my essays prompted me to do even better. On the two days I had no lectures in London, I had the house to myself. In addition, I took the opportunity to study on my 30-minute train journey from Eltham to London, though I had to stand on most days. I made several friends at the college; and discovered a number of inexpensive eating houses around Liverpool Street Station, including a workman's cafe that served the best steak and kidney pudding I have ever tasted.

Ida and I soon settled into a routine. On Tuesdays we spent the evening with my parents. On Friday evening Ida attended choir practice, and on most Saturdays we visited Ida's parents in the afternoon, and later went to the local cinema at Petts Wood. On Sundays my father picked us up in his car to take us to evening worship. In 1949, however, my father-in-law had a heart attack, and for several weeks was in a nearby hospital. After making a nearly full recovery, he and his wife decided to retire to the Isle of Wight where Ida's mother was born and raised. They purchased a pleasant detached house opposite a small airfield just outside Cowes. I remember its long back garden very well, as my father-in-law had converted most of it into a bowling green. Another new game for me to learn!

****

I passed my Intermediary BSc(Econ) examination with good grades and reapplied for admission to LSE and UCL. Several of my classmates had received conditional acceptances from other universities, such as Exeter and Southampton, but having just settled in our new home in Sidcup, I was reluctant to move away from London. I was offered a place in both colleges, and opted for UCL. This was partly because I felt it had more of the atmosphere of a university; and partly that students reading economics at the college were permitted to attend any lectures at LSE they wished. I definitely felt I was getting the best of both worlds!

The Department of Practical Economy at UCL was quite small, but it was staffed by a distinguished Faculty under the leadership of G.C. Allen. Professor Allen was then not only one of the leading industrial economists of his day, but the most prominent British scholar writing on Japanese economic history. During the time I was at the college, he and his research assistant Audrey Donnithorne were in the final stages of completing a seminal two-volume monograph on the role of Western enterprise in Far Eastern economic development. Little did I realize at the time that my own research interests would later so closely parallel those of his. For his part, I do not think he could have anticipated that, within a generation, Japan would become the second-largest industrial nation in the world, and that 40 years on, Japanese firms would be investing abroad ten times the amount of investment by foreign firms in Japan.

University College housed the oldest department of economics (or political economy as it used to be called) in London University, although the college was perhaps best known as being the alma mater of Jeremy Bentham, the nineteenth-century moral philosopher. G.C. Allen's immediate predecessor was Hugh Gaitskell who later became Leader of the Labour Party. During my undergraduate years, I was fortunate to meet and attend the lectures of many eminent economists and political scientists. I well recall the flamboyant and entertaining lecturing style of Lionel (later Lord) Robbins; the gentle but quite incisive teaching of James Meade; the political acumen and brilliant intellect of Harold Laski; the mathematical genius of Roy Allen; the commanding stature of Arnold Plant; and the carefully orchestrated and well-delivered lectures of Ronald Coase and Arthur Phelps Brown. These leading scholars were ably supported by a group of younger lecturers, most of whom later were to achieve academic distinction of their own. I especially recall Alan Peacock, who when he lectured seemed completely lost without a pipe in the corner of his mouth; Jack Wiseman, who was a rumbustious and warm-hearted man; and Ralph Turvey, who most students believed was born clutching an economics textbook in his hand – and an advanced one at that! Meanwhile across London at UCL, Douglas Hague, whose boyish looks fooled many a student into thinking he was one of them, was already publishing in the leading journals.

Although I appreciated the opportunity to attend the lectures at LSE, and to use its excellent library facilities, I found the seminars offered by the Faculty at UCL particularly helpful. Herbert Tout was a particularly well-read economist, as well as being one of the most lovely and gracious individuals I have ever met; while Marian Bowley was as rigorous and demanding a scholar, as I imagine her father – Sir Arthur Bowley, the father of economic statistics and Professor of Economics at University College Reading[1] between 1907 and 1919 – must have been. I was impressed by the kindness and courtesy with which Arthur Stonier treated his students, but less so by the pipe – or rather its contents – which he constantly smoked!

My studying habits at university were very similar to those I had adopted at the City of London College. I must own that, as a newly married man with a home in the suburbs, I took little advantage of the excellent social and cultural facilities of UCL. In retrospect, I regret that I may have missed out on an essential part of the educational process. Yet I still managed to make some good friends, some of whom I remain in contact with today. Those of my fellow students from the City of London College went on to LSE, but none to UCL. One of these was Raymond Croft, who was not only highly intelligent, but one of the most hardworking students I have ever come across. Both of us opted to specialize in economics for the last year of our degree course, which meant that, in addition to the three compulsory courses in Economic Theory, Applied Economics and Economic History, we studied three other specialist topics – in my case, The Theory of the Firm, International Economics and Public Finance.

Looking back to the third-year courses I took at UCL or LSE, most of the contents, which have survived over the past half-century, are now contained in first- or second-year text books. Over the intervening years, the methodology and analytical content of economics has become increasingly mathematical and esoteric; and I have to admit that, on my retirement from Reading in 1992, I could understand less of the contents of many journals like *Econometrica* and the *Review of Economic Studies* than I could when I was a student. In my third year at UCL, Jan Tinbergern's *Introduction to Econometrics* was the latest word in this new branch of the discipline. Now, to appreciate its contemporary counterpart one needs to be not only well trained in mathematics and advanced statistics, but immersed in the subject for several years.

Yet I remain convinced that only about one-tenth of the advanced economics now taught in UK and US universities is of the slightest practical
use. But, lest anyone think I am claiming such courses should be abandoned, I would be the first to acknowledge that the greater part of
commercial research and development comes to nothing, but that without
it, many path-breaking scientific advances and discoveries would never
have materialized! Indeed, some of our foremost practitioners today – one
good example is Mervyn King, the current Governor of the Bank of
England – would be the first to acknowledge the value of a rigorous training in economic theory and econometrics. At the same time, while respect-
ing the work of my more technically sophisticated colleagues, I think my
profession would have better served the national and international community if a much higher proportion of mainstream economists had paid
less attention to the fine-tuning of their technical expertise, and more to a
fuller understanding of the interface between the underlying principles of
their discipline and the political and institutional environment, within
which these principles are put into practice. But more of this later.[2]

****

To graduate from the University of London, and indeed most UK universities, it is necessary to be a registered student for at least three academic
years. But as I had taken my first-year course at the City of London
College, I was ready to sit my finals in two years. Alfred Stonier, my personal tutor at UCL, tried to persuade me to take advantage of the extra
year to gain a better class of degree, but I was anxious to complete my
studies as soon as possible. Moreover, Ida had supported me well for the
past three years, and although she quite enjoyed working and was still
young, she was keen to start a family in the not too distant future.

At the same time, I wanted to graduate formally; and to do this I had
either to pursue some postgraduate studies at UCL – and I was not sure if
I would get a further grant for this – or obtain a research assistantship (RA)
there (or at the LSE), which would earn me some money, yet keep me registered at the University of London. As it happened there was a vacancy for
an RA at UCL. At the time, Douglas Hague was undertaking some research
for the (UK) Board of Trade into the costs and benefits of relocating various
branches of manufacturing industry away from the prosperous Midlands
and south-east England, to areas of above average unemployment (the so
called development areas) in north-east and north-west England, South
Wales and mid-Scotland. He and Peter Newman – his RA in 1951 – had just
completed a study of the clothing industry, but Peter was about to leave to
pursue a PhD programme in the US. So his job became available. I now had

a double reason to do well in my finals. I knew that, unless I got a First or a good Upper Second Class honours degree[3] I would not be in the running for the RA; and I was determined to prove to my tutor that it was not necessary for me to study an extra year to turn in a good examination performance.

Along with 150 or so other students from LSE and UCL, I sat my final exams in June 1951 in the examination hall of the University of London in South Kensington, a mile or so east of the Albert Hall. Most of nine papers were concentrated over a seven-day period. There then followed a gap, when as part of my examination requirements I had to sit and pass two foreign language papers.[4] I chose Italian and French. Since the main purpose of the exercise was to demonstrate a capability of translating foreign economics texts and business literature into English, students were allowed to take dictionaries into the examination. As I had matriculated in French, I foresaw no problem in that language: however, I knew not a single word of Italian. So in the seven days between my last economics paper and the Italian examination I swotted up as much elementary Italian grammar as I could. In addition, armed with a dictionary, I went through the examination papers of the last five years. The strategy worked. Helped by my school knowledge of Latin, I learned all that was needed to secure a tolerable pass in the examination.

****

The months prior to the results of the examination being announced in July were some of the most relaxing of my life. Ida and I went to stay with her parents at Cowes for two weeks, and for most of the rest of July I tried to get my own back garden into some semblance of order. It was a fine, warm summer, and I remember listening to the test matches on the radio. The Australians were visiting the UK, and both teams played some fine cricket with Miller, Bradman, Hutton and Compton each being in splendid form.

But my favourite contest of the year was the annual Gentlemen v Players match, which pitted the finest of Britain's amateur and professional cricketers against each other. Over the past three years, I had attended the Oval cricket ground (in south London) on the last day of this match in July, and I did so again in 1951. But this year was very special as Herbert Tout who was on the Board of Examiners at London University had told me that if I cared to telephone him at 5 p.m. on 20th July – the day of the cricket match – he would tell me my degree result. So shortly after the tea interval at the Oval, I positioned myself beside one of the red GPO (General Post Office) telephone boxes at the back of one of the seating enclosures. At precisely 5 p.m. I placed my 2d in the coin box and dialled Mr Tout's number. He answered immediately. 'John Dunning here,' I said. He replied with genuine pleasure, 'Congratulations, John – you have got a First.' I could scarcely believe it. I thought I had done reasonably well, and would have been disappointed if I had not been awarded an Upper Second class degree, but I had not really expected a First. I walked back to the ground in a daze and watched the last hour's play. I have no idea who won the match – nor did I really care! Later I discovered that my friend Raymond Croft also got a First; but much to his, and my, surprise he had failed his German language paper!

****

My excellent degree results secured me the Research Assistantship at UCL. Having completed a study of the clothing industry, Douglas Hague was asked to turn his attention to the radio and television industry. In the six years since the end of the war, over a score of UK radio and television firms had been encouraged by the government to set up branch factories in the development areas. The Board of Trade wanted to know if the production and transaction costs of manufacturing in those areas were greater or less than those which they might have incurred had they been permitted to expand an existing plant in the Midlands or South East England. The investigation was my first exercise in location economics, and my first experience of field research. I did most of the interviewing with the executives of some 20 or so companies; and visited several government-sponsored industrial estates set up either in the 1930s or since 1945 in South Wales, mid-Scotland, Lancashire and Northumberland. Well-known names of radio manufacturers such as Murphy, Sobell, Philips, Ekco and their component suppliers like Dubilier, GEC and Ferranti suddenly came alive for me, and I travelled the length and breadth of the United Kingdom on British Rail. So also began a love–hate relationship with hotels and guest-houses that remains to this day.

In interviewing the radio and television firms, I was fortunate to receive all the cooperation and information I needed. Partly, I think this was because in the early 1950s academic researchers had not yet begun to flood firms with requests for information; indeed, many of the executives I interviewed were quite flattered that someone wanted to undertake research into their activities. It was also partly because, in this particular case, the senior managers I interviewed were anxious to let the Board of Trade know that, by being compelled to set up branch factories 200–300 miles away from most of their suppliers and customers, they were losing work to their foreign competitors. This is a story which has been repeatedly echoed since that time; but, for good or bad, the facts as given to us by the firms themselves did not wholly bear out their concerns. Many of the additional costs of producing away from their parent companies were, in fact, start-up costs;

and there was already accumulating evidence that, for those firms which had been established the longest, the differences in locational costs between the areas studied were marginal. However, then as now, the inter- and intra-firm communication costs and transport costs of operating a branch unit far away from the parent company were sometimes sufficient to outweigh any savings in rent, labour costs and the like. At the same time, there were significant economic and social benefits, for example a more diversified industrial structure to the regions which before the war were heavily dependent on some of the basic – and now less prosperous – industries.

I did not appreciate it at the time, but this particular research project was to prove an excellent training ground for the kind of scholarly work I have pursued for most of my professional life. I found Douglas Hague an ideal supervisor. Under the guidance of a steering committee organized by the National Institute of Economic and Social Research (NIESR)[5] and chaired by Sir Henry Clay, he set an analytical framework for the project; although apart from supervising the design of my questionnaire he left me very much to my own devices. Almost exactly a year after I began the assignment I placed the finished report on the 'Prof's' desk. It was approved by the NIESR steering committee, and the results were later published under the authorship of Douglas and myself in the *Review of Economic Studies* (RES).[6] This was my first and last article for the RES; I am as proud of it as anything else I have written!

My first year in academia was quite a busy one. However, although the salary of the RA was a little higher than my student grant, I wanted some extra income. More importantly, as my plans were turning increasingly to a university career, I wished to gain some teaching experience. The City of London College was always on the lookout for part-time evening teachers, and because of the good quality of my degree and my previous connections with the college, they were happy to invite me to teach two courses. One of these was a first-year course in Economic Statistics; the other a third-year specialist economics course in the Theory of the Firm. This particular branch of economics has always fascinated me, and in the early 1950s there was a great debate going on among academic economists about the relevance of the marginalist principle to the actual pricing policy of firms.[7] I remember typing all my lecture notes for this latter course at my home in Sidcup. Though there were only six students on the course, I really enjoyed the preparation and the lecturing, although, as often happens with newly graduated young lecturers, I suspect I may have taught above their heads!

I have always believed in maximizing the use made of any academic venture in which I have been involved. In the course of my field research in 1951/52, I had collected a great deal of information about what at that time was a little-known industry. Partly as a result of G.C. Allen's own interest and example, industrial economics was very much in vogue at UK universities.[8] This being so, I decided to write an article on the contribution of the radio and television industry to the post-war UK economy. However, at that time there were few avenues for applied economists to publish in the scholarly journals. But the large joint stock banks helped plug this particular lacuna. Indeed, I can recall that in preparing for my final examination in Applied Economics, I selected 40 topics which I studied in depth. And mostly my sources of data for these were either specialized monographs, or articles published in the quarterly reviews of such UK banks as Lloyds, National Provincial, Westminster, the District Bank, and a group of Scottish banks. Well-renowned economists like Ely Devons, Frank Paish, Lionel Robbins, Roy Harrod and W. Arthur Lewis regularly contributed articles to one or other of these reviews, and I thought that what was good enough for them was good enough for me! As it happened, I shared the contents of the June 1952 edition of the Scottish banks' *Three Banks Review* with Alec Cairncross, an economist who I had long respected and admired, and who, in fact, I had visited at Glasgow University when I was on one of my field trips to Scotland. Over the 40 years until his death in 1998, our paths quite frequently crossed. But it was my proudest moment in 1968 when I was able to present Sir Alec (as he then was) with an Honorary Doctorate of Literature at the University of Reading.[9]

****

I received 25 guineas for my contribution to the *Three Banks Review*. At 2008 prices the equivalent fee in real terms would be £600–£700. But more importantly, I had made my first foray into print – and indeed the article was reviewed in the *Financial Times*. Later I was to publish several other articles on the radio and TV industry. Indeed I became quite a minor authority on the industry, and in September 1953 the BBC asked me to give a 15-minute broadcast on the occasion of the fiftieth anniversary of Guglielmo Marconi's despatch of the first transatlantic radio signal from Poldhu in Cornwall to Newfoundland. I thought the BBC was very brave! I was due to air my talk live at 7.15 p.m. on the Saturday evening but I arrived at Broadcasting House at about 5 p.m. for a rehearsal. My contribution had already been timed for exactly 13.5 minutes, but on the first reading it came out at 14 minutes. So, there and then, I had to cut out three sentences from the script before the producer was satisfied. In the event, I somehow missed reading another sentence and finished ten seconds ahead of schedule! The presenter of the programme – Kenneth Kendall, later to become one of Britain's leading newsreaders – brought the proceedings to a rather slower close than he had expected, but other than that I think all went off quite well.

Over the last half-century, I have given many radio talks and participated in several panel discussions both in the UK and abroad; I have also taken part in numerous television programmes. I well remember an exchange of views I had with Jean-Jacques Servan-Schreiber at the time of his publication *Le Défi Américain*. Most of my interviews for TV have taken place at my home or at the university, or more recently, when abroad, at conferences or in foreign TV studios.[10] On these latter occasions, I rarely get to see the resulting telecast – except perhaps as I did once in my hotel room in Beijing on a news or current affairs programme later that night. But, all in all, I have enjoyed these occasions, even if my rather naive belief about the glamour and excitement of a TV studio or a broadcasting event has been knocked on its head several times!

****

A much more significant portent of my future career – but unrecognized by me at the time – was my observation, on a visit to one of the newer industrial estates in Dundee, that a large number of factories were occupied by American-owned firms such as Westclox, National Cash Register, Burroughs and Remington Rand. Why was this? I pondered. Was it only the Scottish Development Area to which US foreign investors were attracted? I soon found out that this phenomenon, which had yet to catch the attention of post-war economists,[11] was both widespread and quite important. Sufficiently so, at least, for Richard Fry – then the economic correspondent of the *Guardian* and Editor of the *Manchester Guardian Annual Survey of Industry* – to commission a short article from me on the subject. In so doing he was advised by a young lecturer in economics at Aberystwyth University who was unknown to me at our first meeting in 1953, but who was to play an important role in my professional life. His name was Peter Hart.

One sad event occurred during my time as an RA at UCL. On 6th February 1952 I was working in my office, which I shared with James Lanner, a macroeconomist. At about 11 a.m. someone (I can't remember who) put his head round the door and informed us that King George VI, at the age of 57, had died peacefully in his sleep at Sandringham Castle. He had been suffering from lung cancer for some years, but the timing of his death was totally unexpected. The new Queen – Elizabeth – with her husband the Duke of Edinburgh, immediately flew back from Kenya where they were on holiday. Other happenings in the same academic year included the election of the Conservative government under the leadership of Winston Churchill; the end of most forms of wartime rationing; the successful continuation of the Festival of Britain; the reopening of London's foreign exchange market after 12 years; and the detonation of Britain's first atomic weapon on the Monte Bello Islands off Western Australia. In sport, Manchester United were the football league champions in 1951, Australia continued to dominate men's tennis, and, in cricket, the West Indies pulverized England in the test matches. Finally, in the summer of 1952 England experienced some of the worst floods in living memory, particularly in north Devon where the coastal villages of Lynton and Lynmouth were completely devastated.

****

In the spring of 1952, I began to think seriously about my future career. When I had entered university, the thought of becoming an academic had not entered my head. Indeed, it was not until after I had completed my finals, and was well into my research assistantship, that I began to contemplate university research and teaching as a possible vocation. I discussed the various options open to me with several of the Faculty at UCL. In the end, my preferred options were reduced to two: the administrative branch of the Civil Service or a scholarly profession. Opportunities for economic consultancy and international agencies were much more limited than they are today. As I also recognized that neither option might, in fact, materialize, I registered my interest with the Careers Advisory Service at UCL, who arranged a number of job interviews for me with commercial enterprises. I remember one of these being for a trainee manager at Harrods. I was already dressing myself in a black tie and tails[12] when I heard that I was not considered suitable for the post! Thinking back, I believe it to be a blessing in disguise; as was an earlier decision – this time of mine – not to pursue a career in the ladies' fashion industry. This particular opportunity came about in 1948 as a result of a suggestion by the Senior Wren Officer at Arbroath, who was closely associated with a small but very exclusive ladies' fashion house in London. She apparently had been asked to recommend a personable young man who would be willing to train as a purchasing manager. On one of my leaves in London I was interviewed for the position at the Knightsbridge office of her company, and was offered it. Whether it was because I did not want to be associated with the hoary joke that 'he travels in ladies' underwear' I am not sure, but for good or bad, the ladies' fashion world has had to do without my unique talents! This is not to say I was not (and am not) interested in the dressware of the opposite sex; indeed I have quite strong views about it – a fact which the ladies in my life will readily (and sometimes ruefully) confirm!

My choice of occupation being so narrowed, I attended interviews for a position in the Civil Service, and also sought the advice of a student at UCL who was a year ahead of me, and was then working at the Treasury. I think two things caused me to reject this particular career path. The first was a reputably tough entrance examination which I would have to take; the second was that I could just not see myself at an office desk for the rest of my working life. Moreover, there was no assurance that I would be assigned to a department in which I could use my knowledge of economics. Indeed, in recruiting for the senior echelons of the Civil Service, the subject of an applicant's degree is much less important than his or her class of degree, and the university awarding it. To this day, Oxford and Cambridge still supply the majority of the entrants into the administrative branch of the Civil Service, with London coming a rather poor third. As things turned out, I never regretted my decision. Not only are university dons permitted a good deal of freedom in how they allocate their time (though perhaps less so in 2008 than in 1952) but, if they are good enough and wish to do so, they can enter the executive branch of the UK government either as advisors or on secondment from their universities.[13] Entrants to this class may rise to become very top civil servants in the country, including the heads of particular government departments.

So I started to look at advertisements in the *The Economist* and the *Times Educational Supplement* for vacant assistant lectureships at UK universities. Nowadays, it would be unusual for anyone to apply for such a position without first acquiring a doctoral degree, but in the UK in the 1950s few university teachers in economics possessed such a qualification, and apart from Oxford, Cambridge and London, it was unusual for universities to offer doctoral training in that subject.

During the early summer of 1952, I applied for assistant lectureships at the universities of Liverpool, Bristol, and at Britain's newest campus at Keele in Staffordshire where Bruce Williams had just been appointed to the Chair of Economics. I was unsuccessful in each application. I began to look further afield, even applying for a lectureship in Adelaide, South Australia. Then, in July, I was asked to attend an interview at Southampton University.

I recall this occasion as if it was yesterday. The interview was in the afternoon, but I, along with other candidates, was asked to meet some of the Faculty at lunch. I arrived at the university, which had only just received its charter from the Queen,[14] at 11.30 a.m., and was shown to the Senior Common Room (SCR) where the aspiring appointees were assembled. It so happened that the Faculty of Social Science, in which the Department of Economics was housed, was seeking to make two appointments on that day – one in Economics and the other in Economic Statistics. As each new prospective applicant was ushered into the room in which we were asked to assemble, all those present hoped that he (and there were no shes!) was competing for the vacancy they were not! I quickly sized up the opposition, and identified my main competitor as a PhD from LSE. Indeed, I was quite depressed to find that all the other candidates for the Economics post had superior degree qualifications to my own.

Just as I was beginning to think I might as well go home, a small, wiry bespectacled man entered the SCR. 'I'm Ford,' he announced. 'Welcome to the university.' So Peter (Percy) Ford, Professor of Economics (and one-time Professor of Economics and Geography) and Dean of the Faculty of Social Science, took charge of the proceedings. He speedily took us to the Dining Room (everything Percy did was in quick time), where we were joined by Wallace Armstrong, the Senior Lecturer in Economics, and Clifford Thomas, Lecturer in Economic Statistics. The lunch proceeded with everyone being on his best behaviour – each of us not sure whether to open our mouth in case we said the wrong thing, or to keep quiet and be judged an uninteresting and/or ignorant person! I cannot remember much about the interview later in the afternoon, although I recall thinking on the train back to London that I had not done too badly! But I was still not optimistic I would be offered the job.

In the event, two days later a formal letter of appointment arrived from the Registrar of Southampton University. I was offered a three-year assistant lectureship at a salary of £500 a year rising by £50 a year. At the end of that time, provided I performed my duties satisfactorily, I might be promoted to Lecturer, in which case I would secure a tenured position.

Both Ida and I were delighted with the offer – she because, if I accepted it, we would be living just across the Solent from her parents on the Isle of Wight, and myself because I had liked what I saw of the university and the department. Also, the teaching I was being asked to do was exactly what I might have chosen for myself. To this day, I do not know why I was the preferred candidate. My hunch was that Percy Ford wanted to recruit an applied economist, and that my interests fitted in nicely with the needs of the department. In addition, I think the fact that I had already published an article, albeit in a bank review, seemed to appeal to him. In any event, in October 1952 I joined the Department of Economics as its fourth Faculty member. The third was Dick Hodgson who was a Lecturer in Commerce and Accounting. My half-century career as a university teacher had begun.

****

NOTES

1. In 1897 University College Reading, the precursor to the University of Reading, opened its doors as an Extension College of the University of Oxford. Already renowned as an agricultural college, by 1903, the new university college was organized into five disciplinary groups, namely Letters and Science, Agriculture, Horticulture, Fine Art and Music.

2. See Chapter 9.
3. The degree for which I was sitting was an Honours BSc(Econ). Successful candidates were classified into five categories, First, Upper Second, Lower Second, Third Class Honours and a Pass degree.
4. Although the performance in these papers did not count towards the classification of the final degree.
5. Our study was part of a larger programme sponsored by the Board of Trade, but supervised by NIESR. W.R. (Bill) Luttrell – who was then employed by NIESR, and who later set up his own consultancy company – was in charge of the study, and, in due course, he produced a two-volume work. Two additional case studies were delegated to UCL. G.C. Allen asked Douglas to be in charge of both of them.
6. D.C. Hague and J.H. Dunning, 'Costs in Alternative Locations: The Radio and Television Industry', *Review of Economic Studies*, **22**, 1954, 203–13.
7. As sparked off by the work of two Oxford Economists, R.L. Hall and C.J. Hitch in a classic article entitled 'Price Theory and Business Behaviour', published in *Oxford Economics Papers*, **1**(2), 1939, 12–45.
8. See his classic work *British Industry*, London, Longmans Green, 3rd edition, 1951.
9. A reading of his *Who Was Who* entry will give a snapshot of his illustrious academic career, his work in the Treasury as the government's Chief Economic Adviser, and his administrative duties as Master of St Peter's College, Oxford.
10. The most recent (in April 2007) being for Romanian television in Budapest.
11. Although two books – F. Mackenzie's *The American Invasion of Britain*, London, H.W. Bell, 1902 and R.H. Heindel's *The American Impact on Great Britain, 1898–1974*, Philadelphia, PA, University of Pennsylvania Press, 1940 had earlier addressed this subject.
12. The dress normally worn by managers and senior sales assistants at Harrods at that time.
13. On the other hand, as I shall describe in chapter 8, there is much more administration and completion of forms which university lecturers and professor have to put up with today than in the 1950s.
14. Having previously been a university college of the University of London. There were several other universities which attained independent status in the 1950s, and began offering their own degrees. These included Exeter, Hull, Leicester and Nottingham.

Part II: 1952–1987

Summer

5. 'Seeking the bubble reputation':[1] the Southampton years

In 1952, the city of Southampton was still recovering from the devastation caused by the German bombers a decade earlier. The centre of the city around the Bargate and the Town Wall – both of which date back to Roman times – was largely destroyed in a short series of concentrated raids. The port, however, which is one of the largest in the UK, and is the home terminal to the Cunard and Peninsular & Oriental (P&O) shipping lines, remained largely unscathed. The Cunard ship *Titanic* sailed from Southampton on its fateful voyage in 1912. In 1952, partly because of the rationing of foreign currency to the British traveller,[2] and partly because the liners such as *Queen Mary* were only then being decommissioned as troop ships, activity at the port was much subdued.

But, to me at any rate, Southampton was a delightful place in which to live. With a population of half a million people, it boasted some of the finest city parks in the country. Its new library and civic centre were the envy of many city planners. It was (and still is) the gateway to the New Forest, a vast and beautiful area of woodland and open countryside which was home to hundreds of ponies who had (and still have) right of way throughout most of the forest. It was home to a first-rate football team, and to the Hampshire Cricket Club. It was also only one and a half hours from London by express train.

The University of Southampton was located 1.5 miles north of the city. In contrast to many other provincial universities, the main campus was highly concentrated on just 37 acres of land. At the time of my arrival, there were fewer than 1000 students reading undergraduate degree courses, about one-half of whom were accommodated in three halls of residence within a mile or so distance from the campus.

****

After a two-month search, Ida and I moved to a pleasant bungalow in a suburb of Southampton. Although this initially meant a journey on two buses to the university, our new home, which I bought for £2500, overlooked the River Itchen and had a delightful landscaped rear garden backing on to woodland. I had no difficulty in getting a substantial mortgage on the property and, with an interest rate of 4 per cent, the monthly repayments were bearable – particularly once Ida had found acceptable secretarial work.

My office in the university was in a wooden single-storey building which used to be part of a military hospital erected in the 1914–18 war! During my initial academic year at the university, I was asked to teach a first-year economics course to students preparing for a Social Studies Diploma, and one-half of a second-year course in Applied Economics for BSc(Econ) students. The following year, I also taught a third-year Honours course in Advanced Microeconomics. This I particularly enjoyed, as the small number of students on the course allowed me to conduct it as if it were a graduate seminar.

In the 1950s, the public's perception of a (male) university lecturer was largely that of a bespectacled, bookish and absent-minded individual who was normally dressed in a crumpled sports jacket and corduroy trousers! Occasionally, however, it was appreciated that an eminent don might catch the ear of a senior politician or businessman. Such a caricature is frequently to be found in the writings of Evelyn Waugh, C.P. Snow, P.G. Wodehouse and C.S. Lewis. However, this image was shattered by Kingsley Amis in his novel *Lucky Jim*, which was published in 1954; and also by the grant of a charter to several technical or university colleges in the 1950s, and the setting up of a new batch of universities in the 1960s.[3]

It is, of course, perfectly true that some university teachers still fit the public stereotype; and certainly many academics are firmly ensconced in their own ivory towers. But, increasingly, dons are involving themselves in the political, financial or commercial arena. And rarely indeed is an historical or current affairs programme now aired on UK television without some academic specialist being invited to participate. Certainly the twenty-first-century university lecturer is, I think, more realistically portrayed in the novels of Malcolm Bradbury and David Lodge; and by TV presenters such as David Starkey, Simon Schama and Niall Ferguson.

Most of my academic colleagues, friends and acquaintances do not think of me as a typical university don. Neither, for that matter, do I! It is true that my mainstream career has been almost exclusively that of an academic, although I must admit that when I first became a university teacher I had no aspirations of becoming a university professor. By nature, I am a gradualist and an incrementalist; and this was confirmed by an Indian phrenologist in the 1980s, who predicted I would have a steady but increasingly distinguished career!

At the same time, I like to think that I have always had my feet firmly placed in the real world. I greatly enjoy consulting with both business and international organizations, and with governments. Yet, I am sure that had I pursued a career in the commercial world, I would not have had the killer instinct to get to the top.

The fact is that a UK university don's life is very much as he chooses to make it – or at least it used to be. Right up to the 1980s the life of the UK university lecturer was a very pleasant and protected one. Once he or she had tenure – usually after three years as an assistant lecturer – he (or she) could do as much or as little research as he (or she) pleased. This is no longer the case. In the harsher and more competitive world of the early twenty-first century, much more is expected of a university don, including a respectable publications record. Moreover, relative to most other professional occupations, the annual salary of the university teacher is considerably lower than once it was. When I entered the academic world, a university professor earned about the same amount as a senior civil servant, middle manager, doctor or barrister. Today, apart from a few eminent scholars and senior teachers in the leading business schools, most academics earn about one-half to two-thirds the salary of those in other professions. At the same time, an increasing amount of a lecturer's time (and even more so that of a professor) is taken up by administration, committee meetings and form-filling, for which he (or she) has had no formal training or preparation. Even with modern computers, emails and text management, my guess is that the average twenty-first-century university don spends less time teaching and tutoring his or her students, and engaging in research, than his (or her) counterpart 50 years earlier!

It is a fact that much of the distinctiveness and glamour of university life has disappeared. I do not know that, if I were 50 years younger, I would wish to enter the profession. Indeed, in my area, I doubt whether I would have the technical skills now demanded of a young lecturer!

****

In the 1950s I continued to pursue my writing and research interests. As a by-product of my work at UCL I wrote two more articles on the radio and television industry, and two others – both of which were published in the *Manchester School of Economic and Social Studies* – on the changing industrial structure and employment in development areas. But it was the publication of my *Manchester Guardian* article on 'American Factories in Britain' which attracted the most interest, and directly led to the next stage of my research.

****

About a week after my article in the *Manchester Guardian*'s Survey of Industry was published, I was telephoned by a Frances Rogers of the American Embassy in London who asked me to come and talk with him about my work. It transpired that Rogers was in charge of the allocation of a post-war US economic aid programme to the UK, which was part of the Marshall Plan.[4] As an offshoot of this programme, some funds had been set aside for the financing of research into ways in which the UK's industrial productivity might be upgraded. Over the previous two years, a series of Anglo-American teams had studied the comparative performance of firms in the UK and the US in a variety of industries. In his summary of the findings, Graham Hutton – a well-known economics commentator – showed that, on average, US industrial productivity was twice to two and a half times higher than that of the UK.[5]

Frances Rogers asked me if I would be interested in conducting a study of the extent to which, and the ways in which, US direct investment in British manufacturing industry may have aided UK economic performance. I replied that I would. However, I pointed out that since there was very little published information on the subject, a project of this kind could only be undertaken by new and extensive field research. As I would not have the time to visit all of the American subsidiaries myself, I would need funds for a research assistant for at least two years. A programme was mapped out and agreed, and in September 1953 I began the research project.

I appointed a New Zealander, Arnold McKern, to be my research assistant, and between us over the next two years we interviewed 205 of the estimated 240 US manufacturing affiliates then operating in the UK. Over the subsequent half-century I have conducted several research projects, but only in one other case, which I shall describe in Chapter 7, have I had such a high positive response rate to a request for information. I think this was partly because many of the firms had not previously been the subject for investigation; and partly because I was not asking for particularly confidential information. Indeed, most managers of the US subsidiaries were only too pleased to give data on the way in which they believed their presence had helped the post-war recovery of the UK's manufacturing machine.

Besides providing the first account of the extent, pattern and organizational structure of US-owned firms in the UK, my research was directed to identifying and explaining any productivity differences between the affiliates and their parent companies. I then attempted to see how far these differences were due to the location of their value-added activities, and how far to the nationality of ownership of such activities. To do this, it was also necessary to compare the productivity of the US affiliates with that of their main UK competitors. I next went on to estimate the extent to which, by transferring new technologies, management capabilities and a more entrepreneurial culture, these affiliates affected the productivity of other UK firms, for example their suppliers, competitors and industrial customers. Although the results varied between sectors, it was clear that a significant part of the productivity differences between the two groups of firms reflected the superior management characteristics of US-owned firms, even if part of these reflected the location-specific resources and capabilities of the US economy.

The concepts used in this first major piece of research formed the basis of much of my later work on the determinants and effects of foreign direct investment and of multinational enterprise (MNE) activity throughout the world. I have always asserted that the distinction between the (largely) mobile competences and technologies of firms, and that of the (largely) immobile indigenous resources, institutions and government policies of the countries in which they operate, is of critical importance. I would further aver that such a distinction helps us to identify whether inward investment reflects the relatively greater efficiency of foreign-owned, compared with UK-owned firms, or the attractions of the UK relative to those of another country as a location for value-adding activities.

The research also emphasized the importance of the spin-off effects of foreign investment. Thirty years after writing *American Investment in British Manufacturing Industry* I undertook a similar study on Japanese participation in UK industry. Apart from underpinning the earlier investigation with a stronger analytical base, the conclusions were broadly the same. The main benefits of inward investment were: first, the access offered to the host country of new technologies, managerial and marketing capabilities and markets, together with the generally more efficient deployment of resources and capabilities created or acquired by the foreign affiliates themselves; and second, the transfer and diffusion of foreign knowledge, skills, managerial attitudes and entrepreneurship to their indigenous competitors, suppliers and customers. Of course, there were (or often are) some downsides to inward investment, but these I only fully appreciated – not to mention how they might best be minimized – when I later became involved in working for the United Nations in the 1970s.

****

American Investment in British Manufacturing Industry was published by Allen & Unwin on my thirty-first birthday in 1958, and it was the topic of the leading article in the financial section of *The Times* on that date. The reviews of the book in the *Financial Times*, *The Economist*, and later academic journals were generally most favourable. But perhaps more significantly, my interest in the topic of foreign direct investment (FDI) had been so stimulated that I decided to undertake a study of the extent and impact of the reverse flow of FDI across the Atlantic, namely, British investment in North America. To that end, I secured a two-year research grant from the Rockefeller Foundation, which enabled me to visit all the leading UK-owned factories both in Canada and the US, and so prompted my first trip abroad since 1945. In October 1960, I sailed from Southampton to Montreal armed with a brand new UK passport – on a ship of the Holland America line, *Ryndam*. So began the first of my 100 or so visits to the North American continent.

****

I must own that, as far as most things in my life are concerned, I am fairly opportunistic! As my research into *American Investment* proceeded, I thought, why not submit a version of the final report I was preparing for Francis Rogers for a PhD degree in Southampton? This, in fact, I did, and was fortunate to have my former Professor – G.C. Allen – as my external examiner. I received my degree from the Duke of Wellington at a ceremony in the Southampton Guildhall in July 1957. I was delighted not only for myself, but also for my parents. Many years earlier, my Uncle Tom had read Economics for his undergraduate degree at Glasgow University, and had then secured a PhD in Theology. I think it had always saddened my mother that my father had not obtained a degree (why I do not know – except it was the exception rather than the rule for Spurgeon College students to register for London external degrees in the 1910s). In some odd way, I felt I had now at least partly balanced the academic books between the two branches of the Dunning family.

The 1950s saw my streak of opportunism emerging in another way. Earlier I had developed my Applied Economics course at Southampton on the basis of G.C. Allen's classic text *British Industries and their Organization*, but I soon discovered that a rather different tack to analysing the fast-moving developments in UK industry was needed. My own approach was more issue-based, and sought to describe and explain the main driving forces behind the economic and technological restructuring of British industry in the 1950s. Together with a colleague, Cliff Thomas – who was an erstwhile scientist particularly interested in innovations in the energy and chemical sectors – I wrote up the lectures for publication. *British Industry* was published in 1961.[6] The book was well received. One reviewer wrote: 'This book will take its place as one of the main works in its field. It is a good general textbook that comes from attention that it gives to technological change and its effects on the economy' (*Economic Journal*).

The book was later revised and reprinted as one of a Hutchinson University Library series in 1963, but neither Cliff or I were tempted to do further revisions.

****

Outside my teaching and research activities, I played only a limited role in the administrative affairs of the Faculty or the university. I must admit I have always found most university meetings and committees excruciatingly tedious. This may be because rarely did anyone seem to agree with, or take notice of, what I had to say; or because of the triviality – even banality – of most issues which seemed to absorb the time and attention of so many university dons. So, to the undoubted relief of my colleagues, I used to keep my opinions and advice largely to myself. There were a few exceptions however. Jointly with David Rowan who succeeded Percy Ford on his retirement as Dean of the Faculty of Social Sciences at Southampton University, I devised a completely new system for classifying Honours degrees in the Social Sciences. It was warmly accepted, and proved so successful that when I moved to Reading some years later, I introduced it there too.

Like other young university lecturers in the 1950s – and I guess in the 2000s for that matter – I needed to supplement my university salary. As already indicated, my starting annual income at Southampton was £500, about the same as that then being earned by a bank clerk, a coal miner and a secondary school teacher. At the time, there were three main ways in which I could supplement my income. The first and easiest was by marking A level school certificate examinations, or university degree scripts. The second was by writing for the popular press and for some quasi-scholarly journals, for example the *Bank Reviews*; and the third was by extramural lecturing. Contrary to the situation today, the opportunities for consultancy in the 1950s and early 1960s were very limited indeed.

I resorted to each of these routes for earning income. Indeed marking 200–300 GCE Economics scripts each July for about five years, regularly paid for our annual holiday; while a fee of 15 guineas for a 2000-word article in the *Financial Times* or 50 guineas for a 5000-word contribution to the *National Provincial Bank Review* was usually set aside to buy a piece of equipment or furniture for our home.

In the 1950s, extramural lecturing fell into two main categories. One was a presentation at a business conference for which one was paid quite handsomely – even though sometimes the payment was in kind. I well recall a trip to Paris in the early 1960s to give a lecture to the Young Presidents' Association,[7] when for the first time I travelled first class by aeroplane, and was housed at the King George V hotel in Paris. While I enjoyed a glimpse of how the other half lived, I was never tempted to leave academic life for a business vocation. Indeed, it was not long before I found out that, if one was astute enough, it was possible to have the best of both worlds. The secret, I discovered, was to direct one's research efforts to subject areas the results of which were likely to have some commercial as well as academic interest. Throughout my career I have always been extremely careful not to undertake any consultancy or commercial writing unless it was directly relevant to, and helped advance, scholarly research interests. And I am sure those nearest and dearest to me would agree that if my extramural activities were at the cost of anything, it was of my leisure and personal life.

But most of my extramural lecturing took the form of evening classes in economics at Southampton Technical College, and giving courses for the Workers' Educational Association (WEA). While the former involved a similar pedagogy to that which I was involved in my everyday teaching, the latter required a very different approach. This was most forcibly brought home to me on two occasions. The first was when, during one of the courses, a Nottingham miner continually made it known that he thought the whole of economics, as traditionally taught, was absolute nonsense. The second was on one Saturday afternoon following the 1955 Budget statement in the House of Commons, when I travelled to Fareham (about 20 miles east of Southampton) to review the content of the Chancellor of the Exchequer's statement, to a specially convened WEA seminar. I thought I had done my homework quite well and was looking forward to a stimulating couple of hours. I was soon to be disillusioned. My audience consisted of one middle-aged postman and four elderly ladies, one of whom throughout my talk did not put down her knitting or raise her head until it was time (which could not come too soon for me) for tea. Try as I would, I could not raise any real interest or enthusiasm in my small audience, as was particularly well demonstrated by the few questions I was asked at the conclusion of my talk, none of which had anything to do with the Budget, or indeed anything to do with the British economy!

****

As already indicated, my visit to North America in the autumn of 1960 was only the second time I had been abroad, the first being at His Majesty's expense in 1945. The transatlantic voyage was quite smooth and I particularly enjoyed sailing up the St Lawrence River to dock at Montreal – the Paris of North America and the largest city in Canada – on a warm September morning. For my time in the city, I stayed at the University Club of McGill University, from which I set out each day to interview the chief executives of two or three manufacturing subsidiaries of UK firms. Between them, the Canadian provinces of Ontario and Quebec were host to 70 per cent of UK-owned manufacturing establishments in Canada in 1960.

Over the two weekends I was there, I also took the first of many Gray Line Tours I have since taken in Canada and the US. I discovered that Montreal is a thriving and attractive city, which successfully combines the best in Anglo-French living styles and cultures. To the south of its modern downtown area is the St Lawrence River which flows 3800 kilometres from Lake Superior in the US to the Atlantic Ocean. To the north lies the national park of Mount Royal which rises to 650 feet. At its peak overlooking the city and the river is the impressive Cross of Jacques Cartier (the French explorer who first visited Montreal in 1535), which at night is spectacularly illuminated by 850 lights.

From Montreal, I travelled on the Canadian Pacific railroad to Ottawa. I remember Canada's capital city mainly for its gracious Parliament buildings, which could have been transplanted *in toto* from Aberdeen or Edinburgh; for its series of seven stepped locks; for the pageantry I witnessed one Sunday outside the Houses of Parliament commemorating the Battle of Britain; and for the capital's most beautiful parks and tree-lined residential areas.

Toronto was, and still is, the most cosmopolitan of Canadian cities. It is certainly the one most influenced by the culture of its southern neighbour. In 1960, about 60 per cent of the manufacturing output of the region was accounted for by US-owned firms, while the region was also host to the largest concentration of UK manufacturing affiliates in Canada. Here, I gained a first-hand impression of the challenges and opportunities faced by such UK companies as Peak Freans, Yardley, Dunlop, Cadbury, and Albright & Wilson; and of why over one-third of the companies I visited had recorded low profits or losses over the past five years. Poor management, insufficient appreciation of the character and demands of the Canadian market, an unwillingness to adapt UK production or organizational practices to local requirements, an underestimation of the intra-firm transaction costs of operating a subsidiary 3500 miles away from home, and an inability of many affiliates to attain the most economic size of production, were the most frequent reasons given for the disappointing performance of several UK firms.[8]

****

During my time in Toronto, I lived at the home of Dr Emlyn Davies, a long-standing friend of my father, who at the time was Minister of York Minster Baptist Church, one of the largest churches in Toronto.

Being used to attending a new and small suburban Baptist church in Southampton, the experience of worshipping in a cathedral-like sanctuary seating 2000 people, with a processing and splendidly robed choir of 75 – not to mention ushers formally attired in black dress coats – was quite overwhelming! But the hospitality of the Davies household was anything but overwhelming – except perhaps in its generosity. I celebrated my first American Thanksgiving (Canadian-style) dinner of turkey and pumpkin pie with the family and their friends; and the following day I was driven 120 miles to the US border where I caught my first glimpse of the magnificent Niagara Falls. Being transported in a large air-conditioned American car and motoring on an eight-lane freeway was just one of many differences I experienced between everyday living in Canada and England. The supermarkets, the skyscrapers, the enthusiasm and ready friendship of the Canadian people, the gadgetry in their homes, the sense of space – both in cities and the country, the size and content of the Sunday newspapers, and the generally poor quality of North American television, were other differences I found particularly noticeable. No less novel or exciting to me was to watch my first ice hockey match. Never before had I appreciated that it was such an exciting, fast-moving, aggressive and even dangerous sport!

****

In early November 1960 I entered the US by train, crossing the 49th parallel at Buffalo. On my way south to New York I visited the EMI factory at Scranton – a rather depressed and depressing coal mining city in Pennsylvania. EMI's investment in the US was a fairly recent one. It had bought out a defunct American company, together with its recording rights. I then experienced my first meal on an American train, which I ate while passing through the scenery of the Allegheny Mountains and the Delaware valley. My first sight of the Manhattan skyline came in the early evening of a beautiful November day as the train trundled its way across the New Jersey marshlands before descending into the tunnel on its approach to Penn Street at 34th Street.

Many of the large UK companies had (and still have) their US offices in New York City – more often than not in one of the large skyscraper buildings on Park or Madison Avenues. A first-time visitor in 1960 could not fail to be impressed with the sights and sounds of the 'Big Apple'; and during my few days in the city, I took in most of the familiar tourist attractions, as well as attending one of New York's famous nonconformist churches on Riverside, the Minister of which was one of the then giants of the Christian church – Henry Emerson Fosdick. I also visited a dozen or so

UK factories in upstate New York and in New Jersey, before making a short trip to Washington, where I spent three days as a tourist!

From Washington, I boarded the first commercial air flight of my life to Cincinnati, Ohio where I was to give a seminar at the University of Cincinnati. I remember this visit not only for the seminar, but for the fact that later the same evening I watched one of the most historical debates ever shown on US television. This was between the two contenders for the American presidency in 1960 – John Kennedy and Richard Nixon. I was also in the US on election day, and as the results came in from the various states it became clear that the final outcome could go either way. In the event, the contest which Kennedy won was one of the closest in US electoral history.

****

I sailed home from New York on a crisp but fine December evening. My trip home was on the (original) *Queen Elizabeth*, which at that time was the largest passenger ship in the world. Though the Atlantic Ocean produced some of its roughest seas, the Queen's newly fitted stabilizers lessened the worst of the rolling. I arrived in Southampton a week before Christmas, and after clearing customs took a taxi back home.

To this day, it is one of the greatest regrets that I did not complete a book setting out the detailed findings of my field study of over 150 UK subsidiaries in Canada and the US.[9] In retrospect, I believe I made a misjudgement of priorities. In 1961, the spring term was an exceptionally busy one at Southampton University as I had to make up for the lecturing I had missed earlier in the academic year. I then became involved with the Basingstoke project I have already described; and by the time I returned to review my North American data, they had become rather dated. But my research assistant Terry Coram and I did write up some of the history of UK direct investment in the US,[10] while I produced several articles summarizing my conclusions on the extent, pattern and performance of British firms in Canada and the US in the period 1955–60.[11] My findings – that UK firms were, all too frequently, unprofitable and mismanaged – caused quite a stir in the British daily press; one immediate outcome of which was that I was invited to appear on the *Tonight* programme, a nightly television news programme transmitted by the BBC. It was my first TV broadcast, and I quite relished the experience. Geoffrey Johnson Smith was a sympathetic, yet penetrating interviewer, and our allotted six minutes quickly sped by. I do not think I made many friends in British business that evening. In fact, it was the beginning of a rather cool relationship with chief executives of UK firms. This lasted until 1973 when, at that date, as I shall describe in the next chapter, I was appointed as the UK representative to an important UN committee set up to examine the contribution of MNEs to economic development. Suddenly, the doors of British boardrooms became open to me.

As a postscript to the events just described, in 2004 I was invited by Geoffrey Jones, then at Reading University, to contribute a chapter to a book he and Lina Galvez-Munoz were writing on the history of foreign direct investment in the US. I decided, there and then, to revisit the data I had collected 40 years ago, and analyse them in the light of contemporary scholarly thinking. The result was, I think, that the chapter gave a more detailed and rigorous account of the determinants and impact of UK FDI in US manufacturing than what I originally wrote in 1961.[12]

****

Later, in 1962, David Rowan and I were commissioned by the National Economic Development Office (NEDO), a new think-tank set up by the UK Labour government, to undertake two studies. The first was to compare various measures of the efficiency of US-owned subsidiaries in the UK with that of their UK competitors in the period 1958–61. Our results, which were first published in a leading Italian applied economics journal *Banco Nazionale del Lavoro Quarterly Review*,[13] largely confirmed other findings at this time.[14] However, I think the distinctive feature of our own work was that we compiled a new measure of total productivity, which included an estimate of the opportunity cost of capital. We also computed four separate definitions of assets in estimating the comparative profitability of US- and UK-owned firms – data for which were obtained from published sources.

The second study NEDO commissioned from David and myself was to examine the extent, pattern and trends of British direct investment in continental Europe, using both published data and that obtained by interviewing a sample of UK investing multinational enterprises. This study, following my own on British firms in North America, was prompted by the increasing concern of certain sections of the Labour Government about the relatively low rates of return earned by British firms on their foreign direct investments, and their possible adverse affects on the home country's balance of payments. Our own findings, a condensed version of which was published in the *Banco Nazionale del Lavoro Quarterly Review* (**84**, June 1965, pp. 3–32), although lending some support to these concerns, also showed that part of the poor profit performance of UK investors was due to high start-up costs; and also that few of the British firms regretted their decision to enter the European Economic Community which the UK joined in January 1973.

I was fortunate to have David Rowan collaborating with me on both these projects. Along with his considerable charisma and his relaxed and friendly stance, he had one of the most perceptive and logical minds I have ever come across. It was by the deployment of his intellectual talents and organizational skills that he, and his distinguished colleague Ivor Pearce, both enlarged and upgraded the calibre of the Economics Faculty at the University of Southampton. Indeed, by the 1970s it was one of the most highly regarded departments of economics in the UK.

****

In October 1962 I was promoted to Senior Lecturer at the university. The extra salary was welcome as Ida and I had earlier moved from our bungalow in Bitterne to a larger house about a mile away which we had built for us. After the very sad and early death of our first child, Judith, who lived just 48 hours, Philip was born at Southampton Hospital in January 1957. Two years later, we sold our bungalow (for £2400 – £100 less than we paid for it – no house price inflation in the 1950s!) and purchased a new house for £4250. To finance the purchase, I not only had to sell my car, but also had to take out a mortgage five times my yearly income. However, I did so knowing full well that guaranteed increments in my salary, plus my extra income from university examining commitments and publications, would make the repayments bearable. In October 1959 we moved into our new home, backing onto woodland and with distant views of Southampton Airport, and I immediately set about creating a new garden.

****

My everyday life was little touched by the events of the 1950s and 1960s. But it might well have been. The confrontation between the US and Russian presidents at the time of the Cuban Missile Crisis in the autumn of 1962 was in danger of accelerating into a nuclear war. Such a catastrophe was eventually avoided by Nikita Khrushchev agreeing to dismantle the Russian-controlled missile base[15] in Cuba. Almost as traumatic – at least it seemed so at the time – was the assassination of John Kennedy in Dallas in November 1963. I remember the occasion vividly, as the UK TV programmes were being interrupted to break this tragic news. Rather more welcome events in the 1950s included the first scaling of Mount Everest by Edmund Hillary and Sherpa Tenzing Norgay just three days before the Coronation of Queen Elizabeth II on 2nd June 1953. A year later, in April 1954, Roger Bannister became the first man to run the mile under four minutes; while in April 1961 the

Russian astronaut Yuri Gagarin completed the first manned flight into space and back.

Nearer to my own professional interests, the European Economic Community (EEC) came into effect on 1st January 1958; while in December of that year, and for the first time since 1939, the partial convertibility of the British pound and the US dollar was announced. In October 1963, the report by Lord Robbins and his Committee on 'The Future of Higher Education in the UK' was published.[16] *Inter alia*, it recommended the setting up of a number of *de novo* universities, and that, in most existing universities, more resources should be allocated to promoting teaching and research in the Social Sciences. Little did I know at that time, but the implementation of this latter recommendation by a newly elected Labour government, led by Harold Wilson, was to have a significant impact on the path of my own career.

****

NOTES

1. William Shakespeare's fourth age of man, *As You Like It*, Act II, scene 7.
2. £100 a year in 1952.
3. Altogether 15 new universities were created in this period. For 30 or so years following the 1960s there were 45 universities in the UK. Then in the 1990s, this number was doubled, and in 2007 there were 92 universities.
4. The Marshall Plan, named after the wartime General George Marshall, Chief of Staff of the US Army, was intended to help Europe in its economic reconstruction and was initiated in June 1947, and between that date and 1952, $12 billion was pumped into various European economies.
5. *We Too Can Prosper*, London: Allen & Unwin, 1953.
6. Longmans, Green & Co., London, 1951 (third edition).
7. An association of presidents of US companies all of whom were under the age of 40.
8. Further data are recorded in Chapters 5 and 6 of my volume *Studies in International Investment*, London, Allen & Unwin, 1970.
9. In more recent times business historians, notably Mira Wilkins and Tony Corley, have made use of the interwar data I collected.
10. See also his 1967 Reading MSc (Econ) thesis, *The Role of British Investment in the Development of the United States* (unpublished).
11. See again various chapters in *Studies in International Investment*.
12. *Moorgate and Wall Street*, Autumn 1961, 5–23.
13. Reprinted in 1970 as Chapter 9 of my *Studies in International Investment*, pp. 345–400.
14. For example in eight of the industrial sectors we studied, the total productivity of US affiliates in 1961 was greater than that of UK firms, when the opportunity cost of the invested capital was measured as the average rate of return earned by UK firms. Moreover, the profit–capital ratios of US affiliates over the period 1958 to 1961 was higher than that of UK public companies in all industrial sectors except that of textiles and clothing.
15. The particular concern of the Americans was that these missiles were directly aimed at the US. The US responded by placing a naval blockade around Cuba which was lifted on 28 September 1962.
16. Cmnd 2154 HMSO.

6. Towards summer: a personal moment

Every so often in my life I have asked myself such questions as, 'What is it all about, then?' 'What is the purpose of my life?' 'What is – who is – God?' 'Is religion the cause or the cure of the world's social and other problems?' In posing these and similar questions, I am sure I am not alone; although I do not think many people willingly acknowledge that they are spiritual animals! Most either avoid, or rarely think about, the fundamental issues of life. Yet, we are witness to these all the time. Events, and people's response to these, constantly demonstrate and remind us of the complexity of our existence. On the one hand are natural disasters, abject poverty, disease and unspeakable violence. On the other, we see amazing demonstrations of courage, love and compassion. We are compelled to think beyond ourselves and our physical environment.

Perhaps we can never know – or indeed are never meant to know – the full answers to these questions, and, as the Apostle Paul wrote long ago, are only allowed to see through 'a glass darkly'.[1] But I like to believe that if we seek long and earnestly, the veil of understanding will be lifted sufficiently for each of us to draw upon just that amount of help and guidance in how best to conduct our lives, and to do so in a meaningful and worthwhile fashion.

Yes, I believe in God as a transcendent being; and I do so simply because, to me at any rate, the logic, evidence and experience of countless millions of people who across the ages have taken the grand leap of faith is more persuasive than that which denies altogether the existence of a supreme being. At the same time, I accept that our human language can never adequately describe or articulate the concept of a supreme supernatural being. I also believe in a personal God in the sense that the perception of any individual about God and his revealed nature is an intensely personal thing. I would, however, aver that the critical characteristics of God such as love, compassion and justice were supremely expressed in the life and death of Jesus Christ. Even accepting man's evolving concept of God, the fact there is so much love and compassion in the hearts of men and women, coupled with the strong sense of justice and fairness, convinces me that any entity we choose to call God must not only possess but be the original source of these characteristics.

What then of the presence of so much which is – and has always been – unlovely, unfair and unjust in this world? Here logic takes me less far towards an answer – and it is at this point that I need more trust to accept that my God is at one and the same time both all-loving and omnipotent. I must admit that the age-old conundrum, God is either 'all-loving but limited in power' or 'all-powerful but limited in love', is highly persuasive.

The answer of the Christian faith to this conundrum is, I think, twofold. The first is that there is an Anti-God or an Antichrist force at work in the world. For myself, although this is a more cogent alternative to imputing such evil to God himself, I have never fathomed out the existence or character of Satan or the Devil, as this seemed to involve an even more obscure theology than that which debates the existence and nature of God. The second answer is that, although God has created man in his own image, he has also given him a freedom to choose in his beliefs and actions. By definition, this freedom implies that it is possible for him to make not only wrong, but also unlovely choices. While this may not matter in cases where the choice may be the lesser of two goods, in others it may be quite critical and have disastrous consequences not only for the person making the decision, but often for many other people as well. I think, for example, of the devastating effects of the evil choices of some of the world's modern tyrants such as Adolf Hitler, Joseph Stalin, Idi Amin and Saddam Hussein.

I think most people would agree that the majority of the troubles of our contemporary world are man (or woman) made. Most of us, too, accept the notion of the presence of both good and evil. Fewer, however, agree on the reasons for good and bad actions, and right or wrong decisions. At the one extreme there are those who believe in kismet, or that man is a creature of his nurturing and environment and has either no or limited responsibility for his actions. At the other extreme are those who believe that man is wholly responsible for his actions – and must be held accountable for them. For my part, I find that the truth is somewhere between these extremes. I strongly believe that many of the world's ills could be cured, or at least considerably ameliorated, if man chose differently. But right and good choices do not come naturally. Man must be taught to choose sensibly and be motivated to do so. And I believe that God has pointed the way to do just this – to which I shall return later.

****

Yet, even acknowledging that many of life's tragedies can be put down to ill-judged choices and unlovely acts by men and women, it is still difficult to reconcile the concept of a loving God with the kind of natural catastrophes and much personal suffering which we read about in our daily newspapers. From major disasters such as earthquakes, typhoons, floods, drought and avalanches which impinge upon the lives of hundreds or thousands of people, to those affecting just a single individual – micro tragedies such as a deformed baby, a terminal illness striking a young teenager, the murder of an innocent bystander to a crime, the terrible suffering often attached to so many diseases – how, we ask, can a loving God allow, let alone cause, such happenings?

The only honest answer is that we don't know, and perhaps we will never know! This is where, I believe, a healthy agnosticism is needed. If God has created this earth for our fulfilment and enjoyment – yet not to get too attached to, as our lifespan here is limited (why I don't know!) – it is surely no less true that he has given each of us just enough mental and spiritual capabilities to comprehend His nature and wishes for us, and in doing so to take the leap of faith which both stifles many of our worst fears, doubts and anxieties, and gives us an understanding of those things which are beyond the realm of (but not contradictory to) logic and reason.

One thing, however, seems clear to me. That is that the Christian gospel does not promise any of its followers an easy or stress-free life. The fact that some men and women are blessed with good health, a comfortable lifestyle, intelligence and curiosity, and loving relationships, and others are not, is another mystery. But it has nothing to do with whether or not an individual embraces the Christian faith. What the faith does promise – although this may be little comfort to those who feel they cannot accept it – is that in some mysterious way God, through the spirit of Jesus Christ, is with us (or can be called upon to be with us) in all our earthly experiences, good or bad; and that it is not so much the events and relationships which befall us which count, but what our attitude and response to these events and relationships is.

****

I have spent a few pages presenting my personal view of what I believe is one of the greatest hurdles to the concept of a benevolent Deity. In some ways, it is remarkable not that there are so few people who believe in such a God, but that so many *do* so! But, the fact that ever since man first walked the earth there have been a multitude of adherents testifying to the power of love over evil – and that love is indeed the core and radiating force of God's essential being.

There is, however, a second great mystery which is a particular stumbling block to those who might otherwise wish to embrace the Christian faith. Most people who know about the events in Palestine 2000 years ago accept Jesus as a historical figure. Most other religious teachings too – including Islam and Judaism – have little difficulty in placing Jesus on a similar footing as the other great religious preachers and prophets. Most Western culture – implicitly or explicitly – is strongly influenced by the Christian ideology. Many individuals, too, base their own values and behavioural patterns on the principles Jesus affirmed in His various teachings, and the compassion he displayed towards the less fortunate members of society, and His emphasis on the need for social justice.

Fewer, but still many, people believe that Jesus was in some sense different from any other human being who has lived, and that during his lifetime he was able to perform many miracles.[2] A smaller number of people believe in the literal truth of the Resurrection of Jesus, although again the acknowledgement of a presence which *seems* real is by no means unfamiliar, to even the most sceptical of non-believers!

But to my mind, the greatest mystery of all is what occurred at the time of Pentecost, six weeks after the Resurrection, and what, according to the Christian faith, continually happens today. Put in simple terms, the idea is that it is possible for the spirit of Jesus Christ to dwell in our own hearts, minds and souls and so help us to think and behave in a Christ-like way. Now, in the case of some individuals, this may come close to their natural disposition or way of behaving. But for most of us, it is a case of 'being born again'.[3] I like to think that there is a spark of the divine in each one of us, although in some people it may appear nearer the surface than in others. When that divine spark is nurtured by love, learning, the example of others and good experiences, it can begin to dominate our lives. The act of becoming a Christian, however, I believe, needs a conscious acknowledgement of a direct channel of communication between that divine spark and its source.

Again, to a certain extent, each of us is influenced in our attitudes and conduct by those – our families, friends and acquaintances – who cross our lives. How often does one come across someone saying, 'I feel I should not do this because my dead mother [or husband, son, and so on] would not wish it', or going beyond this to: 'I feel my mother's spirit comforting me or pointing me to this or that decision or course of action.' Extend this to the spirit of Jesus Christ, and you have a potent force for good, which I do not believe any other religion has claimed or pretends to claim. In that way, and in a very real sense, a Christian becomes a disciple of Christ within the confines of time and space in which he is placed. This is, in essence, the practice of the Christian virtues which not only Christians, but other religious denominations so highly endorse.

****

My Christian beliefs certainly underpin many of my attitudes and actions in life. Of course, I readily admit that I have failed to live up to these beliefs on numerous occasions. I also appreciate that not always are my values necessarily endorsed by other Christians – let alone to those of other faiths. I, for example, am a strong opponent of capital punishment, but I know many of my fellow Christians uphold it. On the other hand, I do accept the justification for going to war in some circumstances, and that the killing of a person may be the least bad choice. On almost any social or political issue it is quite possible – and indeed acceptable – that equally devout Christians may hold different views.

Similarly, one should not expect Christians to interpret the two golden commands of Christ – to love God and love one's neighbour as oneself – in exactly the same way. I think it was Bernard Shaw who once said that loving your neighbour as you love yourself may not always be appropriate when they have different tastes to your own.[4] Shaw also made the point that embracing the Christian faith does not necessarily turn an unlikeable person into a likeable person – though it might help! Neither does the practice of the fruits of the spirit so eloquently affirmed by St Paul to the Corinthian church[5] mean that you actually have to like everyone you meet. Even Jesus sometimes preferred the company of non-religious people; although this did not stop him from desiring, and where possible doing, the best for even his enemies. Christian love is not primarily concerned with inherited attitudes or social mores, but rather with conducting one's relationships with each person one meets as if both you and they were Christ; in other words, with his or her physical and spiritual well-being in mind.

The Christian has several guideposts as to how he should behave in this world. The Bible is one of these. In my younger days, I used to get very excited in debates about the Bible as a factually correct historical record. At the time, I failed, as I think many people continue to fail, to understand the difference between literal and symbolic truth, between facts and legends, and between actuality and images – each of which may be designed to illustrate reality. It is also necessary to consider the Bible as a whole, and the story it tells of the evolution in the spirituality of mankind, within the context of a particular culture, time and space. *Inter alia*, this is why I find it completely unacceptable for a leader of any advanced democratic and Christian country to seek to impose their twenty-first century values and institutions on less-developed nations with completely different forms of government, ideologies and social mores. Today, I do not really worry about whether there were actually two people called Adam and Eve; whether the Big Bang theory of creation invalidates the story of Genesis; whether Jesus did turn water into wine or walk on the sea; or whether at Pentecost, those present actually spoke in foreign tongues or not! To me the whole purpose of the Bible is lost if it is treated exclusively as factual history. Essentially it is a narrative of man's unfolding understanding and relationship with a transcendent God. It is told by men and women who, insofar as their knowledge allowed, believed passionately that they were close to a supreme being; and were inspired by their communion with Him. They were also fallible human beings; and in the Bible, while an unfolding view of the majesty, justice and love of God comes shining through, one also sees the prejudices, deceit and downright wickedness of man.

Nevertheless, the good book has stood the test of time well; and the New Testament remains not only one of the best-loved stories which has ever been told, but, in my opinion, offers one of the best templates of how best to live one's life, and to do so to the full. That is the core of the biblical message; the poetry, allegory, imagery and vision are all bonuses, but each needs to be placed carefully in the particular situation in which they were written, and by whom, why and for whom they were written.

The task of the Christian in the world is, and always has been, a delicate balancing act. He must be fully involved in the world; and yet his first allegiance is to the teachings of Jesus Christ. He must display the ideals, dedication and enthusiasm of Christ, but not aggressively. He must be God-like without being pious. He must love, try to understand, and show tolerance to all men and women; yet he must be uncompromising in his stand against everything which is un-Christ-like. He must put others before himself, without catering to their frivolous whims or unworthy desires. He must stand firm in his beliefs. Wherever possible, he should eschew religious dogmatism, and respect the opinions and sentiments of others. He must keep a healthy agnosticism on many ideas and issues of the day, without giving ground on the basic tenets of his faith. He must be ready to enjoy himself and share the joys of everything which life has to offer, without being a slave to anything and everything which is of transient value.

****

In these balancing acts, different Christians will veer in one direction or another. It is, I think, my inherited nature to dislike extremes or confrontation of all kinds. I prefer a consensual or middle way. I appreciate that this can sometimes result – or appear to result – in stultifying compromise and lack of action, but when I think back to the terrible acts undertaken in the name of God, for example, in the Crusades of the Middle Ages, and the teachings of some forms of fundamentalism, I think that in most cases my stance is more in keeping with the Christian gospel. I value tolerance – not so much of particular deeds, but of people's values and opinions, and particularly of those that are different to those of my own. As Tony Corley has so kindly implied in one of my Festschrifts,[6] I have sought to apply some of these religious ideas in my professional life. In particular I dislike unnecessary controversy, destructive criticism and abrasive language. Indeed, in my own discipline I usually find that my colleagues are much less likely to say or write something I think (or others think) is wrong, than they are to tackle a slightly different issue, or the same issue from a different perspective. In writing reviews of books or assessing potential journal articles, I try to put myself in the author's shoes; and seek ways and means of adding value to his or her perspective on the subject!

In politics, I rarely take an extreme view on any matter or endorse it in others. But I acknowledge that, on occasions, a marked shift of direction in ideology, policy or strategy may be necessary, and that to achieve this, something approaching a volte-face may be necessary. This is why I think Margaret Thatcher was an excellent choice to lead the UK in 1980, as she was one of the few people prepared to take the drastic steps to get the British economy out of the quagmire of the 1970s. But I was not sorry to see her replaced in 1990. In the everyday hustle and bustle of routine affairs, single-minded and autocratic politicians all too often tend to lose touch with the values and wishes of their constituents – and sometimes, indeed, of their own parties.

As the reader of this volume might well have detected, my politics range from slightly left to slightly right of centre. I have always asserted that if all individuals and organizations behaved according to Christian principles, there would be no need for socialism, as the kind of fairness and justice sought by it would be largely ensured. At the same time, Jesus encouraged each individual to develop and exercise his talents to the full; and this requires a sense of responsibility and entrepreneurship so valued by the more right-wing political ideologies.

It is a fact, however, that such labels as these only become important in an imperfect world; and the most likely consequence is that each in itself is imperfect. This is why it is a good thing not only that individualism and communitarianism are best viewed as complementary to each other,[7] but also that the optimum combination of the two may vary across time and space. The success of Japan and Germany for the first part of the post-war period and of the UK over the last two decades is, in part at least, due to the lack of extreme differences in the economic policies pursued by the main political parties. Hence some kind of economic stability and predictability is assured.

****

Being brought up as a son of the manse, it was understandable – though by no means inevitable – that I would embrace my parents' faith, although in more recent years I have deviated from the mainstream theology of the Baptist denomination. I became a member of Eltham Park Baptist Church in 1942, and remained so until Ida and I moved from south-east London to Southampton a decade later. For much of the intervening time, I was serving in the Navy or studying for my degree at UCL, and was not actively involved in church life.

When he knew I was moving to Southampton, my father put me in touch with the Minister of Shirley Baptist Church which was located just 2 miles from the city centre, and in the first few weeks, during which I was a lodger in a nearby home, I attended evening worship each Sunday. In the event, however, our own new abode was in a different part of Southampton, and the nearest Baptist church was one which had only recently been set up in the midst of a new housing estate at Thornhill, west of the city. The Minister was a young unmarried ex-RAF officer, Frank Keightley, and I can well remember his first appearance when he stood on the front doorstep of our bungalow dressed in full motorcycle gear!

Thornhill became the spiritual home for Ida and myself for 14 years, and I soon became deeply involved in all its activities. I was elected a Deacon (or elder) of the church in 1954, and Treasurer in 1955, positions which I held until I moved to Reading in 1966. I also initiated, and was the first editor of, the monthly church magazine. I started a weekly men's forum to which guest speakers were invited to air their views on a wide range of spiritual and secular subjects. In 1959, I set up and was Captain of the church cricket team. No one was a keener cricketer than our new pastor Gordon Thomas whose aim as wicketkeeper and opening batsman was to be on the field throughout every match.[8] We managed to assemble quite a decent team and usually played about eight Saturday matches each year against other Baptist churches in southern England. I recollect that, in the six years that I was a member of the team, it won or drew about two-thirds of its matches.

****

In many ways, my Thornhill years were the most formative in my spiritual development. Although I had no real urge to follow in the footsteps of my father or uncle into the Baptist ministry, I was quite attracted to lay preaching. I delivered my first sermon near our home in New Eltham at the age of 22, and by my thirtieth birthday I had led Sunday worship at most of the Baptist churches in and around Southampton. I enjoyed preaching both to large congregations in Southampton and Bournemouth; but perhaps even more, I appreciated being part of the intimacy and warmth offered by some of the smaller congregations in the New Forest villages like Lyndhurst, Brockenhurst, Downton and Bransgore.

In the 1950s and 1960s, there were about 300 000 members of the Baptist Church in England and Wales. For organizational purposes, the two countries were divided into eight or so regions, and in each of these a full-time ministerial superintendent was appointed to offer pastoral oversight. In addition, each year, an association president was elected to give general guidance, support and encouragement to the churches in the region. The post of President usually alternated between one of the residing ministers of the area and a layman. By the early 1960s, I had become sufficiently involved and well known throughout the southern region for my name to be put forward as President for the 1964–65 session. Unfortunately the invitation came just a few days after I had accepted an appointment as the Foundation Professor of Economics at Reading University. After a good deal of heart-searching, I decided I could not fulfil both sets of obligations satisfactorily, and had to decline the presidency. As things transpired I am not sure I did the right thing, as Ida and I did not move to Reading until 1966. At the same time, I may well have found the large amount of travelling and week-night engagements, which the presidency demanded, both tiring and difficult to fulfil.[9]

****

My spiritual role models in this period of my life were the great and influential congregational preacher and writer Leslie Weatherhead, and the brilliant Scottish biblical exegist William Barclay. I was not particularly drawn to the evangelism of Billy Graham or to the more conservative wing of the Baptist denomination. I had enthusiastic, but always entirely friendly, discussions with some of my fellow members at Thornhill on a range of theological issues. I was always in favour of a more professional way of administering church affairs. I could never understand (and cannot today) why the same skills applied to running a secular organization should not be used in running a church. Similarly, I believed we should use all the appropriate tools of modern communications to put our Christian message across; although in retrospect my views, which included the showing of religious films as part of Sunday evening worship, may have been a little ahead of its time. However, practically everything I sought after for Thornhill in the 1950s and 1960s is now fairly standard procedure – at least in many of the British and American churches I have visited over the last two decades or so.

****

My faith was well nourished in the Thornhill years although it was severely put to the test in September 1954 when our first daughter, Judith, died within 48 hours of her birth. Ida and I said very little to each other at the time, but we were both greatly comforted in our belief that somehow that tiny spirit had transcended her earthly demise. Without her strong faith, I am sure Ida could have become very bitter – a perfectly understandable, but not a very constructive reaction to perhaps the most traumatic disappointment a woman can have.

Two and a quarter years later, on a cold January morning in 1957, our son Philip John was born. It was indeed a memorable and proud moment for me when he gripped my right index finger as he laid alongside his jubilant mother in her hospital bed in Southampton General Hospital. But within a year or so, both of us were becoming a little concerned as he was not making the progress of a normal baby. It was not long before we learnt that Philip was mentally handicapped – almost certainly as a result of brain damage at birth. Then started a period of many worrying years, especially for Ida. For as well as being mentally handicapped, Philip, had (and still has) his share of physical ailments. He is spastic; for many years he suffered from frequent bouts of sickness; he has petit (and some grand) mals.

And yet for all his many problems, Philip brought with him into the world a lot of joy and love. No less significant, his character and (most of) his behaviour has prompted such love in other people that it is difficult not to see some good coming out of his terrible handicap. One comfort his mother and I have is that, so far as it is possible for us to know, Philip is unaware (in the sense that we are) of his handicap. Philip to Philip is – well – just Philip! Although now at the age of 51 his mental age is still only one and a half or two, he has an almost non-existent memory – except about anything to do with food! He is, for the most part, a cheerful and loving individual, and full of the most impish humour you can ever imagine.

****

Gordon Thomas remained at Thornhill for nine years. During that time a new sanctuary was built, the membership of the church tripled from 50 to 150, and its annual income rose tenfold. I was privileged to preach the sermon at the opening of a beautiful new sanctuary in 1965. I chose as my text, 'Where there is no vision the people perish' (Proverbs 29, v. 18). Though primarily addressed to the congregation of Thornhill, I believe these wise words have more general applicability; not least, I might add, to the teaching and scholarship of international business!

****

The last time I occupied a pulpit was in 1966 on the occasion of Gordon Thomas's induction service at Maidstone Baptist Church, when I had the task of giving the charge to the church.[10] A few months earlier I had preached the Southern Baptist Association sermon at Eastleigh Baptist Church. At that time I based my thoughts on Christ's threefold commandment to Simon Peter, one of his disciples, to: 'Love God, love my church, and love the world' (St John's Gospel 21 v 15–17).[11] As subsequent events were to show, I am afraid I took the last commandment a little too literally! It was not until over 20 years later that I became a regular Sunday worshipper again, and this time it was at the Presbyterian Church in Westfield, New Jersey, USA.

NOTES

1. I Corinthians 13 v. 12.
2. Taking one example. Was the feeding of the 5000 with five loaves and two fishes to be taken literally or did the act of the small boy in handing over his lunch to Jesus inspire many other people who also brought their lunch to share this with other people?
3. As Jesus said to Nicodemus, a ruler of the Jews. John 5, v. 3, 8.
4. There is a similar, and in some respects a readily acceptable injunction originally put forward by both religious and non-religious sages before Christ that one should never do anything to anyone one would not want done to oneself.
5. See especially I Corinthians 12 and 13.
6. M. Casson and P.E. Buckley (eds), *Essays in Honour of John Dunning*, Aldershot, UK and Brookfield, US, Edward Elgar, 1992.
7. As well expressed by Amitai Etzioni in *The New Golden Rule*, New York, Basic Books, 1998.
8. Gordon Thomas succeeded Frank Keightley in 1959. He and I became good friends but saw relatively little of each other when I moved to Reading and he to Maidstone in 1966. Gordon died tragically of CJD (Creutzfeldt-Jakob disease) in 2000.
9. At the time there were around 80 Baptist churches in the southern region, and the President would normally have been expected to visit each of these during his year in office.
10. At the induction service of a new minister in the Baptist Church, there are usually two sermons preached. One is directed to the tasks and challenges of the new minister, and the other to those of the church of which he is now pastor.
11. St John's Gospel, 21 v 15–17.

7. From 'soldier' to 'justice': the Reading years[1]

It is now over 40 years since I was appointed to the Foundation Chair of Economics at Reading University. It seems like yesterday. As one gets older, time seems to encapsulate. Indeed, in a very real sense, the memories which make up one's past life are timeless.

When I received the letter inviting me to attend an interview at the old campus of the university in London Road, Reading, I was delighted, but not optimistic of the outcome. After all, I had not made the shortlist for a similar professorship at Sussex and had just missed out at being offered a second Chair in Economics at Exeter. But after the interview I decided that fortune plays a role in appointments of this kind. There were other equally well-qualified candidates for the Chair, and it may well have been that under a different appointments board, and perhaps on a different day, my good friend and later colleague Geoffrey Maynard would have been chosen.

Or perhaps kismet, or the Almighty, did have a say! I was particularly pleased to be coming to the town in which my father started his ministry; and in retrospect, I do not think I could have hoped for a more congenial environment, and one more suited to my particular tastes and talents!

From the outset, I knew exactly what I intended to do at, and for, the university. Under the vibrant leadership of David Rowan, Ivor Pearce and Gordon Fisher, the Department of Economics at Southampton University was rapidly gaining a reputation as one of the leading UK schools in southern England in theoretical economics and econometrics. I decided to try and persuade my colleagues to develop Reading, which was just 50 miles away from Southampton, into a first-rate teaching and research centre in applied economics.[2]

The challenge was also an exciting one. As I have already recounted, it was as a direct result of the Robbins report that the UK government had pumped large additional amounts of resources into higher education. Seven new universities were created[3] and several existing universities were allocated funds specifically to develop research and teaching in the social sciences. Reading was one of these. Until October 1964, it housed no separate Department of Economics, and all teaching in economics (apart from agricultural economics) was undertaken in the Department of Political Economy, headed at that time by Peter Campbell, a political scientist. This department was now to be split into two new departments – Politics and Economics – and another new department, that of Sociology, was to be created.

And so, it was on my arrival at Reading in September 1964 that I inherited a group of just four economists: Eric Budden, who sadly died shortly after my arrival (no causal relationship I think!), Tony Corley, Mike Utton and Roy Thomas. I shall ever be grateful for the friendship and cooperation of these colleagues, and particularly so in the early years of my appointment. Our first departmental meeting took place in November 1964. Mike Utton was appointed as minute secretary. The meeting lasted an hour, and the first set of minutes ended with the immortal words: 'The meeting closed at 3.45 p.m. and everyone adjourned for tea'!

****

My initial strategy for the Department of Economics was to attract one or two renowned senior scholars who might be persuaded to come to the university, and help put the department on the map.[4] One major incentive, I believed, was our location: Reading is only a 30-minute train journey from London, where there were many opportunities for economic consultancy of one kind or another. A year after arriving at the university, I managed to entice Geoffrey Maynard – a macroeconomist then working with the Ministry of Overseas Development – to join the department. At the same time, I was delighted to recruit Geoffrey Denton, a former colleague at Southampton University who was now working with John Pinder at an influential think-tank, Political and Economic Planning, in London. My senior team was completed in 1967 when Peter Hart, a quantitative economist from the University of Bristol, and consultant to the London-based National Institute of Economic and Social Research, accepted the second Chair in Economics. At the time of his appointment Peter's external assessor Professor Ronald Tress, of Bristol University, referred to him as being 'pure gold'. And so he turned out to be.

****

I have every reason to suppose my initial strategy was successful, as the department's teaching programme became more ambitious, with the launch of a single Honours degree in economics and several new combined Honours degrees in the later 1960s.[5] Specialists in various branches of economics were appointed. These included David Robertson (international economics), Peter Reed (transport economics), Colin Ash and Mike Barron (microeconomics), Matt McQueen (development economics), Mark Casson and Nick Robinson (macroeconomics), George Yannopoulos (European regional economics) – all of whom were appointed between 1965 and 1969. Backed by a sympathetic Vice-Chancellor – Harry Pitt – and generous funding, by the late 1960s I had managed to assemble an excellent and congenial team of colleagues, each of whom became quickly and actively involved in a variety of research projects. By September 1968, when I took a year's leave of absence to visit North America, the student numbers in the department had more than trebled and the teaching and research staff had increased from five in 1964 to 14 in 1969. By that latter date, the Faculty was also supported by two full-time and two part-time secretaries. In my review of the work of the department in the academic years 1967–69, I identified 49 books and journal articles which had been published in those two years. When I look back at this phase of expansion, I am amazed at how this was achieved on such a minimal budget. Excluding salaries and hardware paid for by university central funds, our department funding was a miniscule £25 in 1964/5 and £180 in 1968/9. By 1985 this had risen to £90 000, and at the time I relinquished the headship of the Department, to a six-figure sum.

****

While I quite enjoyed departmental meetings, for the most part I found most Senate and Faculty meetings and committees excruciatingly boring and time-consuming. I rarely expressed an opinion at these meetings, and this was obviously observed as I was never appointed to any influential university committee. I did not really mind this as it released my time for departmental work and my own research; but I believe the university was the loser! In the Faculty of Letters, I sensed that the Economics Department was not generally liked! In the early years, at least, I felt that it was regarded as a cuckoo in the nest by several of the arts-based disciplines. But this view changed in the later 1970s when economics became a popular subject of study, and in the case of those departments participating in combined Honours degree courses, helped recruit for them additional students. However, because of the initial disquiet (which was never openly voiced) I and my colleagues tried to set up a separate Faculty of Social Sciences. This ploy was unsuccessful, mainly because of some of the other departments of the proposed Faculty, such as Politics, who were deeply embedded in the Faculty of Arts. By the time Law began to be taught in Reading in the later 1960s, it was too late – the chance had been lost! In retrospect, however, I do not think it proved a hindrance to the growth and development of the Department of Economics.

If Senate and Faculty meetings were tedious, my dealings with the university administration were frustrating – and particularly so when anything to do with money was concerned. While I found the Registrar and his colleagues always very helpful, I could not say the same for the Bursar's department. In many private and public organizations, there is an ingrained tension between spending and funding departments, and universities are no exception to this. But what I found difficult to suffer was the presumption by some parts of the administration that it was their task to control and manage the academic departments rather than to serve them. Of course this attitude is not confined to national administrations. Indeed, perhaps the most blatant example of inhibiting bureaucracy I have ever come across is in the financial division of some parts of the United Nations (UN). Also, all too frequently, especially in the public sector, customers are treated as if they are a nuisance! So often in our Western culture, service seems to be confused with servitude. Not so in the Confucian ethic of the Far East, which I have encountered first hand in my travels. Anyone, too, who has taken a sea cruise cannot have failed to be impressed by the efficiency and cheerfulness of the Filipino or Thai waiters and room attendants.

****

In my early years at Reading, I soon came to distinguish between two groups of students who wished to read economics. The first were those who wanted to become professional economists in government, academia or a business enterprise, or were fascinated with economic analysis and quantitative techniques as an intellectual challenge. For these students, we devised a single-subject economics degree programme. The second were those who wanted a reasonable grasp of economic principles, but were primarily interested in the application of these principles to tackling real-life problems and issues. For the most part, this second group of students had their main interests in the other disciplines they studied with economics. For these students, we offered a series of joint Honours degrees.

To make economics interesting and relevant to the students reading a combined Honours degree, the department tried to devise tailor-made courses to suit the other discipline, and to encourage the other disciplines to reciprocate our efforts. In this respect, we were not entirely successful. One notable exception – of which I remain proud – was to initiate and implement a first-rate degree course in Regional and Urban Economics. This was helped enormously by the appointment of Peter Hall to the Chair of Geography in 1974, and the transference of the College of Estate Management from London to Reading a year earlier.[6] A particular bonus to our own department was that the college brought with it a number of economists with particular interests in land and urban economics. With the appointment of Alan Evans in 1977 as Reader in Environmental

Economics, the future of this part of the department's work was assured.[7] Alan, who was later promoted to Professor of Environmental Economics, was ably supported by Paul Cheshire – now Professor of Economic Geography at the LSE – Graham Crampton, Jack Harvey, Mike Stabler and Geoff Keogh. It was due to the intellectual expertise and hard work of these colleagues, and of Frank Stilwell, Manfred Streit, George Yannopoulos and George Norman from the core of the Economics Department housed in the Faculty of Letters and Social Sciences, that by the early 1980s Reading had established a reputation as a centre of international excellence in regional and urban economics, second only to that of Cambridge.

****

By the mid-1970s, a decade after I had come to Reading, it was clear to me that not only was the department gaining an international reputation in applied economics, but that this was especially noticeable in two main areas, namely regional and urban economics, and international business. The department was also becoming recognized for its contribution to the work of the Graduate School of European Studies;[8] and also, led by Peter Hart and Mike Utton, for its teaching and scholarly research in industrial economics.

These strengths, however, rested, at least in part, on there being a strong and vigorous intellectual infrastructure in mainstream economics. Here, as witnessed by their publications and consultancy work, Peter Hart and Geoffrey Maynard were joined by new colleagues such as Jim Pemberton, Kerry Patterson, Dorian Owen, Charles Sutcliffe and John Board, each of whom later achieved professorial status.

At the same time, in a relatively small university, the efforts of individual scholars – however brilliant they may be to embrace most aspects of macro or micro economics – do not necessarily make up a coherent and distinctive school or programme of scholarship. Only amongst quite a large nexus of such scholars – as housed, for example, at Cambridge, Oxford and London, and also at a couple of the newer universities, for example, Essex and Warwick – has this proved to be a viable proposition. In each of the other new universities and in the burgeoning economics departments of the most established provincial universities, niche strategies, directed to build up a comparative advantage in a particular branch of economics, were evolving. The classic case of such a strategy was that pursued in public finance and health economics by Alan Peacock and Jack Wiseman at York University.

I have already written about one of the niche strategies Reading came to pursue in the 1970s and 1980s. Partly by *force majeure* and partly by the research interests of several colleagues in the Department of Economics prior to the arrival of the College of Estate Management, Alan Evans and his colleagues managed to create one of the most renowned centres for regional and urban economics in the UK. By the time I retired from the headship of the Department of Economics in December 1987, the annual publications of the department on regional and urban economics were approaching 30, and were accounting for a quarter of all its publications.

Serendipity also played some part in the founding of the Reading school of international business scholarship. Contrary to the belief of some of my colleagues at the time, I did not initially set out to create such a school. Though my own research interests were increasingly concentrated in the field of foreign direct investment (FDI) and the multinational enterprise (MNE), I never took advantage of my position as Head of Department by appointing additional Faculty specialists in that field.

However, a set of circumstances in the 1970s and 1980s combined to give Reading the reputation of being one of the world's leading research centres on the economics of FDI and MNEs. The first was my own translation from the Foundation Chair in Economics to a Professorship in International Investment and Business Studies in 1974. This latter Chair was initially financed by the Esmee Fairbairn Trust. I had earlier applied to the trust for funding, because I wanted to secure (in my place) an additional senior appointment in mainstream economics, and seeking external financial support for a specialized Chair in my own subject area seemed to me as good a way as any to do so. In the event Victor Morgan from Manchester University was appointed to the Chair of Economics which I had relinquished in October 1974.

The second trigger was the evolving interest of my other colleagues in international business. Little did I know that when Peter Buckley joined the department as my research assistant in October 1973, his influence, enthusiasm and friendship with Mark Casson would draw Mark's interest to research on the MNE. As is now history, the seminal monograph of Peter and Mark, *The Future of the Multinational Enterprise*, appeared in 1976.[9] The same year also saw the first presentation of my own closely related eclectic paradigm at a Nobel Symposium in Stockholm.[10] It was also during the 1976/77 academic sessions that Alan Rugman visited the Department of Economics.[11] In his PhD thesis, Alan had already written on MNEs and risk diversification, in which he used the elements of internalization theory. But, at least partly as a result of his time at Reading and his friendship – not to mention some collegiate rivalry – with Peter, Mark and myself, Alan developed his own perspective on internalization which has well stood the test of time over the subsequent 40 years.

So the Reading school of international business was born![12] Over the following years, the Department of Economics benefited from a succession of new Faculty, research assistants and visiting scholars working in this area. Foremost among these, I would single out Bob Pearce, who began helping me with my research on UK FDI in developing countries in the late 1960s, and has been an enthusiastic and productive researcher ever since! No one was more pleased when Bob's talents were appropriately (if not tardily!) acknowledged in 2007 by his being awarded a Personal Chair. Others who spent time in the department and helped further its reputation in international business research included John Mellors, Graham Bird, Eleanor Morgan, Tom Parry, David Paxson, Len Skerratt, Seev Hirsch,[13] Peter Gray and Martin Gilman.

The growing interest of several colleagues in international business (IB) prompted me to widen our graduate teaching programmes. In 1978, the department began to offer (and was among the first UK universities to offer) three one-year MA courses. Again, these were intended to promote the interests of colleagues who were not normally IB researchers, but the content and scope of whose own sphere of interest was being increasingly influenced by the global spread of FDI and MNE activity. These were respectively MAs in International Business in Economic Development (which was convened by Matt McQueen), International Business and Financial Management (convened by Brian Quinn) and International Business in European Integration (convened by Geoffrey Denton). At the same time, we launched a PhD programme in IB. While the initiative took longer to attract students (there were very few national government grants to UK students at that time) it gradually proved to be attractive (particularly, I remember, to Portuguese and Greek students), and by the mid-1980s it was one of the largest (if not the largest) of its kind in the country.

****

The final development of the 1970s I wish to mention was the introduction of accounting and financial studies into the department. Two young lecturers, Brian Quinn and Charles Sutcliffe, were appointed in 1973, and our first Professor of Accounting, Michael Bromwich, in 1977.

I must own that some of my departmental colleagues were none too keen on introducing accounting into the undergraduate curricula. Earlier in the late 1960s the department had been approached by Henley Management College (HMC) to help give their teaching programmes a stronger analytical component, and possibly to set up joint Masters and PhD programmes with them. But this came to naught, partly because of the uncertainty about the financial position of the university, and partly because several of my colleagues were uneasy about the department widening its economics curricular to embrace management-related subjects.

In retrospect, I think this may have been a mistake. Not only has the HMC gained an enviable international reputation over the years,[14] but in the 1980s the Department of Economics was virtually forced to broaden its curriculum to embrace business studies, which were increasingly being demanded by overseas students, each of whom at the time, and unlike students resident in the UK, paid the full tuition fees. Much of the subsequent development of management studies occurred after I had relinquished the headship of the department. A major restructuring of departments in the university occurred in 2002 with the launching of the Reading Business School. The school has two unique advantages. One is that it is closely associated with the ISMA (now called the ICMA) Centre,[15] a world-renowned financial learning centre; another is that it embraces a combination of well-reputed departments such as Land Management, Geography and Business History. Its main drawback – at least prior to the proposed merger with HMC – was that it lacked a set of business-related disciplines, most noticeably in marketing and organizational studies. I believe that had the niche strategy I (and later Mark Casson) adopted in the 1970s and 1980s continued, and had the focus of management studies had been on global studies, this together with the work of the prestigious ISMA Centre would have enabled Reading to become a major world player in international business studies. But, as I write in 2008, this potential is yet to be fully realized.

****

The financial atmosphere in the university changed dramatically in the 1970s. In contrast to the expansion of the earlier decades, UK universities began to be targets for government cuts, a situation which continued right up until the 1990s. Along with other departments at Reading, the Department of Economics was finding it increasingly difficult to promote staff, or to obtain replacements for them when they left. Staff–student ratios worsened dramatically, and as Head of Department I found myself increasingly competing with other departments for scarce resources. Morale throughout the university started to fall, and as real salaries declined, there were an increasing number of resignations and it was difficult to recruit good staff (when this was allowed). The lowest point in this saga of retrenchment came when the UK government introduced an early retirement scheme, and the universities were forced to lose Faculty they could ill afford to lose. The Department of Economics was no exception, and all of us were extremely sorry when one of our most loyal and talented colleagues, Peter Hart, decided to retire early.

Looking back, however, it is clear that in the 1970s and 1980s there was a lot of 'fat' in universities – among both the academic departments and the administration. Yet, until adequate incentives were given to individual departments to raise more external resources – for example from research councils, foundations, international agencies and individual businesses – they were loathe to spend their time doing so. This again was an area where the views and actions of the administration of the university and heads of department often clashed.

The Department of Economics fared better than most other departments in the University. It did so partly because its Faculty were good enough to obtain funding from research councils and private foundations, and partly because of its aggressive strategy in attracting foreign students. This strategy was focused on building upon its comparative research advantages, and developing a series of graduate courses in the particular scholarly areas earlier described. Such a strategy, together with the excellent publication record of most of the Faculty, helped the department to be highly ranked by the University Grants Committee in an exercise on research and teaching quality it conducted in 1985.

****

In 1978, Dr Harry Pitt, a benign and distinguished scholar, retired as Vice-Chancellor (VC). He was replaced by Ewan Page a computer scientist who was a much more abrasive, demanding and ambitious individual; and who valued getting his own way more than most. Neither did the new VC suffer fools gladly, and in his early years he was anxious to stamp his mindset and authority over all departments. But, to his credit, he did have a fighting spirit, and a determination that Reading would win through its difficult times. He was also astute enough to know which of his senior colleagues could best help him in his quest. I often felt the biblical expression, 'The Lord chastiseth those whom he loves', particularly applied to Ewan's dealings with the Department of Economics. The reaction of most colleagues to the sometimes draconian methods of the VC was either to lie down and accept them, or seek out alternative sources of finance, and so partly escape his control! The Department of Economics chose the latter route, which bore some fruit while I was its Head, but which flourished more after Mark Casson took over in 1987.

At the time of my resignation, the department was the largest in the university and was well respected in the wider economics community. I felt my own strategy had been vindicated; and that the policy of Ewan Page, though it caused much heart-searching, had probably been justified. I was also delighted that several younger Faculty who had been recruited to the department in the 1960s and 1970s now had senior appointments at other UK or foreign universities.

****

As the university went through a series of financial cutbacks, more accountability was required of it. This meant that, to be successful, heads of department and their colleagues needed not only to be entrepreneurial, but also to devote a lot more time to administration, financial matters and paperwork of one kind or another. As I shall describe in more detail in Chapter 10, the main tasks of a head (or chairperson) of a department had changed dramatically since the early 1960s. No longer were they solely focused on recruiting the most deserved students, designing the best teaching programmes, and encouraging research excellence. In any case, I felt I had lost some of my earlier drive and enthusiasm. At the same time, I was confident that there were several very able colleagues who could step into my shoes. By the mid-1980s, the Department boasted five full professors, and after over 22 years I considered it was time for a change. In no way did I sense that my colleagues were wanting me to resign; but this might be because they had got used to me, like a worn glove – and, in any case, I was in the middle of my four-year cycle as Head of Department. But, in January 1987, I resigned from the headship of the Economics Department, and then immediately left for a year's leave of absence at Rutgers University in New Jersey, USA.

But before turning to this period of my life I would like to retrace my steps and describe some more personal events of my time at Reading, and my various travelling experiences in that era.

****

NOTES

1. The fourth and fifth ages of man as described by Shakespeare in *As You Like It*, Act II, scene 7.
2. In the 1960s there was a much clearer distinction between theoretical and applied economics than there is today.
3. At Essex, Kent and Sussex in the south of England. Warwick in central England and Keele, Lancaster and York in northern England.
4. Although at the time Reading was well renowned for its Department of Agricultural Economics which was housed in a completely different part of the University.
5. For example Economics and (various) languages, Economics and Sociology, Politics and Economics and Geography and Economics.
6. Which then became a fourth Faculty of the university, namely the Faculty of Urban and Regional Studies, and which was housed in a new and purpose-built building on the campus.

7. Earlier in 1975, David Metcalf had been appointed, but he resigned in 1977 to take up a Chair in Political Economy at University College London.
8. Geoffrey Denton was elected Chairman of that school in 1976.
9. Published by Macmillan.
10. Elsewhere I have acknowledged the contribution of Peter and Mark to my own thinking. See my article for example 'Perspectives on International Business Research: Fifty Years of Research and Teaching International Business', *Journal of International Business Studies*, **33**, 2002, 817–35.
11. Alan was among the first of 12 of the leading foreign scholars in international business to visit Reading University between 1975 and 1978.
12. A 'school' (of thought) refers to a group of scholars following a similar methodology or approach to their subject. In a perceptive recent review of the reputation of a number of eminent economists, John Kay has argued that while Keynes and Friedman established schools of thought, Schumpeter, Galbraith and most of the recent Nobel laureates were best renowned for their own work rather than for the schools of thought they established. See J. Kay, 'Economists of Scale', *Financial Times Magazine*, 8/9 September 2007.
13. Whose classic paper 'An International Trade and Investment Theory of the Firm' published in 1976 in *Oxford Economic Studies*, **28** (2), 258–70 was first published as a Department of Economics Discussion Paper in 1974.
14. It now offers a joint Phd programme with London's Brunel University. On 1st August 2008, however, a merger took place between the university's Business School and Henley Management College.
15. International Securities Market Association.

8.   The Reading years: family and related matters

Things were going extremely well for me in the mid-1960s. I had achieved, at a comparatively young age, a professorship at a prestigious UK university. I was given the challenge of building a new Department of Economics – and at a time when ample funding was available from the University Grants Committee.[1] Together with four other professors and under the chairmanship of Victor Morgan, I was a partner in a newly formed London-based economic consultancy (Economists Advisory Group, EAG). I was deeply and happily involved in Hampshire church life, and an active lay preacher.

For the first two years of my appointment at Reading, I commuted most days from Southampton. However, in 1966, Ida and I moved to a lovely new house in Henley, which we had built for us. If there was a cloud on our horizon it was that our son Philip was now severely mentally retarded, and there was little sign that he would ever have a mental age of more than two. In Oxfordshire we found what were reputed to be, at the time, the best day-care facilities for his needs. To begin with, Philip went each day to Borocourt Hospital near Henley just 5 miles away from his home. Later, he became a resident in the hospital for part of the week. But for all his physical and mental impediments, Philip was growing up as a loving and cheerful boy. Most important to us, he seemed contented in a world of his own, at least for the majority of the time.

****

Yet, often, when the balloon of life is full, it is badly pricked. Sometimes the burst is caused by a sudden illness or the death of a loved one; sometimes by a change in working environment or unemployment; and sometimes by a burglary, a car accident or a financial setback.

In my case, two events occurred – each within the space of three years. The first was that my mother and father died within a year of each other – in 1965 and 1966 respectively. My mother had been unwell for some time, but in the spring of 1965 the cancer in her stomach took its grip, and she died that June – at the comparatively young age of 72. My father, who although retired was preaching most Sundays and was enjoying his hobby as a bee-keeper, developed prostate problems during the following year. After an operation in Sidcup Hospital (in Kent), he unexpectedly collapsed, and died of a heart attack. He was buried alongside my mother in Chislehurst cemetery in June 1966, almost exactly a year after he had stood by her graveside. He was nearly 78, and had much to live for!

It is usually long after one's childhood that one can look back with any objectivity, and properly appreciate the critical role parents often play in shaping one's life. By their love, example and sacrifice, my parents could not have given me a better upbringing, education or sense of direction and values. Moreover, each parent imparted to me priceless assets. From my father I inherited the value of tolerance, a logical and enquiring mind, the gift of teaching and public speaking, and a generosity of spirit. From my mother I learnt initiative, a sense of adventure, pragmatism and a joy for the ordinary things of life. If I lacked anything – and this is not a criticism of their parenting – it was exposure to the world outside that familiar to my immediate family. As a teenager, I was emotionally sheltered; and until I joined the Navy in 1945, I knew little of how people outside my own walk of life lived, or behaved.

If I am honest with myself, for the first 37 years of my life I faced no real personal crisis, in the sense that I was unchallenged to make a decision, the result of which might not only fundamentally affect the trajectory of my own life, but also adversely affect those closest to me.

But, in the autumn of 1967 this happened – and it happened unexpectedly. I fell in love with another woman. As it happened, the other woman (a distasteful expression!) was Christine, my secretary at the university. The story is an all too familiar one. It happens every day, every year, and I imagine will continue to do so. But I really did not expect it to happen to me.

I do not intend to recount the way in which my relationship with Christine evolved in 1967 and 1968. Suffice it to say that, in September 1968, I left my home in Henley to take up a one-year visiting Professorship in Economics at the University of Western Ontario in London, Canada.[2] Christine accompanied me. On our return to England, Christine and I moved into an apartment in Streatley (near Reading), and later bought a house in Goring. In the hope that my feelings for Christine might burn themselves out, Ida was disinclined to grant me a divorce under the two-year 'mutually agreed' clause. Instead, we had to accept a full five-year separation, after which either party could claim 'an irretrievable breakdown of marriage', even if the other objected. Ida and I were eventually divorced in March 1975, and Christine and I were married in the following August.

Even if divorce is quite a common occurrence in most Western societies, I am still very sad when it happens to friends and acquaintances, however amicable the conditions surrounding a marriage dissolution or its aftermath may be; and it has meant a lot to me that, over the last 40 years, Ida and I have kept in close touch with each other. Divorce involves tremendous upheavals and damaged relationships which often extend well beyond the immediate parties concerned. I regret, for example, that I lost the respect and friendship of Ida's mother; and that, for many years, I was even reluctant to contact my own relatives for fear I would be ostracized. (I was probably harsher on myself than they were.) In fact, it took me more than ten years to contact my cousin Tom (on the Dunning side), and 15 years to introduce Christine to my aunts Doll and Vi, who were two of my mother's younger sisters. With the passing of time, Christine and I also built up a friendship with Derek (Ida's brother); and in June 1992, on the occasion of my sixty-fifth birthday, Christine gave me a surprise party to which both my and her relations were invited. As both Ida and Philip were present at the celebration, I felt that after such a long time of being in the dark familial shadows I had created for myself, I had come out into the sunlight again, and was delighted that the two families appeared to get on so well together!

The other cost – to me at any rate – of my divorce was that I felt I could no longer undertake lay preaching. I know there are many divorced clergy who still occupy the pulpit, but to me, since I had broken a solemn vow made before God on the sanctity of marriage, I decided that if I could not preach the complete Christian gospel I was not worthy to preach any of it! I do not regret my decision, but I do miss the opportunity of leading Sunday worship, which I did quite frequently between 1953 and 1966. Had my life proceeded on its earlier trajectory who knows what might have been? Indeed. I might well have followed in my Uncle Tom's footsteps and become the President of the Baptist Union in the UK.[3] But let bygones be bygones; and though, as I set out in Chapter 6, my faith has not diminished over the years, it has shifted ground. Moreover, a sense of my own unwillingness and/or inability to live a life which, in my better moments, I think I would like to live, has increased greatly.

****

One of the alleged attributes of an individual born under the sign of Cancer is a great devotion to home and family life. Certainly, I am a home-loving person. Nothing gives me more pleasure than just relaxing in my home or garden, or on the terrace of our apartment in Cornwall overlooking the sea. This is particularly the case after a long and arduous trip abroad. As fate would have it, Christine and I have not been granted our own family; and certainly I feel my life is the poorer for it. But again, I must acknowledge the joy Philip has brought me. Indeed at the start of my ninth decade I rather envy my contemporaries who extol the happenings of their grandchildren – and sometimes their great-grandchildren – and the warmth and happiness (along with occasional trials and tribulations!) which family get-togethers obviously bring them.

In retrospect, I must admit that as a child of the manse my early experience of family life was very confined. I have already recorded that apart from holiday times, it was quite rare for my mother, father and myself to relax as a threesome. I can remember many outings and treats with one or the other of them – but not with both. The fact that my father was at meetings most evenings, and at church functions most Saturdays – and, of course, he was 'on duty' all of Sundays – did not make for family togetherness. I do not think I was conscious of minding this very much, as I always found something to occupy myself; but it almost certainly framed the kind of attitude which I now have to other people's family life.

Moreover, although my mother was one of 12 children and my father one of six, I cannot recall a single occasion when there was a really big family party at our home. The Dunning and Baker cultures did not easily mix with each other, although both my parents were extremely hospitable people. In particular, my father had quite a devilish sense of humour, and loved to play tricks on one or another of my mother's sisters when they visited us in our homes at Walthamstow and Harrow. Yet, apart from the occasional visit to my father's brother (Tom) and to my mother's sisters' families, I cannot recall spending much time outside my own home. Certainly this would never occur at Christmas, as my father would always have been conducting services on that day. While I am convinced that my mother and father were devoted to each other, as far as their respective families were concerned, 'each to his (or her) own' seemed to be the posture adopted by both of them. And I was caught somewhere in the middle!

In both my marriages, I have been fortunate with the in-laws I inherited. Both families warmly welcomed me into their folds, and I was shown nothing but kindness by both sets of parents-in-law. Ida was one of three children and Christine one of four. After my marriage to Ida, and while we were still living near to both sets of parents, we visited each of them once a week: but after we moved to Southampton, our main contact was by letter or telephone, and by occasional visits to each other. Though always friendly with her sister and brother, Ida was not in frequent touch with either of them, and – apart from weddings and funerals – I can only recall one or two occasions when her family were all gathered together.

By contrast, Christine's family were, and still are, very closely knit; and each takes his or her pleasures and responsibilities of being a member of the family very much to heart. Again, I think this partly reflects the impressive tapestry of togetherness woven by Christine's mother and father. But whereas my parents' tapestry was limited in the way I have described, theirs was both wider – embracing part of Christine's mother's family – and deeper, in the sense there was much more day-to-day intimacy (not to mention the rough and tumble) of family life than that with which I was familiar.

My reaction to being drawn into a new and warmly cohesive family was (and still is) somewhat ambivalent. While part of me welcomed the opportunity of forging closer family ties, another part drew back from being fully involved in this tightly knit form of bonding. Whether this was because I could not enthusiastically embrace the values and belief systems of my new in-laws; whether it was because their closeness reminded me that I did not have the same intimacy in my own family; whether it reflected my streak of independence and ingrained sense of being a 'loner'; whether it was because, over the years, I had had little experience of small-talk among family members; or whether it was a combination of these factors, I do not really know. But sometimes I get quite upset when I know I am not bringing as much conviviality to family gatherings (or for that matter other social gatherings) as I should.

This is a pity, because I like my extended family and particularly Susan (Christine's sister) and Edward (Christine's brother), and greatly value their love and friendship. But at heart, I think I am a one-to-one person. Should I be offered a choice between attending a cocktail party or banquet or an intimate dinner with two or three friends, I would opt for the latter every time. If on occasion this makes me behave unsociably, I apologize for this, but that is the way I am!

****

Over the past four decades, I have lived a privileged and rewarding life, not least because I have been given the opportunity – largely at someone else's expense! – to visit 85 countries in many parts of the world, and to meet a large number of interesting and delightful people. I have always thought that one of the perks of a university don and international scholar is the opportunity to traverse social, cultural and religious boundaries; and although my travelling experiences have not been without an occasional social gaffe or insensitivity to local cultural mores, for the most part I have managed to adapt quite easily to whatever circumstances in which I find myself. Fortunately, I have fairly catholic tastes in my eating and drinking habits, although I have frequently disappointed my friend and colleague Louis Wells for refusing to eat such delicacies of the East as snake, sheep's eyes and fried alligator!

Moreover, in spite of my earlier remarks on social gatherings, I have enjoyed many wonderful and memorable experiences. Indeed, it would be astonishing if I did not relish dining well with a UK prime minister (James

Callaghan) and his guests at 10 Downing Street; or attending one of Queen Elizabeth's garden parties at Buckingham Palace; or being entertained by the Lord Mayor of London at the Mansion House; or being hosted in the magnificent splendour of the Guildhall to a banquet honouring the Portuguese President; or being invited to receptions given by foreign heads of state or dignitaries such as the King of Lesotho, the presidents of China and South Korea, Prince Bertil of Sweden, the Governor of North Korea, the Indian Ambassador to the US and the US Ambassador to the UK. Even so, to be truthful, more often than not the splendour of my surroundings left a more lasting impression on me than did the social chit-chat of my fellow guests!

At the same time, although academic and professional conferences frequently take place in towns or cities best forgotten, there are some delightful exceptions. Recollections of a dinner of the International Economic Association in the magnificent dining room of a floodlit castle on the outskirts of Madrid; of an al fresco candlelit supper at a restaurant overlooking the orange groves of Spoletto in Umbria; and of several most splendid banquets in Taipei, Beijing and Seoul, readily come to mind. But, of my most enduring memories, none surpasses the beautiful surroundings of, and exquisite hospitality offered by the Rockefeller Foundation's Villa Serbelloni in Bellagio. I have visited the villa – which is set on a promontory overlooking Lake Como and Lake Maggiore in North Italy – on four separate occasions. The villa dates back to the fourteenth century, and was donated to the Rockefeller Foundation in 1923. Since that date, it has been used as a conference centre, and a haven for individuals to spend up to six weeks in the pursuance of scholarly research and writing. The grounds of the villa comprise 25 acres of landscaped and terraced gardens which rise to 400 feet above Bellagio. These contain an abundance of Mediterranean fruit trees, including oranges, lemons, olives and persimmons. Paths wend their way upwards between fragrant oleanders, hibiscus and bougainvillea bushes, and many species of deciduous and pine trees.

The Rockefeller building itself consists of 15 bedrooms, some of which have their own balconies, and five reception rooms, including a conference venue which comfortably seats 30 participants. But it is the dining arrangements which particularly impress the guest. Each evening, drinks are served on the terrace overlooking Lake Como, or in one of the reception rooms. Dinner is formal, and everyone is allotted a place at table. Usually one or two scholars in residence – which include musicians, artists, statesmen, writers and academics – will join the conference participants, and conversation is lively. The food is delicious, wine flows freely and everything is gracefully served on the best of china. After dinner, the participants usually adjourn for further conversation and occasionally a piano recital; and until around 11 p.m. whatever one wishes to drink is available. The bedrooms, too, are of the standard of a first class hotel; and with the sweetness of the lakeside air and a balmy climate – at least for most of the year – one can usually expect to sleep very well.

Villa Serbelloni is a place I could return to again and again. Indeed I myself organized two conferences – one in 1972 the other in 1985 – not least to recapture the ambience of the idyllic surroundings. But the same cannot be said for some university quarters and hotels in which I have stayed. On opening the door to my bedroom at the East–West Centre in Hawaii in the 1970s, I was greeted by a stream of cockroaches creeping their way to the kitchenette, where the last (human?) occupant had left an opened tin of fruit. In a third-rate hotel in Florence, I spent most of a sweltering hot night swatting mosquitoes – but I was still terribly bitten and my life's blood splattered the walls! At another hotel in Fiji – as I shall recount later – a hurricane tore apart my bedroom ceiling in the middle of the night. At the prestigious InterContinental Hotel in Maui I found myself, on getting out of bed one morning, ankle-deep in seawater swept in by an overnight storm. Finally, in 1995 at an allegedly three-star US hotel in Baltimore, I returned from dinner one evening to find a note for me: 'We are sorry but there is a large hole in your bath and we shall have to move you to another room'.

Quite often, when I am lecturing, consulting or attending conferences outside the UK, I do quite a bit of work in my hotel room. Nothing annoys me more when I return to my room in the late afternoon than to find it has not been made up. In my experience, this is most likely to occur in US and European hotels, be they three, four or five star. By contrast, in many upmarket Asian hotels both the quality of room service, and the size and facilities of the rooms themselves, are usually quite superb. In Beijing, New Delhi, Kuala Lumpur, Taipei, Jaipur and Bangkok, I have been given a taste of how the really well-off live. (I have not yet stayed at a top hotel in the Arabian Gulf.) Not only have I enjoyed a suite of rooms, complimentary champagne, fresh fruit and chocolates, but also, luxury on luxury, a warmed toilet seat and TV in the bathroom! No wonder that I do not choose to participate in some of the social activities as much as my colleagues would like. In any case, as I have already written, I am not very good at small-talk, nor, for a variety of reasons, do I enjoy late-night drinking or exploring the nightspots of the cities I visit.

****

Finally, at this point in my story let me write about my hobbies, and my likes and dislikes. When I am not working (which Christine will tell you is not very often – even in my early eighties!), how do I occupy my time? Well, until recently my favourite recreations have been gardening – shaping and pruning shrubs I find especially therapeutic – walking, particularly on the Cornish headlands, reading and watching my favourite TV programmes (which I find, as I get older, are becoming fewer and fewer), dining out, going to the theatre and concerts, and river cruising. At the same time, the hassle of contemporary road and rail travel and mixing with teeming crowds in large cities is such that Christine and I usually prefer to frequent restaurants and theatres nearer to home; in both these respects we are well served around the Henley and Windsor areas. Both of us, and particularly Christine, enjoy a day out organized by (a local branch of) the National Trust. By such means we have also visited several of the cathedrals in England and Wales (I would like to visit all 44 in my lifetime), as well as several country estates and gardens. I also very much enjoy train journeys, particularly those powered by steam engines, and which are off the main line routes.

Our second home in Cornwall, which is right on the south coast near St Mawes, is our most treasured haven. After visiting this part of the world and renting a National Trust cottage for 20 years, the opportunity arose for us to purchase one of the apartments of a converted hotel building. As I write these words, at 10.30 a.m. on a beautifully sunny morning overlooking a calm and serene sea, with no other building in sight, but just a view of sheep and cattle grazing in a nearby field, and cormorants, kittiwakes, oystercatchers, and seagulls trying to prise out small fish and crustaceans from the rocky beach immediately below me, I am as content as I possibly could be. But, of course, being exposed on a promontory on the south-west Cornish coast, we are also subject to horrendous storms; and then it is a case of battening down the hatches, and watching the angry and swirling seas from the safety and comfort of our living room.

I love Cornwall – and particularly the Roseland and the Cornish people. Within an hour of our flat, we can motor to any part of the county, from Land's End in the west to Looe in the east, and to the artists' paradise of St Ives and the small fishing port of Padstow on the north coast. But I think our favourite harbour resort is that of St Mawes, from which we can catch a ferry across the entrance to the Carrick Roads (where large cruise liners are frequently moored) to the bustling, but charming port of Falmouth. Since 1999, I have aimed to spend at least 90 days writing and relaxing in the most idyllic and inspiring of surroundings. But the Roseland is a 260-mile drive from our home in Henley, and I fear it will not be too long before this might become too much for me![4]

****

What next of my likes and dislikes? As I have already written (in the previous chapter) I have fairly eclectic culinary tastes, although I prefer relatively plain food, made from the best ingredients and expertly cooked, to elaborate dishes in which (in my opinion) the sauces and other embellishments, rather than bringing out the taste of the main ingredients, often stifle them. I am a 'middle of the road' music lover, and enjoy particularly the more popular works of the classical composers, especially those of Handel, Mozart, Tchaikovsky, Beethoven, Vivaldi and Strauss; those of the early twentieth-century musicians such as Elgar and Vaughan Williams; and, on a lighter note, the melodic masterpieces of Gilbert and Sullivan, and Andrew Lloyd Webber. I prefer reading non-fiction, and particularly biographies and political memoirs, though I am not averse to the writings of more popular novelists like Ken Follett, Anita Shrieve or even Jeffrey Archer! Although I believe UK TV to be the best in the world, I like only about 10 per cent of the programmes screened, preferring the documentaries on the natural world (those of David Attenborough in particular) and those recounting our rich historical heritage. I also avidly watch political and religious debates, and anything to do with different cultures and social mores.

As to my dislikes, I hate anything to do with cruelty and gratuitous violence; and deplore much of the belligerence and anger which seems to infuse so many TV programmes and films. I know that war and brute force are part of our everyday life, but I am convinced that much of what our children are exposed to every day is all too easily considered as the norm rather than the exception. It is here where, in our celebrity- and media-obsessed culture, our societal norms – for good or bad – are shaped.

My other pet aversion is that of man (and child)-made noise – of almost any kind! I certainly have a love–hate relationship with mobile phones. I regard most of the conversations I am forced to hear in airport lounges, on public transport, in restaurants or at any social gathering an intrusion into my liberty *not* to be exposed to such noise – which in nine cases out of ten, is no more than idle chit-chat. Yes, of course, I fully appreciate the benefits of mobile phones – particularly in emergencies of one kind or another. But like most forms of modern consumer technology – including car radios, and computers – they can be deployed in an antisocial way.

I must own that I am an intellectual dinosaur as far as computers are concerned. Since I authored my first article in 1952, right up to the present day, the first draft of everything I have written (including that of this volume) has been prepared by hand. 'Why?' you may ask. Well, the short answer is that over the past 40 years, I have been blessed by having a succession of efficient (and very patient) secretaries, who have typed all of my single-authored works. My present, and most valued helpmate is Jill Turner, who

for part of my time as Head of the Department of Economics was my secretary, and who since her retirement from the university has both done most
of my typing and looked after my emails. More recently, in my jointly
written books and papers, my co-author – who, almost invariably, has been
younger than I, and weaned in the computer age – has done all the typing.
One example of how much I owe to these colleagues and friends is that of
the initial typing of the 1400 pages of the revised edition of my magnum
opus *Multinational Enterprises and the Global Economy* which was done
entirely by my joint author, Sarianna Lundan. At the same time, I must own
that my pen and pencil have never let me down, even on my various airline
journeys, though to the flight attendants and nearby passengers my mode
of writing must appear anachronistic!

What, finally, do I regard as the most fulfilling part of my life? On a personal level, it is the life I share with Christine. Though very different in a
number of ways, our tastes and personalities complement each other very
well. She, like my mother, is a very practical, sensitive and loving individual, who cannot do enough for her family and friends, and particularly for
her sister. I, on the other hand, am more like my father – quite hopeless with
anything mechanical or electrical, and viewing all problems and challenges
as objectively and logically as I can.

Christine is particularly blessed with an enviable fund of emotional intelligence and generosity. Such personal attributes as I possess are more
directed to helping those in need to understand the underlying causes of
anything which may concern them; and how best they might deal with such
causes in a morally acceptable way. We are really quite perfect for each other!

Outside my personal life, teaching, research, consultancy and writing
have given me almost complete fulfilment. I enjoy my leisure pursuits,
though I am not passionate about any hobbies. Cricket and tennis are my
favourite sports, but (and this might be heresy to some of my readers) I am
neither a soccer nor a rugger enthusiast. When I go to bed each night, I
judge the worthwhileness of my day by the quality of the relationships I
have had with other people, and the ways and extent to which I feel I have
made a positive contribution to anything – work, charitable causes or
leisure – in which I might have been involved that day.

****

NOTES

1. The main university financing arm of the UK government.
2. Details of which I set out in Chapter 9.

3. Earlier in 1965 I had been elected as President of the (UK) Southern Baptist Association which I was forced to decline as my time was fully taken up with my new appointment at Reading.
4. In fact, we disposed of our Cornish property in July 2008.

Receiving Honorary
Doctorate
at Autonomous University
of Madrid
1990

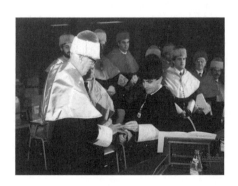

My retirement
party at
Reading University
1993

With John Cantwell,
Rajneesh Narula and
PhD students
at Reading
1997

PhD students at Rutgers
and Mrs Miller (secretary)
1995

With Peter Gray
at EIBA Meeting
Maastricht 2005

With Danny Van Den Bulcke
2005

Singing (!)
at Chinese Culture University
Taipei 1996

9. Shakespeare's fourth age continued: a peripatetic professor

At the time of my childhood, it was unusual for children to travel abroad. Nowadays it is commonplace. Several of the 85 countries I have visited in the last 40 years, I had never even heard of in the 1930s: and, of course, since gaining their political independence in the post-Second World War era, most erstwhile British territories have changed their name. Even in my wildest dreams, I could never have imagined that I would be spending such a large part of my working life outside my home country.

I have already described my first foray abroad in 1945, which was taken courtesy of His Majesty. After that, it was not until 1960 that I acquired a passport. In the 1950s, Ida and I spent our holidays in England – mostly on the Isle of Wight where Ida's parents then lived.

Both my first two overseas trips were by sea or overland, although in October 1960 I did take my first commercial flight from New York to Columbus, Ohio. But since then, beginning with various speaking engagements and consultancy commitments on the European continent, I have travelled mostly by air.

As I described in the previous chapter, in 1968 I was invited to spend nine months at the University of Western Ontario in London, Canada. Accompanied by Christine, the journey to Toronto by a Boeing 707 was my first transatlantic air crossing; we then boarded a twin-engine propeller plane to take us to London, 120 miles to the west of Toronto. It had been eight years since I had been in Canada, and I was looking forward to my return visit.

The university had arranged for Christine and I to rent a very pleasant apartment just ten minutes walk from the Department of Economics. The Department was centrally situated on a most attractive campus. My immediate impression was how similar the architecture and stonework of the buildings were to that of many Scottish universities.[1] The apartment was also conveniently located on a bus route just 15 minutes away from downtown London.

After a week or so in London, Ontario I bought a second-hand car – a Triumph 2000, similar to the model I owned at home. It was a dreadful mistake. The British-made car was completely unsuited to the rigours of a Canadian winter. It was off the road more than on it, and it frequently failed me just when I needed it. I paid (Canadian) $2000 for the vehicle in September 1968, but could only sell it for $400 a year or so later.

****

During my time in Canada, I travelled to each of the Canadian provinces. I visited the University of Winnipeg in Manitoba, in deep midwinter. I recall that the temperature was 0 degrees Fahrenheit, and that the cars in the university's parking lot were plugged into a heating stall to prevent their windscreens from icing up. In Calgary, after a lecture at the University of Alberta, I was taken by car 90 miles north and introduced to one of the most beautiful national parks in North America at Banff, the gateway to the Canadian Rockies. I spent another weekend in Vancouver in late spring 1969, during which time I enjoyed seeing the spectacular floral displays in Stanley and Elizabeth parks. I revisited a revitalized Toronto, this time with Christine, and we were both impressed by the many new and exciting downtown developments, and those bordering on Lake Ontario. We were also charmed by a Chelsea-like redevelopment scheme off Bloor Street, called the Hampton.

In a warm, but fragrant, Canadian summer, Christine and I also travelled east from London by Canadian Pacific railroad through some delightful countryside to spend a pleasant weekend in Canada's cradle of modern history, Quebec City. This was the site of the epic battle in 1759 between the British and French armies, in which the British, led by General Montcalm, scaled the Heights of Abraham which surrounded the city. This action, which led to the British gaining command of the French stronghold in Canada, is played out in miniature each day in a museum in Quebec. I also recaptured my memories of Ottawa, and was reminded of how similar the architecture of the parliamentary buildings there is to the Houses of Parliament in London, while that of the major university buildings in Toronto and Hamilton (like those in London, Ontario), were not only influenced by Scottish architecture, but were often built by stone imported from north-east Scotland.

While in Canada, I also ventured south of the 49th parallel on three occasions. The first was to New York to present a paper (recently co-authored with Max Steuer of the London School of Economics – LSE) at a seminar organized by the National Bureau of Economic Research (NBER).[2] It was on this occasion that I first met Charlie Kindleberger, and it was at his invitation that six months later I paid a visit to the Massachusetts Institute of Technology (MIT) at Boston to attend a symposium he organized on The International Corporation. It was also at that time that I was introduced to Stephen Hymer, and came to know about – and indeed acquired a copy of – his seminal 1960 thesis on the *International*

Operations of Firms. Immediately, I was attracted by the serious vitality of the black-bearded Canadian scholar. Here was a man with a scholarly mission; and in his comparatively short professional life[3] he made several path-breaking contributions to the theory of foreign direct investment, and to the role of multinational enterprises (MNEs) in economic development.[4] Hymer had been Kindleberger's PhD student some years earlier, as indeed had several other attendees at the conference including Bob Aliber. A year later, both Hymer and Aliber were among the North American participants at a small workshop organized by myself and sponsored by Shell International, at the University of Reading on The Multinational Enterprise.[5]

****

Throughout my professional life, I have often found that unexpected benefits come out of conferences and symposia in which I have participated, but which, at the time, I viewed more as a duty than as a pleasure. Certainly both the NBER and Kindleberger conferences encouraged me to continue my research on foreign direct investment (FDI) and the MNE. And so it was, in 1972, that at the invitation of Shell International I was invited to attend an international seminar in Dusseldorf, Germany on the legal implications of the growth of FDI. The only time I spoke at that seminar was to make a five-minute intervention summarizing the economist's view of the costs and benefits of international business activity.

But the intervention caught the attention of Philippe de Seynes, Under Secretary-General of the Economic and Social Council of the UN. Earlier in 1972, this charming Frenchman had been charged by the Secretary-General to convene a panel of high-level experts (later called the Group of Eminent Persons) to examine the role of MNEs in economic development and international relations.

At the time, Mr de Seynes had appointed most of his 20-member team, but needed to find a British representative as his first choice, Roy Jenkins – a distinguished politician and author – was not able to participate. However, rather than seek out another politician or statesperson, he decided to recruit a British academic; and to my honour and delight he requested permission from the UK government to submit my name to the Secretary-General. I shall recall later, in more detail, some of my subsequent associations with the UN, but as a direct result of my short intervention in that seminar in Dusseldorf, my professional life took a path I am sure it would not otherwise have taken.

****

Sometimes, too, one visits a country, city or organization which at the time seems to have no special significance, but later, in a totally unanticipated way, comes to play an important part in one's life. Such was my first visit to Rutgers University in New Jersey in the spring of 1969. Little did I know at the time, that 30 years later I would be spending half of each academic year at that university.

Nevertheless, my visit was memorable in another respect. My teaching schedule at the time was such that I could only manage a day's visit to the university campus at New Brunswick. I left London (Ontario) at 6.00 a.m. on a lovely Friday morning in late April and motored the 90 miles to Toronto Airport in a high-powered hire car (my Triumph 2000 was having one of its regular hospitalized treatments!). I then took an Air Canada flight to JFK Airport in New York, from whence I flew by helicopter across New York to Newark Airport in New Jersey. There I was met by my host, and driven through the racially tense (and, at that time, quite dangerous) city of Newark[6] and then another 30 miles or so to the New Brunswick campus, where we arrived at lunch time. After my afternoon lecture (I seemed to recall my subject was the comparative profitability of US and UK overseas investment) I joined the Economics Faculty for drinks. For the first time, I met Peter Gray, – who, throughout the past 40 years, has been a valued colleague and a good friend.

Around 6 p.m. my host drove me back to Newark Airport, and there I again boarded a helicopter, this time for a breathtaking trip above Manhattan just as the skyscrapers were being turned into a fairyland of twinkling lights. After dinner on a Canada-bound jet, I arrived at Toronto at 10.30 p.m. and began my long drive home. The night was fine and the roads were almost empty as I speedily drove my way to London. I was about halfway along the Queen Elizabeth highway when a police car caught up with me. I had to admit I was exceeding the 60 mile an hour speed limit (by a margin of 35 miles it turned out!). I tried to use my British accent, and professed innocence of Canadian motorway regulations to avoid being given a speeding ticket but the police cop, polite as he was, was having nothing of it. The penalty was an on-the-spot fine. I had a choice of punishment: pay $30 within seven days, or go to jail for two days! I was almost tempted to add to my Canadian experiences by choosing the latter option, but thought better of it, and duly paid the fine. I arrived back in London just before 1 a.m. on the Saturday morning, feeling that I had really lived the previous day to the full!

****

In June 1969, Christine and I left London, Ontario for San Francisco and Berkeley. I had enjoyed my time at the University of Western Ontario and the experience of teaching Canadian students. I also respected the high intellectual calibre of the Faculty, and their friendliness to me. However, in the absence of Grant Reuber, who since inviting me to the Department of Economics had become Dean of the School of Social Sciences, there was no one else working in my area of research.[7] Both Christine and myself found the North American lifestyle easy and comfortable. Many things which are now quite commonplace in England – like half-gallon plastic cartons of milk, multiflavoured ice creams, a huge range of breakfast cereals, waffles and syrup, and clam chowder soup – were all quite new to us, as were the large and well-stocked supermarkets and the large weekly shops done by the average Canadian housewife. But for the most part, we ate – as we continued to eat when we later lived in the US – much as we did in England. Over the years, with improvements in refrigeration techniques, the speed of transportation and the advent of the microwave, most out-of-season or nonindigenous foods have become available to shoppers throughout the world. Fortunately, however, there remain variations in culinary tastes between national consumers, so that wherever one travels there are different things to eat, or different ways in which dishes are prepared. This, however, was not so much the case in 1968. Certainly, at that time, unlike the situation in the UK, the US supermarkets were truly an Aladdin's cave, offering a huge and tempting range of packaged food items.[8] Neither, of course, was there then any concern about the environmental consequences and rising fuel costs of transporting goods over long distances, which in 2008, is causing UK shoppers to favour locally grown food products.

****

Our three months at the University of California at Berkeley were quite eventful. We were able to rent not only a modern and unfurnished apartment about a ten-minute drive from the campus, but also (and separately) the furniture we needed. We also managed to borrow crockery, kitchen utensils and the like from a rolling store organized by the students. We rented a Volkswagen Beetle car, which we used not only for shopping and other local trips, but to do some sightseeing elsewhere in California, and also in Nevada where we experienced US-style casinos and high-profile entertainment for the first time.

However, perhaps most memorable at the time were the student demonstrations and various love-ins and flower power festivals for which San Francisco and Berkeley became particularly well known in the late 1960s. This was also the time of the Vietnam War, while the introduction of the contraceptive pill was having a quite dramatic affect on young people's attitude towards gender-related issues. Almost every day, the city of

Berkeley was the scene of some kind of student activism, which climaxed in September 1969 in a lengthy sit-in against the policies of the Californian government towards the war, and cutbacks in university finances. Though these events only marginally affected our everyday lives, they did provide us with a real glimpse into the evolving youth culture in the US, and the strong reactions of the vibrant and more educated Americans to events unfolding in both their own country and across the globe.

****

For some three years after my return from my year's leave of absence in North America, I was occupied in completing several research projects, which left little time for foreign travel. These included a two-year study of the economic structure and likely future of the City of London. The results of this study were published in a volume co-authored with Victor Morgan on behalf of the Economists Advisory Group.[9] I also put together a book of essays which contained some of the results of my earlier researches into UK FDI in North America;[10] and edited another volume which contained the papers presented at the Reading conference on MNEs to which I have already made reference.[11]

At the same time, other interesting opportunities for travelling abroad were opening up. The first was in April 1970 when I testified before the US Foreign Affairs Committee of the US Senate in Washington on the role of US-owned affiliates in the UK economy. I remember this especially because it was my first experience of travelling in a jumbo jet across the Atlantic – and travelling first class at that! Since my visit was financed by the US government I was required to travel on a US airline, in this case on Pan American. My return flight particularly sticks in my memory as I was one of just six first class passengers looked after by six flight attendants! I certainly got the taste for upmarket air travel on that flight, and when, a year later, an opportunity for travelling first class around the world came about, I took it with both hands. This opportunity arose as a result of a second event which occurred in my travelling itinerary in the 1970s.

****

In 1972 I was asked to be External Assessor of the Department of Economics at the University of the South Pacific (USP) in Suva, Fiji. Lest anyone thinks that this was a ticket to sunny paradise, let me hasten to disillusion them. Suva, the capital of Fiji, is one of the wettest places on earth. It boasts (if that is the right word!) an annual rainfall of 264 inches a year – and most of this seemed to descend the first time I visited the island in April

1973. My visit was financed by the Inter-University Council in London. At the time, the University of the South Pacific was only four years old, and was under the guardianship of the Ministries of Education of the Australian, Canadian and UK governments, which *inter alia* required each department of the university to be externally assessed. Each assessor was appointed for three years, and was expected to visit the department in at least one of these years.

The Inter-University Council provided me with an economy round-trip fare from London to Suva which – in 1973 – amounted to £1200. But I soon found that I could buy a first class round-the-world ticket from Pan Am for £1100. The routing of the ticket was from London to San Francisco, and then on to Honolulu, Hong Kong, Bangkok and London. Apart from San Francisco, I had not visited any of these places, and although I was unable to spend more than a couple of days in each, I sampled enough of their delights to tempt me to return.

The Hawaiian Islands became the fiftieth state of the USA in 1950. With an indigenous population of 700 000 in 1970, the islands (previously known as the Sandwich Islands) were much less developed than they are today. Honolulu, the capital and leading tourist centre, is situated on the south coast of Oahu island. The islands have one of the most equable and warm climates in the world, although occasionally they suffer from hurricanes, as was the case in September 1992 when a devastating storm destroyed most of one of the northern outer islands, Kaui. I stayed at the Hilton Hawaiian Village, a five-star hotel right on Waikiki Beach, and surrounded, in its own grounds, by a village of five restaurants and 30 shops. There I enjoyed a 48-hour rest after my 20-hour flight from England, first across the Atlantic to San Francisco and then across the Pacific to Honolulu. Early on a sunlit morning, I found the approach to the volcanic islands, which rose out of the Pacific some 40 000 years ago, was quite magical.

Waikiki Beach is perhaps the most famous surfing beach in the world. Between it and Honolulu Harbour (Pearl Harbour is about 5 miles further north) is the delightful south side park which is a favourite picnic spot of the local residents. From there, a coastal road winds its way through Diamond Head around the island, though a quicker way to the less-developed north shore of Oahu is through the mountains. The latter route takes in spectacular Hawaiian scenery full of lush tropical vegetation. Compared with about 40 inches of annual rainfall around the coast, the middle of Oahu has over 125 inches, and the top of the mountain is usually enveloped in mist.

The University of Hawaii is situated on the southern slopes of the mountain, about 5 miles north of Honolulu, and within an easy bus ride of the city. Its mainly white contemporary buildings, which blend well with the landscape, are set midway between the East Asian coast and western coast of the US. Not surprisingly, being set on an island midway between East Asia and the US, the university has established an outstanding reputation in its teaching of Asian–US studies. It also houses a prestigious international research unit – the East–West Centre. It was to this Centre that I was to return three times over the next decade.

****

In my overnight air journey from Honolulu to Fiji, I crossed the international date line, and lost a day of my life! While the international airport is on the south coast of one of the largest of the Viti Levu Islands, Suva, the capital is on the north coast, and in the 1970s could only be reached by air. After a half-hour flight in a small 12-seater Fokker plane crossing a range of hills covering the centre of the island, I was met at the airport by the Vice-Chancellor's chauffeur who, like most Fijians, was a giant of a man! My accommodation was in a wooden bungalow located at the entrance to the campus of the university. My small bedroom housed a wardrobe which had an electric heater in it – a necessary piece of equipment to prevent one's clothes from getting mildew in one of the most humid climates I have ever experienced. I, and another visiting professor – Eric Hobshawn, the eminent historian – were looked after by an ebullient and extremely welcoming Fijian housekeeper. Both Eric and myself remember her particularly for the size of her breakfasts and evening meals. We both felt she was doing her best to fatten us to become as large as the average male Fijian!

****

My task as External Assessor at USP was to review the syllabi of the Department, read some sample examination scripts, consult with each member of the Economics Department, with some of those from other departments within the Faculty of Arts, and with the Vice-Chancellor. At the end of my week's stay, I was required to submit a report to the Senate of the university. In the event, under the leadership of Ashok Desai, a most likeable and competent Indian economist and excellent administrator, the Department was offering a creditable portfolio of economics courses, and was trying to establish its own niche by focusing its teaching and research interests on the economics of the west Pacific islands.

Some 90 per cent of the students reading economics at the university came from Micronesia – and especially from Tonga, Samoa and the Gilbert and Ellis islands. For the most part, they got on well with the indigenous students, half of whom were native Fijian and half of Indian origin. But on social occasions, when sometimes things were apt to get out of control, relationships between the Fijians and other South Sea Islanders became extremely strained. On one of the evenings when I was in Fiji, there was a party given to introduce me to the students. On this particular occasion, the drink – including a particularly potent home-brewed beer – flowed freely, and by the time I left at about 10 p.m. the party was really swinging. The following morning I was told that, by midnight, things had got quite nasty between the red-headed Tongans and the large native Fijians. Fighting had broken out; there were several injuries; and a lot of broken furniture! Ashok Desai was quite calm about the whole affair, indicating to me that it was not unusual, and put it down to 'high spirits'. The culprits were never identified – not formally at least!

I enjoyed my time in Suva, though I disliked the humidity – only the cupboard housing the mainframe computer had air conditioning in the university! I was also very concerned about an outbreak of dengue, a particularly virulent and painful kind of fever similar to malaria that frequently led to anyone catching it becoming extremely depressed and frequently suicidal. While I was in Fiji, more than one-third of the foreign students and Faculty succumbed to the bug! Unfortunately, at the time there was no known immunization or cure for it. Daily mosquito bites were commonplace, but there was no way of telling whether one had been bitten by a dengue-carrying insect; that is, not until about ten hours afterwards when the symptoms of the malaria, including acute stomach pains and diarrhoea, became all too apparent. Not until I was well on my way across the Pacific to Hong Kong did I relax!

****

I returned to Fiji three more times. The first two were again as External Assessor. Normally, the Assessor makes only one visit to the University of the South Pacific (USP), Suva, but as two new heads of department in economics were appointed in quick succession to each other (Ashok Desai returned to India in 1973) the university asked me to provide some continuity to the affairs of the Department. On my second visit to Suva, I lived for four days at the home of the Vice-Chancellor – a New Zealander – and his charming family. On my third visit I put myself up at a hotel in Suva and commuted the short distance to the university each day. I also did some sightseeing around the beautiful island of Fiji with some colleagues from the Department. However, the most memorable tourist expedition occurred on the last day of my third visit.

I had left Suva airport at 7 a.m., and arrived at Nadi airport 40 minutes later. I had decided to take a day-long boat trip to one of the coral reefs off the south coast of the island. This initially involved a 5-mile taxi ride from the airport to the seaport of Luto Ka. Before I did this, I deposited my luggage in one of the lockers at the airport. The day, which had begun fine and sunny, turned overcast by mid-morning, and before we had completed an hour's boat trip to the out island, it had started to rain. And it continued to rain off and on until early evening.

It was hardly the ideal visit to a dream island, and things – for me at any rate – did not improve on the return boat trip when a group of extremely merry and half-drunk Australians proceeded to entertain (!) the rest of us with a succession of bawdy songs. The boat docked at Luto Ka at 9.30 p.m. A taxi I had earlier ordered was waiting to transport me back to the airport. I had plenty of time, as my plane was not due to leave for Honolulu until 2 a.m. I arrived at the airport at about 10 p.m. to collect my luggage, only to find that I had lost my locker key! Later, I decided it must have fallen out of my pocket when I was sitting on the beach of the out island (in the rain) at the coral reef. There followed two hours of almost complete panic, which only ended around midnight when the Chief of Security – the only person who had a duplicate key, and who himself was partying in Nadi – arrived at the airport to help rescue my suitcase. But my (and his) troubles were not quite over, as without my key I could not remember in which locker I had left my luggage! Eventually, after opening five lockers, we found the right one, and more in pity than in anger the long-suffering Chief of Security – perhaps the largest Fijian I had ever come across – handed the crazy Professor his suitcase. And as he did so, he still managed to smile!

****

My fourth and final trip to Fiji was in 1978 under very different, but no less traumatic circumstances. In the mid-1970s and early 1980s I was doing a lot of travelling for the UN Centre on Transnational Corporations (UNCTC).[12] On this occasion, although my journeying (another round-the-world trip) started well in Sri Lanka and India, by the time I reached Singapore I was feeling distinctly unwell. I think I must have picked up a stomach bug in Delhi or Madras. I managed to give a seminar at the Singapore National University, but on the night flight to Sydney I spent more time in the toilet than in my seat! Somehow or other I got through the lecture I had to give at the University of New South Wales in Sydney before boarding a plane later that afternoon to Canberra, where I was to spend a couple of days with my friend and erstwhile colleague David Robertson. I well recall that Geraldine, his wife, had arranged a lovely dinner party that evening, but in the event I could not eat a thing! The following day I decided I had to see a local doctor as I was becoming completely dehydrated. After

36 hours of Lomatil and salt tablets, I started to greet life once again, and was even able to enjoy a meal on my plane journey from Sydney to Nadi.

On this occasion, my visit to the USP was to consult lecturers from the departments of Economics, Geography and Sociology about the incorporation of material on transnational corporations (TNCs) into their undergraduate or graduate courses; and to establish what interest they might have in attending an intensive three-week course on TNCs and economic development, which the UNCTC was planning to arrange. After three days of unusually lovely weather, I took an afternoon plane back to Nadi. Rather unexpectedly, it turned out to be one of the bumpiest flights I have ever experienced, and by the time I arrived at the international airport the clouds had rolled in and there was a 60 mph gale blowing. When I checked in at the Quantas desk, I was informed that a hurricane was approaching Viti Levu, and that there was a possibility that my flight from Sydney to Honolulu might not touch down at Fiji. Two hours later, with winds increasing all the time, I and about 50 other passengers were informed that the flight to Honolulu had been cancelled; and we were each advised to seek accommodation in a nearby hotel to see us through what promised to be a rough night.

Naturally, by that time, all the hotels nearest the airport were fully booked, but the Fijian tourist bureau did manage to find me, and a couple of other passengers, rooms in a newly opened motel about 5 miles outside Nadi. I was given a room on the second (and top) floor of the building, and after a light meal I retired for the night. The wind was really getting up, and by midnight it had reached over 120 mph. The rain was torrential; nobody now dared venture outside; every moveable object had been stowed away and only the buildings of the motel and the surrounding palm trees were exposed to the brunt of the storm. By 3 a.m. the winds had peaked at 150 mph and the first power lines were down; the lights went off in my room. Half an hour later, the rain started to come in from the ceiling just above my bed. As there was a kitchenette attached to my room, I managed to catch the drips in two saucepans!

The storm continued with increasing ferocity for another two hours, and then began to abate. By early morning, the worst was over, and I and my fellow guests were able to assess the damage it had caused. Further along the road, several bungalows had had their roofs ripped off, cars were on their side or upside down, palm trees had been flattened, and there was a mass of debris where electrical cables had once been. All telephone lines were inoperable, and there were no mobile phones at the time. We were completely cut off from the outside world.

Later, we heard that Nadi Airport was closed as the storm had damaged the air traffic control tower. However, early that evening, after kicking our heels all day we were informed that the airport was once again operational. We were also told that an unscheduled Quantas flight would be diverted to Nadi later that night. So 24 hours later I finally left a hurricane-ravaged Fiji. As far as I am aware, there were no deaths or serious injuries that night, but there was a lot of structural damage and several families had to be evacuated from their homes.

****

My troubles were not over yet! I was working to a tight schedule. I left Fiji early on a Tuesday morning. Crossing the date line, I arrived in Honolulu on Monday at midday, and reached San Francisco later the same evening. By that time, I should have been in Fort Collins in Colorado; indeed, I had arranged for my good friend Teretomo Ozawa to meet me at Denver Airport at 6 p.m. on the Monday. Fortunately I had managed to telephone him from Honolulu, and inform him of my new arrival time of 9.30 a.m. on the following day. This meant I had to leave San Francisco at 6.30 a.m. So when I arrived at the airport just before midnight, I simply made myself comfortable on a bench seat and tried to get some sleep. It was the first time (though not the last) in my life that I had been forced to spend the night in an airport lounge!

By the time Teretomo and I arrived at Fort Collins after a two-hour drive from Denver airport, I was completely exhausted, as I had not slept properly for over 48 hours. And at three that afternoon I was to give a seminar, and at six a public lecture. After a couple of hours, sleep at the hotel, I was feeling absolutely awful. But the adrenalin eventually took over and I managed to stagger through both seminar and lecture! The following day I left for New York for a couple of days' work at the UNCTC, and then home!

****

The third factor which influenced my travelling arrangements in the early 1970s resulted from an invitation by the Secretary-General of the UN to be the UK representative of a 20 member Group of Eminent Persons (GEP) to study the impact of multinational corporations on economic development. As I have recounted earlier in this chapter, my appointment was one of the unexpected happenings in my professional life which directly led, over the following 30 years, to a variety of consultancies with several UN agencies.

The work of the GEP was undertaken at a time when there was a great deal of unease about the role of MNEs in economic development. Indeed the UN enquiry was prompted by the alleged interference of a powerful US MNE, ITT, in the political affairs of the Chilean government. At its first meeting in New York in April 1973, the Group appointed C.K. Jha, a former Indian Ambassador to the US, as its Chairman, and decided on its agenda. It was agreed that a Secretariat, comprising three of the staff of the Department of Economic and Social Affairs, were to assemble as much data as they could on the then extent and structure of MNE activity throughout the world, and its impact on economic and social development. It was further agreed that, at a later meeting, the Group would discuss drafts of the documents prepared by the UN Secretariat and listen to the views of a number of selected statesmen, scholars, business practitioners and representatives of special interest groups. In addition, the GEP drew upon the advice of two resident consultants, one of whom was Nat Weindberg, who had earlier served as Secretary of the leading auto union in the US.

About four months after the Group's first meeting, it convened again – this time at the Palais de Nations of the UN in Geneva. It spent five days listening to a wide range of testimonies about the ways in which MNEs were thought to impact on the economic and social welfare of the different constituents of the countries in which they operated. I remember in particular the eloquent, and often quite persuasive, presentations given by such distinguished scholars as Stephen Hymer, Oswaldo Sunkel, Joseph Nye and Ray Vernon; by such powerful business executives as Giovanni Agnelli (of Fiat), Jacque Maison Rouge (of IBM) and Gerry Adler (of Shell); and by leading consumer activists such as Ralph Nader.

A couple of months later, the Group repeated this exercise in New York, at the end of which it spent three days reviewing both the testimonies and the documents assembled by the Secretariat. It was at this point that a three-man subcommittee was appointed to prepare a draft of the report of the Group of 20, and I, along with the Chairman and Julian Somavia – now Secretary-General of the International Labour Office (ILO) – was charged with the responsibility.

****

The subcommittee, together with a three-man Secretariat from the UN, agreed to meet twice in the next two months – the first time in Rome, and the second in New Dehli at the Kashmir Embassy. In the event, because of illness, Julian Somavia was unable to attend on either occasion, so it was left to the Chairman and myself to prepare the draft report. While we were both very much of the same mind and took a broadly positive stance towards the role of MNEs in economic development, we recognized that among our group and those testifying to it, there were those who took a very different view, particularly with respect to the social and political implications of MNE activity in small countries, and/or in those pursuing socialist policies. Our task, then, was a tricky one. It was to prepare a document which was descriptively accurate, analytically sound, and sensible in its policy recommendations, yet was sufficiently in accord with the opinions of each member of the Group if he was to append his signature to it.

I also recall that, even among the Secretariat trio who were responsible for the actual drafting of the report, there was some discord, particularly with respect to the impact of MNEs on such culturally sensitive areas as labour and industrial relations, transfer pricing and the environment. One thing was agreed, however: that the report should recommend that the activities of MNEs – which the Group were later to rename transnational corporations (TNCs) – should be regularly studied and monitored by a specially appointed Commission of Transnational Corporations. It was envisaged that such a Commission would consist principally of civil servants appointed by national governments. However, it would be aided in its deliberations by academic and other experts, and be served by a full-time Secretariat. Gustave Feissel, one of the Secretariat and assistant to Philippe de Seynes, drafted much of the proposal; and he subsequently played a major role in the administrative affairs of the Commission and its supporting Secretariat.

The other two members of the Secretariat were a well-respected Chinese economist, N.T. Wang, and a young Greek economist, Satirios Mousouris – who earlier had completed his PhD degree at the Harvard Business School. Sitoris was inclined to be much more critical of MNEs than N.T. Wang, and I well remember having to tone down some of his more extreme drafts – particularly with respect to the impact of inbound FDI on employment and wages in host countries. However, by and large C.K. Jha and I were well satisfied with the Secretariat support we had, and our draft report was submitted to the GEP on time.

Both in Rome and in New Delhi, there was time for some sightseeing. Of the two capital cities, New Delhi more impressed itself on my memory, partly because it was so different to any other city I had ever visited, and partly because of the widespread and abject poverty which was so blatantly in evidence. The sheer number of destitute and frequently maimed small children and elderly men and women, not to mention those of working age in enforced idleness, overwhelmed me.

The UN team was housed at the Ashoka Hotel, a three-star government-owned establishment on the outskirts of New Delhi. I can well remember spending time with Sitoris and N.T. Wang drafting our report in the garden of the hotel (it was the Indian winter) around an empty swimming pool which was being repaired. I observed, with both interest and concern, that while the men did most of the actual construction work, it was the women – again, of all ages and clothed in traditional Indian garb – who acted as the carriers of the materials!

****

I spent most of one day in New Delhi taking a coach tour around both the new and old parts of the city. I visited Gandhi's tomb, the Red Fort[13] – to which I returned later that night to see one of a most memorable son et lumière which traced the history of the British involvement in India up to the time of independence. It was in that part of the old town that many of the city's street beggars congregated, converging on the tour buses as they disgorged their customers. Our tour guide advised us that, however much we might be moved by the plight of these unfortunate people, we should not give them any money. Although on this occasion I took their advice, on another I did not. I was in another part of New Delhi doing some shopping when a young boy – about nine years old I would think – approached me. He did not say a word. He just looked at me with his huge, sad and lovely brown eyes, and held out his hand. I did my best to ignore him, but he trotted beside me as I made my way back to the taxi rank. Eventually I put my hand in my pocket and gave him a couple of rupees. This was very unwise. Suddenly, out of nowhere it seemed, a score or more of young children descended on me, all thrusting their hands out and pleading for a few coins. Even when I got into the taxi, they surrounded it and ran beside it until it drew away from them. The taxi driver – although a resident of New Delhi – repeated the guide's advice to me.

Later – although my heart and soul spoke a different message – this advice stood me in good stead when I encountered even more soul-destroying poverty in Bombay (now Mumbai) and Madras (now Chenai). I have travelled to many developing countries, but none has presented so much a contrast between affluence and poverty, beauty and ugliness, hope and despair than has India. With the possible exception of Singapore (which today cannot really be thought of as a developing country), the urban areas of all poorer nations contain a distressingly large number of exceedingly poor people, many of whom are sick or disabled. But from Bangkok to Buenos Aires, Harare to Manila, and Jakarta to Lesotho, I have never come across the kind of poverty which so robs man of his dignity as I have in India. Although in part this may be a cultural phenomenon, it also has much to do with a long history of the caste system, British rule and, until the later 1990s, inappropriate economic policies.

And I believe it will take years – perhaps generations – of careful nurturing to imbue the average Indian with any real sense of self-respect and optimism. Fortunately there are now signs that under the leadership of Manmohan Singh, India is embracing the challenges of globalization, and is on the path of strong economic growth and social reform.

****

The annual round of conferences and seminars sponsored by universities, businesses, international agencies and scholarly associations have taken me to many places in Europe, North America, Australia and Asia since the early 1970s. Looking back, among my most vivid (non-conference) memories of those years were the majestic and stunning beauty of Sydney Harbour, the largest natural harbour in the world; the chilling and sinister edifice of the Berlin Wall, and the drabness of the environment in East Berlin; the unrestrained licentiousness of the Pat Pong district of Bangkok; the contrast between the sterility of the architecture of much of modern Stockholm, and the charm and character of the old city; the incredible treasures of the Hermitage museum in St Petersburg and the magnificent sculptures and artefacts of the Florentine museums; the orderly behaviour, movement and conduct of people in the densely populated and traffic-polluted city of Tokyo; the pristine and picturesque beaches of North Kaui, at the foothold of a dramatic volcanic mountain; the intricate network of canals in Amsterdam; the awesome grandeur of the Grand Canyon in Arizona; the proud, yet poor people who eke out their living in such a clean and dignified fashion at Aberdeen Harbour in Hong Kong; the idyllic setting of the Rockefeller villa which towers over the confluence of Lakes Como and Maggiore in North Italy; the most excellent restaurants of Montreal and Bangkok;[14] the exuberant and infectious *joie de vivre* of the people of New Orleans at the time of the jazz festival; in the 1970s, the thousands of Chinese all bicycling to work at the same time in Tianjin, China's third-largest city;[15] and the watching of a mock air-raid (supposedly from North Korea) at dead of night from the fourteenth floor of a hotel building in Seoul.

Finally, in July 2006, I dined with my friends and colleagues of the Academy of International Business (AIB) in the huge and magnificent banqueting room of the People's Palace in Beijing. No less fresh in my memory was the privileged viewing (with Christine) a year earlier of the life-sized Chinese terracotta warriors and horses of Emperor Qin Shi Huang's Mausoleum near Xian City; and, in 2007, our tour over the ornate, ostentatious, marble-built and largely unoccupied Palace of Parliament,[16] which was built by Nicolae Ceausescu in Bucharest as the showpiece of the

Communist world, and now reputed to be the second-largest building in the world.[17]

****

In June 1975, I received the totally unexpected honour of being awarded an Honorary Doctorate in Economics by Uppsala University in Sweden. My presenter was one of Sweden's most distinguished economists, Sune Carlson. The occasion was an auspicious and memorable one. The ceremony took place in a majestic, oval-shaped auditorium which seated around 2000 people. Uppsala is the oldest university in Sweden, and in 1977 celebrated its 500th anniversary. Each June, it confers three kinds of doctorate degrees. The first are for those students who have just graduated from the university; the second are contemporary Honorary Doctorates, and the third are for Uppsala alumni who gained their Doctorates 50 years previously. Unlike in most academic institutions, the graduates were not clad in academic robes. Instead all the prospective doctorates wore black tails and waistcoats and white bow ties. On their heads, they wore a top hat. The only academic insignia presented to each graduate was a gold ring, personally inscribed, together with a small laurel wreath.

The great hall of Uppsala University is situated at the top of a 500-foot hill overlooking the city. Immediately outside the main entrance to the building there is a large tree-lined terrace, which was later to be packed with proud relations and friends of the graduands. When I arrived for the ceremony, I noticed a group of about 20 Swedish soldiers standing around four large cannons – with a huge stack of shells beside them. When I asked Jan Eric Vahlne – one of Sune Carlson's students, and now an eminent scholar in international business – what was going on, he explained that each time the first of the three kinds of graduands received his (or her) degree, one shell was fired; when the Honorary Doctorates were received a salvo of two shells was fired; and when the 50-year doctorates were received a salvo of three shells was fired. I later learned that there was someone strategically placed at one of the upstairs windows of the auditorium, whose job it was to signal to the officer in charge the precise moment when the degree was conferred by the President of the university by crowning the head of the graduand with the laurel wreath.

The ceremony was a long – a very long – one. It lasted over three hours as there were more than 200 Doctoral degrees being awarded. Each of the 20 or so Honorary Doctors was introduced by the Dean of the Faculty, who had originally nominated them. I and Gunnar Ohlin – the nephew of the Nobel prize winner Bertil Ohlin – had to wait until near the end of the ceremony before Sune Carlson presented us. He rose, put his hat over a novel he had been reading for the past two and a half hours, and proceeded to recite our respective academic merits – in faultless Latin! (Later he sent me an English version of what he said!) As I received my degree I heard the two-gun salvo go off; I only wished I had asked for the empty shells, as many of the new graduands had done!

The night before the ceremony I had been splendidly entertained by Jan Eric and another student (both of whom did their best to expose me to the nightlife of Stockholm!) and I remember walking in the centre of the city at 2 a.m. as if it was daytime! How different from my next visit to Uppsala two years later when, on a bitterly cold December day, there were over 14 hours of darkness! Some two decades later Christine and I took a cruise up the Norwegian fjords, and for 72 hours experienced no darkness at all. By contrast I remember a couple of visits – to Singapore and to Arusha in Tanzania[18] – to places where on each day in the year, there are equal hours of daylight and darkness.

****

To say that I have always enjoyed travelling is untrue. Anyone who has taken more than a dozen air trips – and some who have taken only one – has suffered from flight delays, cancellations, bad food and indifferent service, noisy and obnoxious fellow passengers, obstreperous children, shrieking babies, cramped seating, bad weather, diverted flights and mislaid baggage. I have endured each of these experiences. These have ranged from a 15-hour delay on a BA flight from Montreal; to flying through a frightening thunderstorm across the Pacific; to more than a dozen cancelled flights – the most memorable being at Tianjing Airport in 1977 when no one had the slightest idea of when the next flight to Beijing was likely to be; to several forced stopovers in Los Angeles, Nadi and Hong Kong, because of missed connections; to the almost impossible task of getting a ticket changed at the Jakarta office of Indonesian airlines; to being grounded by fog for several hours at Heathrow, Milan and Aarhus airports; and to almost not being allowed to leave New Delhi Airport in the 1970s because a customs official was expecting a bribe if he was to permit me to carry on board some Indian brassware. But on this latter occasion, when I showed him a document confirming that I was working on for the UN, his aggressive – not to mention expectant – attitude changed to one of ungracious resignation in allowing me to leave the country. And, of course, I like other travellers, have had to suffer quite regular irritations of arriving at airports where there is no vacant reception bay for the aircraft; or when it is parked away from the terminal and there are no readily available steps or buses; or, when one gets outside the airport building, huge queues to get through immigration and long baggage delays. In each of these respects, I think that prior to the opening of Terminal 5 in 2008, Heathrow Airport must have the worst record.[19]

However, when things go smoothly and one is travelling business or first class, air travel can be both luxurious and exhilarating. I enjoy the facilities and quietness of the airport lounges – or rather I did, before the mobile phone was invented. I appreciate the more spacious and comfortable seats and ample leg room of the more expensive seating. I relish the anticipation of a first class meal – particularly on Singapore, Thai or Gulf carriers, but very rarely on any US airlines! I like being pampered and addressed by name – as happened when Christine and I travelled by Concorde between London and New York in April 1995. I also value the opportunity of disembarking from a 747 before most of the 400 people on board, which usually means I am among the first through immigration and customs.[20]

I enjoy all these things, but most of all I appreciate them because they allow me to work quietly, particularly on day-long trips. Perhaps the oxygen at 35 000 feet does something to my brain. Perhaps it is because I am away from the telephone and other interruptions, but I do find airline journeys quite conducive to writing. This means that usually I am not a very sociable travelling companion – not, at least, until the meal is served. Over the years, my secretaries have also told me they can gauge how much I have had to drink on a particular journey, as the more I imbibe the more flowery and difficult to decipher my writing becomes!

****

If air travelling has its hazards and hiccups, so does road and rail travel. In Mexico in 1975, I was travelling by road from Mexico City to a conference centre about 30 miles away when the engine at the rear of the bus caught fire. There was a quick evacuation of the passengers, and we all stood at the side of the road in temperatures of 95 degrees Fahrenheit waiting for a replacement vehicle. Another time, I was abandoned by a New York taxi on the main freeway between J.F. Kennedy Airport and Manhattan; although the alternative option – of continuing the journey in his cab with unreliable brakes – seemed to me even worse. And anyone who has travelled in one of Danny Van den Bulcke's cars knows that it more than likely to break down, as it did on one occasion when he was driving me to Brussels airport to catch a flight to Johannesburg. Hardly less scary was a 10-mile police-escorted taxi journey from the centre of Athens to Piraeus. On this occasion, Christine and I were travelling in a convoy led by the President of Greece. With all horns blowing, and loud screaming by the drivers, who ignored all red traffic lights, we sped our way at an alarming rate from city to port!

But I think my most memorable foreign car journey was in South Korea. In 1977, I was invited to that country as a guest lecturer at King Sojan University in Seoul. This was a private university at which the mother-in-law of a PhD student of mine at Reading was President, and his brother-in-law was Professor of Economics. The student's name was Hyaun-Du Park, and his father Inn Gack Park was Governor of the North Province of Korea (South Korea has never acknowledged the annexation of the northern part of the country by the North Korean government), a post which included responsibility for the refugees who chose to migrate from the north of the 38th parallel.

At the end of my lectures, I had a couple of days to spare and Governor Park suggested I might like to accompany him on a visit he was about to take to the province of Chinju, some 150 miles south of Seoul. Apparently, every six months, as many of the male descendants of the Park dynasty as possible gather at a shrine of their ancestors in a park-like setting in one of the oldest parts of Korea, where many of the past generations of Parks (and other families) are buried. The Governor and I were comfortably transported in a chauffeur driven-car along a motorway through beautiful hilly countryside rather like Somerset or Devon. On our arrival in Chinju, I was given a guided tour of the district, although I learned very little as the Governor could speak little English, and I knew absolutely no Korean. Yet, somehow, we managed to communicate – I think mainly by sign language – during the evening we spent together. After breakfast the following morning, we made our way to the burial ground of the Parks. All that identified the place was a large green mound, into which there was a door into a series of burial chambers. Just in front of the mound there were several tables on which was placed some food and drink. I was introduced by the Governor to a handful of the 200 or so Parks present, and then a service of thanksgiving and remembrance (which rather resembled Holy Communion in the Anglican Church) started – and this lasted for about an hour. Immediately afterwards, we adjourned for lunch and then started our return journey.

The time was then 2 p.m., and I was to be driven directly to Seoul Airport to catch a flight to Tokyo which left at 7 p.m. The journey to Seoul was expected to take about two and a half hours so I had plenty of time to spare – or so I thought! All went well until we were about 60 miles from the airport and the car started misfiring. We stopped at the side of the road, and the chauffeur got out of the vehicle, opened the bonnet and peered inside. He cleaned the distributor head, adjusted a lead or two, shut the bonnet and returned to the car. For the next 25 miles, there was no other sign of trouble; then not only did the engine start misfiring again, but it began to lose power. As time was getting on, we had no real alternative but to continue our journey. The next 10 miles took nearly an hour to cover, and our rate of progress was getting slower and slower. Eventually, just 5 miles from the airport and 70 minutes before my plane was due to leave, the car came to a complete halt on a very busy highway. By this time, Governor Park was quite beside himself. The possibility that his distinguished visitor might miss his plane because of *his* car breaking down was beyond his comprehension. I was then to witness an extraordinary sight. Governor Park got out of his car, and standing first at the side, and then gradually moving to the middle of the road, he began to thumb a lift. Even more astonishing was what followed. A milk float came along, stopped, and picked us up. There was no room in the front for both of us. The Governor insisted I sat beside the driver, and he deposited himself at the back, surrounded by milk crates with his legs dangling over the rear bumper. The chauffeur was left with the beached car!

It was in this style that we arrived at the airport with about 45 minutes to spare. With Mr Park by my side I checked in, and we made our way to emigration. Here we were greeted by an extremely lengthy queue. I thought there was no way I was going to catch my plane. At this point the Governor took direct action. Summoning the highest official he could lay his hands on (literally!) he explained the situation and who he was. Suddenly all doors opened! I was immediately given the VIP treatment and the last I saw of my Korean friend, as I was personally escorted through immigration, was a very relieved man mopping his brow!

****

In 1976, Christine and I spent the first four months of the year at Boston University. The university found us a pleasant apartment in an older residential district overlooking the Charles River. It was just five minutes' walk to the School of Management, and a ten-minute subway ride from downtown Boston. The time away from Reading University was the first leave of absence I had had for eight years, and I used it for two purposes. The first was to prepare a 40-hour lecture course on MNEs in the global economy. This later provided the basis for a similar course I was to teach as part of our MA degree programme in International Business at my home university. As it later transpired, these same lecture notes also provided the first draft of my volume *Multinational Enterprises and the Global Economy* published 16 years later.

I also used my time in the US to prepare a paper for an important symposium – the Nobel Symposium – on 'The International Allocation of Economy Activity' which was to take place later in the year in Stockholm. It was indeed at Boston that the eclectic theory (later renamed 'paradigm') was conceived. It attempted to combine some of my earlier work on the ownership (O) advantages of firms and the locational (L) advantages of countries with the burgeoning internalization (I) theory of the MNE. A seminal article on this latter subject by the economist J.C. McManus was brought to my attention by Edith Penrose on an aeroplane journey between London and Milan in 1973. At the time, she was reading an article by the Canadian scholar who was possibly the first economist to put the theory explicitly on the scholarly map. I well remember Edith saying to me that she thought there was little particularly new in the theory. Preferring the word 'integration', she asserted that she had analysed most of its characteristics and predictions in her 1959 book *The Theory of the Growth of the Firm*.[21]

In my paper, I traced the history of the post-war development of both FDI and trade theory, and then put forward a framework for a generalized model of trade and international production. The core of that framework rested on a trio of interrelated propositions, namely: (1) foreign-owned value-added activity would most likely take place when firms of one nationality had privileged access to unique income-generating assets over those of another; (2) their preference for accessing or utilizing these assets outside their national boundaries; and (3) the extent to which they found it in their best interests to create and use these assets themselves (that is, internalize the markets for their rights), rather than to lease the permission to do so to foreign firms. It was a relatively simple concept, the genealogy of which could be traced back to the PhD thesis of Stephen Hymer which he completed in 1960, and an article which he first published in 1968 in a French journal but was not translated into English until 1990.[22] But, it attracted the attention of the profession, and by the mid-1980s was perhaps the dominant economic explanation of the extent, pattern and organization of MNE activity.[23]

****

The winter of 1976 was an exceptionally cold one, and I can remember that the snow did not clear from the Boston streets until mid-March. So Christine and I did not travel much during this time. We did, however, get to know Boston very well – and in particular the Italian district downtown. At the time, the waterfront had not been rebuilt but that did not stop me from making regular visits to the shellfish market where one could then buy live lobster for $2 (about 80p a pound at the then current rate of exchange). 'New' Boston consisted of two areas; the first was uptown, the centre of which was a new Sheraton Hotel and an impressive 24-storey glass-walled building named after the founder of Boston, John Hancock. The other new buildings were downtown, and comprised a complex of State of Massachusetts administrative offices.

Together with Williamsburg in Virginia, Boston is the cradle of post-revolutionary American history; and a lot of that part of the city which surrounds the spot where the Boston Tea Party took place in 1776 is still standing, as is the church graveyard in which some of the first emigrants from the UK – including John Winthrop, one of the founding members of the Massachusetts Bay Company – are buried. Christine and I also crossed the river to visit the Harvard Business School, where I presented a paper to a graduate seminar organized by Ray Vernon. At the time, Professor Vernon's son-in-law was on the Faculty at Boston University, and later in the spring, we enjoyed a delightful evening at the home of the Wortzels.

****

By the time we left Boston in early May 1976, the spring flowers were in full bloom, and the rowers from Harvard and Massachusetts Institute of Technology (MIT) were actively practising on the Charles River. Open-air concerts in the park alongside the river were about to start; and the street cafes were attracting custom in the Italian quarter. On our last weekend in the city we watched the end of one of the earliest Boston marathons from a vantage point just a couple of blocks away from where we lived. In the previous month, we had been taken, by some newly found friends, to visit Stourbridge, a replica of an eighteenth-century New England village. It was good to be reminded of how the ancestors of the modern Bostonians lived and worked.

****

In the later 1970s, I took various trips abroad, mainly to present papers at conferences. In 1978 I revisited Hawaii, where at the East–West Centre, and at one of the first conferences on Third World MNEs, I introduced the concept of the Investment Development Path (IDP) to explain the connection between inward and outward direct investment and a country's stage of development. But, as it turned out, I became better remembered at the conference for what seemed to me a minor incident at the time but, over the years, has ballooned into a classic 'Dunning' story. In the basement of the Halls of Residence adjacent to the East–West Centre was (and probably still is) a 'do-it-yourself' laundry. I am ashamed to say up to that point I had never used a washing machine before, but as I was away from England for a month, needs must! I put the detergent in the machine as instructed, followed by the clothes, and after switching on the machine, sat down and waited. The clothes spun happily round and round and round! After about ten minutes, I thought they should be thoroughly washed. I stopped the machine, opened the door; and behold, everything was as I had put it in, but warmer! Only then did I realize that I had put my clothes in a dryer and not the washing machine. Tom Parry, an ebullient Australian friend who was with me at the time, made sure my blunder quickly became public knowledge. However, I am sure I was less embarrassed by the incident than was a Swedish friend who, when he got back home, found in his luggage some soiled underwear belonging to one of the ladies attending the conference!

From Hawaii, I travelled to Australia to give some seminars at the University of Sydney, where Bruce Williams (who had formerly been Professor of Economics at Keele University) was Vice-Chancellor, and an ex-student of mine, Frank Stilwell, was a teacher. Frank showed me around Sydney, and I really fell in love with its spectacular harbour. From Sydney, I flew westwards to Bangkok, where for a couple of days I joined other tourists and visited the floating market, the King's palace and innumerable temples or *wats*. As I mentioned a little earlier, I especially enjoyed being taken to a huge fish market-cum-restaurant where you could choose and pay for the fresh fish of your choice, which was then cooked and served to you at your table.

****

A couple of years before the Hawaiian seminar I attended the Academy of International Business (AIB) annual conference. It was in New York City. I have grown to know Manhattan Island very well over the last 30 years, and I still have a love–hate relationship with it. New York is a city of complete contrasts. On the one hand the 'Big Apple' is sophisticated and pulsating with energy, with world-class hotels and restaurants and gourmet entertainment. On the other hand, in 1976 it was host to 2000 murders and many muggings; a rapidly deteriorating infrastructure, and quite disgraceful slums not a stone's throw from the delights of Central Park; it was not exactly America's flagship of capitalism.[24]

I remember well my first trans-Atlantic air crossing to New York. I had travelled on an early evening flight in June and arrived at New York at 9 p.m. just as it was getting dusk. As was not unusual at that time of day, taxis were in short supply; and so I shared one with a very noisy and aggressive American couple. It was not long before the man began arguing with the cab driver over the fare he wanted to charge for the journey to Manhattan. The disagreement got increasingly heated, and eventually the cab driver drew out a kind of truncheon he had concealed at the side of his seat, and told the couple to get out of his vehicle. By this time, we were on the outskirts of Kennedy Airport, but his manner was so threatening that the couple did as they were asked. I remained in the cab, and in spite of his swearing and grumbling most of the way to Manhattan, he charged me a considerably smaller fare than he was asking of the evicted passengers. This is New York cab drivers all over – brash, quick-tempered, often rude, very basic, but often (and unpredictably) gregarious and generous. But like all big cities, a visitor has to know his way around to get the most out of Manhattan Island; and there still remain no-go areas – particularly at night.

****

Over the years, I have been fortunate to stay at some of the best and grandest hotels in the world, with the most magnificent views. Among my favourites are The Oriental in Bangkok, the Shangri-La in Kaula Lumpur, the Nassau Beach in Nassau, the Oberoi in Jaipur, the Plaza in New York, La Residencia in Majorca, The Mandarin in Hong Kong; and, nearer home, The Chewton Glen Hotel in Hampshire. But I have also stayed in less salubrious lodging-houses, and in the most unappealing of rooms – often shared with one or more species of insects. I remember one night in a Florence two-star hotel spending most of it night swatting mosquitoes. By the morning my blood – as purloined by several of the wretched creatures – was splattered all over the wall. I can also recall the several times I have been unable to open a window in my room and have been practically stifled to death. When I once asked the concierge at a five-star hotel in New Orleans why the window was sealed, the reply was, 'For your own protection, sir'. 'Protection from what?' I asked. 'From your wishing to jump out of the window', was the reply! Bedrooms which reeked of stale smoke, and noisy neighbours, are another bane of my hotel life. Many a time I have been kept awake by a family squabble in the next room to me, or some raucous confrontation in the corridor. Occasionally, I have been woken up in the middle of the night by a 'lady' on the other end of the telephone offering to avail me of her services.

****

Thankfully, apart from three occasions, I have not experienced any medical emergencies in the 800 or so air and sea journeys I have taken outside the UK. Earlier in this chapter I referred to the time I was unwell and suffered from a stomach bug and dehydration on my visit to Singapore and Australia in 1985.

The second occasion followed a brief visit to Zimbabwe in October 1990. The purpose of the visit was to conduct a series of seminars for African University lecturers on how TNC material might be injected into their courses on economic development.[25] These went well, and I remember, too, being introduced to Robert Mugabe, who had recently been elected as President of Zimbabwe. Mr Mugabe was at pains to express to me how he and his newly formed government welcomed inbound FDI and the contribution it could make to his country's economic development. I must own that, at the time, I was quite impressed with his sincerity and understanding of the issues at hand. How wrong could I be!

Whenever I travel to different countries, where possible, I try to bring back some lasting mementoes. At our home in Henley, these are displayed in the living room and in my two studies. Zimbabwe is especially well known for its stone carvings, and I was taken by my host to one of the more prestigious of the showcases of such art. I was particularly attracted to two sculptures – a modern representation of an elephant's ears, and the head of an elderly Zimbabwean man. I quickly discovered that these were extremely heavy to handle. However, on my return home, since I did not want them to be damaged by placing them in the hold of the aircraft, I decided to carry them (for some distance I might add) at both Zimbabwe and London airports.

As it happened, on this occasion I was scheduled to fly on to New York just four hours after my arrival in London. As, at that time, Christine was not staying with me in the US, we agreed to meet at the airport, and that she would take my Zimbabwean purchases back home. A little later, my wife told me that she thought I looked more than usually fatigued, but put this down to the lengthy overnight air flight. As it happened, I was not feeling 100 per cent well, but it was not until Christine had left me, and about one and a half hours before my plane left for New York, that I began to feel an ache in my right groin. I then discovered I had quite a lump there. Over the next 45 minutes or so, the discomfort increased so much that I began to question whether it would be wise for me to take my transatlantic journey. But when the flight was called at 12.30 p.m. I proceeded down the walkway to board the plane. Just as I was about to step onto the aircraft, I began to realize that all was really not well, and that I would be foolish to risk an eight-hour flight – at least without first gaining medical advice. So quickly – very quickly – two senior male nurses were summoned from the medical centre in Heathrow (to this day I cannot remember where this was)! I was taken to a small room near the departure lounge and briefly examined. Neither of the nurses was completely sure what was wrong with me, but both strongly advised that I should not board the plane to New York. Instead an ambulance was arranged to take me to a nearby hospital, about 5 miles away in Ashford.

****

At the hospital I telephoned a surprised and somewhat anxious Christine to tell her my whereabouts; and then I waited for about half an hour before the duty registrar could see me. (This, I remember, was a Sunday afternoon.) He quickly diagnosed that I had all of the symptoms of a hernia – but not only this, he thought it could be a strangulated hernia that needed immediate surgery. So he telephoned the Chief Surgeon who happened to be playing golf, and within an hour, a charming South African was quietly informing me that I needed an operation within the next hour . . . or else! He himself did all the preliminaries, and by five that afternoon (when, had I caught my plane I would still have been 30 000 feet above the Atlantic) I was back in a private ward – which was to be my home for the next week or so. Later I was informed by the surgeon that had I chosen to travel on that plane the chances that I would have arrived alive at Newark were quite slim!

****

My third extra-UK medical emergency is worth recalling less for its contents than for the situation in which it occurred. In spring 2005, Christine accompanied me on my annual visit to Rutgers University, and on this occasion we decided to travel home by sea. In 2004, *Queen Mary II*, the largest flagship of the Cunard fleet, came into service, and Christine and I decided to sample the delights of the floating hotel of 120 000 tons which carried nearly 3000 passengers. Our cabin was on the thirteenth deck, and we spent much of the transatlantic crossing trying to find our way to the main dining-room, several specialized restaurants, theatre, library, entertainment lounge and shopping arcade, each of which seemed to be located on different decks, and in different parts of the ship. But the place I did not expect to visit was the doctor's surgery on the first deck! On the third morning of our voyage, and in mid-Atlantic, I woke with a stabbing pain in and around my kidneys. Within an hour this had got so bad that we had to call the doctor to the cabin. After half an hour or so he – a laconic Frenchman – arrived and diagnosed my problem as a kidney stone. He gave me an injection which was intended to relieve the pain. It did not do so, and after another 30 minutes of my writhing on the floor, Christine telephoned the doctor again. 'Bring him down to the surgery', was the somewhat brusque response. So a nurse came to the cabin with a wheelchair and I was transported lift-wise down 12 decks. There I was re-examined, given a further injection of painkillers, and told to rest on one of the beds in the surgery. Almost immediately, I went to sleep, and three hours later I woke up with no pain at all. On returning home I had various tests, but everything seemed fine. But in the middle of the Atlantic, 1500 miles from the nearest land, this particular emergency was a little scary!

****

I hardly like to tempt fate, but in the hundreds of aeroplane journeys over the past 40 years, my luggage has arrived at the appropriate carousel on all but three occasions. On the first, it came by an earlier flight, and was waiting for me in another part of Heathrow Airport. On the second, it missed the plane I just managed to catch, but it was delivered to my home the next day. On the third occasion – at Johannesburg Airport in 2006 – after I had reported that my luggage had not arrived, I discovered that it had been mistakenly placed on another carousel! Today, I try and avoid such mishaps, and long delays in retrieving bags and cases stored in the aircraft hold, by travelling light, with only luggage I can take on the plane with me.

While I am usually pleased to return home after my travels, I am usually pretty unsociable for the first few days. The adrenalin has disappeared, household or office chores have piled up, and especially on a long flight coming from the west, jet lag takes its toll. Often, too, after a difficult and long-delayed journey, I vow to myself that I will not travel again – or at least not as much – in the future. But within a few weeks, I am rummaging through the airline timetables trying to seek out a better way of getting from Lisbon to Lima, or Colombo to Santiago, than that which the computer, travel agents or the airlines have come up with. And what's more, I usually succeed!

****

NOTES

1. Later I discovered that Scottish architects helped design the campus, and that some of the granite stone for the buildings was imported from Scotland.
2. The paper was one of the earliest attempts to evaluate the conditions under which the transfer of technology by MNEs would be likely to benefit the host country. It was first published in 1969 in *Moorgate and Wall Street*, and later in my *Studies in Overseas Investment*, London, Allen & Unwin, 1970. See also my article 'When I met Hymer: Some Personal Recollections', in *International Business Review*, **15**(2), 2006, 115–23.
3. Hymer met an untimely death in a motor car accident in 1972.
4. These contributions are well summarized in a series of articles published in the *American Economic Review* in May 1985. For further details of Hymer's contribution to IB theory see a special issue of *International Business Review* edited by Christos Pitelis in 2005, and an article by myself and Christos Pitelis in *Journal of International Business Studies*, **39**(1), 2008, 167–76.
5. A volume of that title edited by myself was published in London by Allen & Unwin in 1972.
6. 1969 was at the height of the racial disturbances in the US.
7. Most of the teaching and research on IB issues was undertaken by the Business School which was housed in a different part of the university campus. Although I presented a couple of papers in the school, the relationship between it and the Department of Economics were rather distant – to put it mildly! It is also true that in the late 1960s, my own researches were firmly directed to the causes and consequences of FDI, rather than to the organization and strategies of MNEs.

8. I must, however, own that in 2008 I do not think any US supermarket can come close to beating Marks & Spencer for its range and quality of packaged food products!
9. An economic consultancy set up by Victor Morgan in 1966. See Chapter 11.
10. *Studies in International Investment*, London, Allen & Unwin, 1970.
11. *The Multinational Enterprise*, London, Allen & Unwin, 1971.
12. My work for the UNCTC is more fully described in Chapter 11.
13. The Red Fort, so-called because of its colour, was the headquarters of successive British battalions stationed in New Delhi.
14. Particularly the fish restaurants, where you could choose the fish or crustacean you wanted to eat, and it was cooked for you on the spot.
15. Today most of these bicycles have been replaced by cars, but in Taipei the main mode of transport currently used by young people – especially university students – is the moped.
16. Formerly called the People's Palace. The pharaonic project took several years to complete, and *inter alia* involved the destruction of a whole district of old houses.
17. The first being the Pentagon.
18. Each being on or very near the Equator.
19. And even on the opening days of this airport, in March 2008 the luggage loading system broke down and many BA flights were cancelled.
20. But not if another jumbo jet had landed 15 minutes earlier!
21. Oxford, Basil Blackwell.
22. The English version of which first appeared in Mark Casson's edited volume on *The Multinational Corporation* published in Aldershot, UK and Brookfield, US by Edward Elgar in 1990.
23. But not necessarily of the multinational enterprise per se, where the internalization theory, and particularly the work of Peter Buckley and Mark Casson was, and still is, highly influential.
24. The crime rate in New York has been drastically reduced over the last 25 years; and is now lower than that in London.
25. As part of a UNCTC programme more fully described in Chapter 11.

Part III: 1987–2007

Autumn

10. 'And so he plays his part':[1] the Rutgers years

As I have described in Chapter 8, by the mid-1980s I was finding the headship of the Department of Economics increasingly frustrating and unrewarding. The financial cutbacks, which began in the 1970s, showed no signs of abating. At the same time, universities were being subject to the most intense scrutiny from a variety of sources, and having to justify every pound of the income they received. The University Grants Committee (UGC), which distributed the central government grant between the 45 UK universities,[2] was becoming increasingly selective in its allocative strategy, and was demanding the most detailed information on the teaching and research programmes of university departments. Performance targets were now the name of the game – for example, with respect to the deployment of Faculty time; the range of and content of courses taught; the justification for purchasing new, or upgrading existing equipment; and the content and quality of degree results. Almost every new or replacement teaching post seemed to bring demands for numerous referee reports and masses of information of one kind or another; or for the monies so allocated to be drawn from other resources, for example secretarial facilities, administrative overheads or research funds. Committee meetings at various levels multiplied. Appointment and promotion committees became increasingly paper-driven, and more formal; and staff–student meetings took on an ever widening agenda.

There was, however, one bright side to these events, but even this was a two-edged sword. One of the first actions of the newly formed Conservative government in 1980 was to charge all foreign (for example non-EC) students full (economic) tuition fees. This immediately tripled the income coming to the university, which the administration was willing to share with the teaching departments. The Economics Department benefited considerably from this kind of 'soft' money. This was partly because, as I described in the previous chapter, most of the students on its graduate courses came from overseas; and partly because a large number of foreign students pursuing undergraduate degrees wanted to take at least some courses in economics.

However, all the UK universities had the same idea. In consequence, the 1980s saw a quite dramatic increase in competition for students and resources between universities; and some spent a good deal of their budget in marketing their wares to potential clients and donors. All departments and research centres were encouraged to be more entrepreneurial in their efforts to raise revenue and reduce costs. As the UGC was beginning to allocate income on the basis of the research excellence of departments, new and more vigorous efforts were directed to securing grants for such research, and for Faculty to publish its results in the top-ranked journals. In 1986, an exercise was conducted by the UGC to establish the quantity and quality of the research output of each of the UK universities. On the basis of such factors as number of postgraduates, research grants obtained, published papers and monographs of the Faculty, departments in various disciplines across the UK were ranked on a 1–5 scale – 5 being reserved for the outstanding departments. The Department of Economics at Reading was awarded a '4' in this exercise; a reasonable result, we thought, as only six of the 45 universities were awarded a '5'.

Departments were also urged to undertake more commercial consultancy – a dramatic volte-face on the attitudes and policies of the 1950s and 1960s, when it was generally thought to be a second-best to research and teaching, and not at all to be encouraged. Some universities – and particularly those with business schools – became highly successful in offering consultancy services in their own right. As the 1980s proceeded, there was a noticeable increase in both university and private research institutes.

****

Universities were certainly becoming different places to when I started my academic career. Perhaps it was bound to happen, but the change in the duties and responsibilities of heads of department from those almost exclusively directed to creating and encouraging scholarly excellence in teaching and research, to those of management and administration, and of entrepreneurship in fund-raising, was something most university dons had not anticipated they would have to do; nor, indeed, had they been trained to do. However, because of their professional background, and the popularity of their subject, economists were often better equipped to deal with a difficult financial situation than some of their arts and science-based colleagues. I was also fortunate in that most of the Faculty in my department were highly research-oriented, and were also frequently involved in the kind of applied or policy-oriented projects the UK government, through such avenues as the Social Science Research Council, wished to encourage.

Partly by good judgement, and partly by good fortune, the research and teaching strategy I had sought to deploy over the previous two decades provided a firm and selective basis from which to expand and diversify further.[3]

The Department's reputation in international investment, in regional and urban studies, in European integration and in industrial economics, were attracting both good students and lucrative research grants. But it was becoming clear that if we were to do even better in an increasingly competitive world, we had to branch out further, and strengthen our mainstream economics teaching and research.

Besides the increasing extra academic demands placed on heads of department, I reckoned the time I spent on pure administration had increased from the average of one day a week to two and a half days, between 1964 and 1986, and by the summer of 1987 I felt I had lost something of the zest I had only five years earlier. Twenty-two years is a long time to run a department; and it must surely be an exceptional person who can, at one and the same time, efficiently embrace the myriad routine and managerial demands placed on him (or her) and sustain or increase the scholarly reputation of his (or her) department.

****

Throughout my time as Head of the Economics Department at Reading I had experienced nothing but complete loyalty and support from my colleagues. If there were rumblings that a change in leadership was desirable, they did not reach me. In some ways, I would have liked to continue to oversee the Department until I was 65, but an inner sense told me that, for all concerned, it was time for a change.

My decision to relinquish the headship early in 1987 was prompted by three things. The first was that by then there were several very able people who could take over from me. I do not think I would have felt this two or three years earlier. Second, a unique opportunity came my way to accept a four-year research professorship (at Reading) which would take my academic career almost up to my retirement. Third, in the summer of 1986, I was invited to spend the whole of 1987 as Seth Boyden Distinguished Professor in International Business at Rutgers University in Newark, New Jersey.

During my life, a series of serendipitous events have shaped my career. I have described some of these in previous chapters, but one which well illustrates that timing and personal relationships can both be of critical relevance came about late in 1985. The initial trigger which led to my Research Professorship at Reading was an article I wrote in the *Lloyds Bank Review* in July 1985 entitled 'Multinational Enterprises, Economic Restructuring and British Industry'. In this article I tried to assess (in layman's terms) the contribution which both outward and inward foreign direct investment was currently making to British economic welfare; and to suggest the strategies the UK government should pursue if that contribution was to be optimized. The ideas set out in the article struck a chord with Sir John Harvey-Jones, the ebullient, unconventional, yet highly effective Chairman of Imperial Chemical Industries (ICI) – at that time, Britain's largest manufacturing company. He invited me to one of the small lunch parties he gave from time to time at ICI's London office. We talked about the factors influencing the competitiveness of British industry, and particularly the incentives offered by the UK government to British firms to upgrade their competences, and to penetrate global markets better. Sir John took a 'centrist' view of the strategy, and suggested I might like to explore how the leading Western industrial economies were responding to the challenges of globalization; and what, in particular, the institutions and policies of the British government should put in place if its own companies were to be among the most competitive.

I mapped out a research programme for two parallel studies. The first consisted of a major review of the role of multinational enterprises (MNEs) in the global economy, and the second, an analysis of the way in which institutions and policies of the governments of the leading Organisation for Economic Co-operation and Development (OECD) countries were affecting the productivity and globalization of their MNEs. Sir John approved of these projects, and it was agreed that ICI should finance a Research Chair in International Business (for myself) at the University of Reading, for a four-year period beginning at a time to be agreed with the university.

The letter of confirmation of the ICI Research Chair came at the time I was negotiating a one-year appointment at the Graduate School of Management (GSM) at Rutgers University. The idea of my spending some time at the State University of New Jersey was initially aired by Farok Contractor in October 1985 at the AIB meetings at New York. In order to advance its reputation as the leading state university, the New Jersey government had made available some funds to Rutgers with the explicit purpose of attracting a limited number of 'World Class Scholars' in different subject areas. David Blake, the then Dean of the Graduate School of Management (GSM) was anxious to recruit such an individual for the school; and Farok was one of his senior Faculty designated to identify some possible candidates.

Though attracted to the idea, I did not want a permanent or full-time appointment in the US. But I informed Farok that I might be tempted by a one-year visiting appointment. In the next few months, David Blake considered this proposal, and in due course secured funding from an endowment trust set up by the widow of a renowned and wealthy New Jersey citizen, Seth Boyden, to finance visits by distinguished overseas scholars. So, after some protracted correspondence over the spring and summer of 1986, it was agreed that I would spend the calendar year of 1987 in New

Jersey, and that I should take up the ICI research professorship on my return to Reading in January 1988.

I was now almost ready to relinquish my Esmee Chair at Reading – but not quite, as my four-year research grant from ICI was due to end in December 1991, and that left me with a nine-month gap before I was due to retire. To close that gap I applied to the UK Economic and Social Research Council (ESRC) for a personal research grant for nine months, to start writing the first of the two volumes I had suggested to Sir John Harvey Jones. The proposal was accepted, and it was agreed that the grant would run from 1st January to 30th September 1988. This meant that the university was to receive the ICI research funding from 1st January 1988, but would not start paying my salary until 1st October 1988, and I would then be able to receive my monthly salary cheque up to 30th September 1992 – my due retirement date.

****

In October 1986, the annual conference of the AIB was held outside the US for the first time in the Academy's history. Together with Art Stonehill of Oregon State University, I was elected Joint Programme Chairman for the meetings which were to be held in London. All worked out well, although I think the conference was less remembered for its academic content than for its social programme, the highlight of which was a lavish cocktail party hosted by the Lord Mayor of London in the magnificent ballroom of his residence at the Mansion House, right in the heart of the City of London.

Just a few days after the AIB meetings, during which I had preliminary discussions with Sarah Mallen of Addison Wesley about the publishing of *Multinational Enterprises in the Global Economy*, my arrangements for the next five years had been finalized. I now felt free to inform my colleagues at Reading, and resigned from my tenured Chair. Although the Vice-Chancellor (VC) asked me to consider continuing the headship of the Department until 1989, when my current four-year stint was due to expire, I thought it was best to make a clean break. At the November meeting I announced that I would resign the headship on 31st January 1987, just 22 years and 4 months after I had arrived at Reading.

In the six weeks before Christmas, the VC and I both took soundings from my colleagues of who they thought should succeed me. Just before Christmas the VC informed me that he had appointed Mark Casson – a choice which, at the time, I thought entirely appropriate, and which subsequent events proved to be well justified.

Originally I had intended to say goodbye to my colleagues at a departmental meeting in mid-January. However, Mark thought there would be little business which could not wait until later in that term, and he arranged an informal farewell party for Christine and myself at one of our favourite local hostelries. In retrospect, I regret my decision not to hold that particular departmental meeting, as I would have liked for it to have been formally minuted how much I had appreciated the loyalty and friendship and support of my colleagues over the previous two decades.

****

At the end of January 1987, Christine and I boarded a Virgin Atlantic flight for Newark, New Jersey. We spent the first ten days or so at the Westfield Inn,[4] on the recommendation of a realtor who David Blake had arranged to show us some apartments in different parts of New Jersey. In that time we saw a lot of the state, which we soon discovered had many attractive characteristics. Outside the large conurbations of Newark, Union City, Hoboken and Trenton, the countryside resembles that of Surrey in the UK. Its vegetation includes an abundance of oak, beech, ash and elm, and a host of flowering trees and shrubs, including cherry blossom, azaleas and the Florida dogwood – a beautiful small tree which yields a profusion of salmon-pink and white flowers each spring. Not for nothing is New Jersey called the 'Garden State'. It supplies most of Manhattan Island in New York with its vegetables and fruit.

I had decided not to buy a car, but to use the train to get to the Graduate School at Newark. Christine and I were then looking for an apartment within walking distance of the local station, and about a 30-minute commute from Newark; and also close to a good shopping area. With this brief in mind, the realtor took us as far north as Montclair and as far south as Princeton. In between, there were a host of very pleasant suburban communities like Summit, Chatham and Maddison. Each of these locations had their pluses and minuses, but none could offer both the kind of housing and the ease of commuting to Newark that I was seeking.

At the end of our first week in the US, the university housing officer offered us a modern furnished apartment at a very reasonable rent in New Brunswick, the town which housed the main campus of Rutgers and at which 45 000 students were taught. But the apartment was isolated, and a bus ride away from both the train station and shops. After two weeks of commuting in particularly atrocious weather conditions – on one evening, I had a 45-minute walk in the snow back from the station – Christine and I decided we could not stand it any longer, and resumed our search for something more suitable. About a week later, we saw an advertisement in the local paper for one of the very few rental apartments in Westfield. We inspected it, and although it was quite small we liked it, and agreed to lease it for a year.

So our domestic life started at Trinity Gardens, Westfield at a one-time Catholic school and nunnery, which had recently been converted into 55 delightful condominiums, some with their own patios and small gardens. Although our apartment was carpeted and blinded, and had a fully fitted kitchen, our first task was to find some furniture. This we did quite speedily by hiring most of what we needed from a furniture rental company in Elizabeth, about 10 miles away. We then rented a car for a couple of days, and stocked up with bedroom and bathroom linen, kitchen equipment, cutlery, a tea and dinner set, a colour TV and a telephone! And before we knew it, we had set up home!

****

One of the main purposes of David Blake's inviting me to Rutgers was to help him internationalize some of the GSM's curricula, and to start a PhD programme in international business (IB). In my first two semesters, I taught two PhD courses, and an MBA course on International Business and Economic Development. At the time, the GSM did not offer a major specialization in IB, but doctoral students could take a minor specialization, consisting of (up to) three IB courses. But such was the enthusiasm of the students that, in the autumn of 1987, Farok Contractor and I were prompted to seek ways and means of offering a full PhD programme in IB.

The GSM at Newark consisted of a number of teaching departments, one of which was Business (later renamed International Business) and the Environment. This was the department to which I was assigned, but I was also hoping to encourage the internationalization of some of the other disciplines in the Faculty, notably Economics and Finance, Marketing, and Organization and Management. In this quest I was not very successful as the Faculty of most of these departments were disinclined to move in this direction.[5] I was soon to discover that, if Rutgers was to enhance its reputation in IB teaching and research, the Business and the Environment Department would have to do it largely by itself.[6]

Towards the end of 1987, I decided I would like to spend the first few months of my ESRC research grant period in the US, and to supplement my income by repeating one of my PhD courses. Moreover, since in October 1986 I had been elected President of the AIB for 1987/88, it was desirable for me to spend as much time as possible in the US. About halfway through the spring semester, David Blake asked me to reconsider his earlier invitation to join the Rutgers Faculty as a 'World Class Scholar'. After giving the matter further thought, and consulting ICI and the VC at Reading, I agreed with David that I would accept an appointment at

Rutgers, but only spend alternate academic years in the US. In this way, I could continue my English citizenship, and re-establish residence in the UK after a two-semester stint at Rutgers.

****

I agreed to start the new arrangement in September 1989, after having spent the previous one and a half years in England. Christine and I decided we wanted to continue living at Trinity Place in Westfield. However, on this occasion we had the choice of renting or buying a condominium. I estimated that, quite apart from the hassle costs of finding new accommodation and furniture each time I came to the US, and assuming property prices rose by 5 per cent or more per annum over the following five years, it would be worth taking out a mortgage and buying a property. As it happened, in the summer of 1989, an ideal south-backing condominium with a small patio garden came onto the market. Since we could not personally inspect the property, we asked some US friends to do so. They kindly agreed, and reported favourably on it. So sight unseen, I became a property owner in the US. I gained possession of IBS 519 Trinity Place on 15th September 1989, and on the same day took delivery of two beds. On the following day, Peter Gray, who had kindly stored various items of bedlinen, cutlery, and so on from our earlier flat, brought these back to Trinity Gardens. So for the first week or so I worked, ate, watched TV and slept in the bedroom.

Over the next two months, I completely furnished the condominium. Christine was not with me at the time as she was supervising the final stages of some building extensions to our home in Henley. On most weekends, I hired a car and scoured the district for furnishings. But in the event, most of our major items of furniture came from a couple of Danish-owned outlets in Manhattan. Not only did I like their furniture – all of which was imported from Scandinavia – but they were able to deliver it quickly from their large warehouses on Long Island. I changed the carpet but kept the window dressings, which were included in the sale price. With accessories like lamps, cushions, pictures, pot plants, mirrors and sundry ornaments, the condominium was completely furnished by the end of November. Fortunately, when Christine joined me shortly afterwards, she broadly approved of my various choices.

I quickly settled into a comfortable routine, and became a regular train commuter into and out of Newark. At the GSM, I had a pleasant office with ample storage space. Earlier, as a condition of my appointment at Rutgers, it was agreed that I would be provided with a senior secretary. I have never regretted making this condition, as a good secretary is worth her (or his) weight in gold; and Phyllis Miller was to prove this time and time again.

****

During the first three years of my appointment at Rutgers, I helped set up a PhD programme in International Business; and by the mid-1990s the GSM had one of the largest initiatives of this kind in the US.[7] There were just four members of staff specializing in IB – and an earlier promise to me of an additional Faculty never materialized! Farok and I decided to adopt a niche strategy, and designed a PhD programme which was of contemporary relevance, yet directly related to our research interests and those of our colleagues. The area we chose as our specialization was the interaction between governments, international business and competitiveness in an increasingly globalizing world. We also decided to give special attention to the strategies of MNEs and the policies of host governments in the creation and deployment of such 'created' assets as human competences, innovations and technology, institution infrastructure and entrepreneurship. We designed each of our courses to instruct the students in the latest and cutting-edge methodologies and empirical findings; and to motivate them to work with the Faculty in their research projects. This strategy was generally successful. With the valuable help of Peter Gray who had just retired from Rensselaer Polytechnic Institute in upstate New York, and Briance Mascarenhas, who had been appointed a Professor at Rutger's Camden Campus,[8] we built up an excellent network of senior and junior Faculty within three years of my arrival, and also launched a series of departmental research papers in IB. In the 1990s, several of these papers were co-authored by Faculty and PhD students; and most were later published in scholarly journals or as monographs. Our first graduating PhD student in IB was Rajneesh Narula – now Professor of International Business at the University of Reading – who graduated at the end of 1992. He was the first of 18 students Farok and I had the pleasure of supervising between that date and my retirement in 1998. Since graduating, ten of these students have become university teachers; and six are full or associate professors at well-respected business schools in the US or Europe. Several – notably Summit Kundu of Florida International University, Rajneesh Narula of the University of Reading, and Sarianna Lundan of Maastricht University – have had research papers published in the leading IB journals.

In addition to my two PhD courses, I agreed to teach one MBA course each year. I decided to entitle this course 'Issues on International Business', and to expose the students to the work of scholars undertaking cutting-edge research on topical issues. This proved very successful the first time round in 1990, and I repeated it again in 1992 and 1994, but with a different group of visiting lecturers, and focusing on the theme of Globalization and International Business.

During my time at Rutgers, I was also fortunate to benefit from the support services of two graduate students each year, and a generous travelling budget. This budget enabled me to attend all the conferences I needed, and also to finance the expenses of visiting speakers to my MBA course and to my research seminars. I found my graduate students of great help in a variety of ways, such as checking references and assembling statistical data for my new book; but also, as I have already mentioned, in the preparation of jointly authored papers.[9]

****

Coffee and pastries served by the newsvendor at Westfield Station; supermarkets open day and night; 50 or more channels on cable TV; seven-lane highways with a 55–65 mph speed limit; an imaginative variety of ice creams; gasoline at less than £1 a gallon; fully air-conditioned cars, homes and offices; buckets of popcorn consumed by most cinema goers; perpetual sales at departmental stores and other retail outlets; the distinctive yellow cab taxis of Manhattan; colonial-style architecture of Westfield; bitterly cold winters and stiflingly hot summers; glorious autumn foliage; inexpensive food at takeaway outlets; Thanksgiving; turkey and pumpkin pie; the expression 'Have a nice day', the skyscrapers of downtown New York City; the Virginia Slims tennis championship at Madison Square Garden; free local telephone calls; a plethora of junk mail; screw-in light bulbs; the US presidential elections in 1992 and 1996; these are just a few of the remembrances Christine and I have of our experiences of living on the East Coast of the US in the 1990s.

****

During the 1980s, I could find no spiritual home in England in which I was able to feel completely comfortable. While I appreciated the tradition and dignity of an Anglican service and was awed by the beauty of our local parish church at Rotherfield Greys, at heart I continued to be a nonconformist. At the same time, I did not want to become a regular worshipper at any church at which Christine, who had been brought up in the Anglican faith, could not feel at ease. We sometimes attended a small and friendly local non-denominational church in a nearby village at Stoke Row, but neither of us felt inclined – or indeed had the time – to be actively involved in its day-to-day affairs.

Shortly after arriving in Westfield we began attending the Presbyterian church. With its impressive 100-foot steeple, the building dominated the town and was adjacent to a delightful park with a lake. Dating back to 1640 – although twice since rebuilt – its style of architecture was classic colonial. The exterior of the edifice was mainly clad with white weatherboarding, and decorated with large, but plain, oblong windows. The inside of the sanctuary was bright, airy and dignified, with choir stalls positioned behind the pulpit. The decor was mainly off-white except for a full-length red curtain at the rear of the church, in front of which was the communion table. The sanctuary seated 1500 people, and during our time at Westfield the 10.30 a.m. service was normally attended by about 600 worshippers.

Sunday worship was dignified, and carefully orchestrated to meet the needs of the contemporary American worshipper. At the time of our arrival in Westfield there were three ministers, the senior of whom, Jeffrey Wampler, was one of the finest preachers I have ever heard. One Sunday he delivered a sensitive and memorable sermon, told in the first person and in allegorical style, of Simon, who was a traveller from Cyrene caught up in Christ's crucifixion, and was forced to carry his cross (Mark 15 v. 21). I felt I had found my spiritual home in the US.

In June 1987 I went home to the UK, but on my return to Westfield, I was sorry to hear that Jeffrey Wampler had accepted a post in Princeton Seminary – the leading theological college for the training of Presbyterian ministers in the US. For the following two and a half years, the church searched for a new senior minister, although for much of the period, Dr Jim Angel, a retired minister from San Francisco, ably filled the position of interim Senior Pastor.

My return to Westfield in September 1989 coincided almost exactly with the induction of Dr William Ross Forbes as the Senior Minister of the Presbyterian Church. Bill, an amiable pastor and highly talented preacher, was returning to New Jersey after ministering to a large Presbyterian church in Atlanta, Georgia. Rather unusually for a Presbyterian, Bill had taken his Doctorate in church liturgy, and soon after he came to Westfield he introduced several novel changes to the order of worship. Bill's teaching ministry was quite outstanding. *Inter alia*, he also made good use of sacramental and other symbols to help put over his views. His preaching, though lightened by many stories and anecdotes, was firmly based on scriptural insights; and he was never afraid to pull his punches, or make demands on his congregation whenever he thought it necessary.

For most of 1992 I was by myself in Westfield, as Christine stayed in the UK to look after her parents; and I attended the Presbyterian church whenever I could. By that time, Bill Forbes had been joined by two new members of staff. The first was Jeffrey Chesbrough, a dynamic and extraordinarily friendly man in his late thirties; and the second was Helen Beglin, a native of Georgia but a Princeton graduate, who was appointed Director of Education – a task to which I quickly found she was excellently suited.

I soon discovered that there were very few things within the Presbyterian Church to which I, brought up as a Baptist, could not wholly subscribe. One, perhaps, was infant baptism – but even here I could happily identify myself with the meaning behind the symbolism. I also found the Presbyterian system of governance rather strange, and never quite got used to the idea of a church meeting after the morning service, to which all the congregation were invited.

Certainly my spiritual life was enriched by my time at Westfield. I also had a lot of time for thinking, and tried to evaluate my life's journey as I was now approaching Shakespeare's seventh stage in the life of man. But that is a story for another chapter.

****

One of my more notable achievements at Rutgers, which I look back on with some pride, was to obtain a CIBER[10] grant for the GSM. But, of course, I was not able to obtain this funding without the active cooperation of my colleagues in the Department of International Business and the Environment, and also J.C. Spender from the Department of Management. We based our application to the US Department of Commerce partly on our comparative research strengths, and partly on our intention to introduce new IB-related courses – particularly in Economics, Finance and Management – to the existing curricula of the school. We also proposed to initiate a series of conferences and seminars, which would highlight a number of international business issues, and would hopefully attract interest from the business community in New Jersey. Finally, we flagged our desire to broaden the base of our language teaching for business students.

In the event, we were successful in obtaining an $800 000 grant for a three-year period from 1992 to 1995. We believed this would act as a catalyst for providing funding for the programme we had set out in our proposal, including the enlargement of our research paper series, and the financing of several research projects by Faculty.

J.C. Spender was appointed the Founding Director of the Rutgers CIBER, and I took on the role of Research Director. Both of us were assisted by a Dutchman, Hugo Kline, who was not only our hands-on manager, but who also helped organize conferences, liaised with Faculty members wishing to offer new courses, and collaborated with the Dean's office on all data collection, finance and reporting matters. It was Hugo's initiative and his contact with the Netherlands government that helped provide the necessary financial support and speakers for our first one-day conference which we held in 1993. The title of the conference was Foreign Investment in the New Jersey Economy. A second conference was arranged a year later on New Jersey in a Global Economy, and a third on Globalisation: A Two Edged Sword in 1997. The proceedings of each of these events were later published as books by Rutgers University. During my time as Research Director, CIBER also published 25 research papers. These were authored not only by Rutgers scholars, but also by those from other universities in the region.

In 1994, J.C. Spender left Rutgers to become Dean of a business school in New York City. For the last 18 months of our CIBER grant I took his place, and Farok Contractor became Research Director. We then began preparing our submission for a new grant for the next three years. I must admit I was not optimistic about our chances of a renewal, although I believed our research proposals were outstanding (and were, indeed, acknowledged to be so by our assessors). However, as it was apparent that I would be retiring in the course of the next three years; as there was only a tempered enthusiasm of Faculty to extend their teaching programmes to embrace more IB-related topics; and as there was no one in the Faculty ready and willing to give the time and energy necessary to developing a really worthwhile outreach programme, our bid failed. While I think the GSM administration was disappointed about the outcome of our bid, and Hugo found himself without a job,[11] I sensed that the reaction of most of my IB colleagues was one of indifference. They could now 'plough their own furrows' as they had done prior to CIBER coming into existence. For myself, I was disappointed at the decision, mainly because it signalled the inability of the Rutgers Faculty to build an integrated nexus of international business scholarship that I believed it was both possible and desirable for it to achieve. Instead, until very recently at any rate, the GSM at Newark continued to be known for the research excellence of its individual scholars[12] rather than for its reputation as an establishment where IB occupied a premier position in its curricula.[13]

****

The decade following my conversations with Sir John Harvey Jones at ICI was among the most productive in my academic life. Relieved of most administrative duties, and with my teaching responsibilities mainly confined to the PhD programme at Rutgers, I not only completed my magnum opus, *Multinational Enterprises and the Global Economy*, in 1992, but also fulfilled the second commitment I made to the Chairman of ICI – namely to undertake and complete a project on the interface between the activities of MNEs and the actions of governments to promote the international competitiveness of their economies. In 1994, I organized a conference in Washington, DC, which was funded by a grant from the Carnegie Bosch Foundation, at Georgetown University on this very topic. The conference was well attended by political scientists, strategic analysts, economists, government representatives and business executives. The proceedings were published by Oxford University Press (OUP) in 1997 in a volume edited by myself entitled *Governments, Globalisation and International Business*. Case studies of the ways in which a selection of developed and developing countries' governments considered their competitiveness might be enhanced by inbound and outbound MNE activity comprised the core of the book. A subsequent and related volume, which was the outcome of a symposium held at Rutgers University in 1998, was published under the title *Regions, Globalisation and the Knowledge Economy*, again by OUP, in 2000.

At the same time, after completing *Multinational Enterprises and the Global Economy*, I contributed several papers on the implications of globalization for the interface between national governments and MNEs. Several of these essays were set out in my 1993 book *The Globalisation of Business* (Routledge, 1993). During this period of my scholarly career, my research interests moved away from the activities of MNEs to that of the challenges and opportunities of globalization per se; although, in my 1993 book, I did attempt to introduce more dynamic and strategic elements into the eclectic paradigm.

****

Finally, in the late 1980s and early 1990s, I began to be a more frequent participant in international business conferences. At the conclusion of the London AIB meeting in 1986, I was honoured to learn that I had been elected as the first UK President of the Academy for 1987–88. As the annual meetings for these years were to be held respectively in Chicago and San Diego, it was most convenient that I was living in the US at the same time.

One of my aims as President of the AIB was to identify and emphasize the unique contribution IB could make to scholarly thought. In my presidential address[14] I urged the need for more collaborative and interdisciplinary research. Increasingly I argued that the kind of issues now challenging IB scholars needed to be approached by an amalgam of different methodologies and analytical techniques, some of which were not part of the mainstream curricula of business schools. In the late 1980s, for example, economic geographers, business historians, sociologists, political scientists, lawyers and economists were increasingly presenting their views and explanations of the growth of MNE activity; and I considered that the AIB was an organization which had a critical role to play in leveraging and integrating these different perspectives.

I think that in the 1990s some of these aspirations came to fruition; but I must own I was less successful in a third objective I set myself – namely to engage more interest of the business community in the work of the AIB. In the early 2000s, there are some signs that this interaction is now improving – both in respect of AIB and its sister organizations, and between IB scholars and business practitioners. Partly I see this as a reflection of the increasing number of IB Faculty that are consultants to business enterprises; partly because successive Programme Chairs of AIB have done their best to invite some of the leading business executives to participate in its annual meetings; and partly because, as the analytical content of managing a global company has become more complex, practitioners have found it beneficial to work more closely with academic researchers. But, for the most part, there still remains a large gap between the mindsets of most business practitioners and scholars. To my mind, it is largely the responsibility of educators to help narrow the gap. This, in itself, might involve a rethinking of our business models and methodologies about which, in his writings, Sumatra Ghoshal has been the most critical.[15] At the same time, some of my colleagues – notably C.K. Pralahad and some of the most cited IB scholars – are doing a great job of linking the interests of the business and academic communities.

****

My stint as President of the AIB came to an end just as I was elected President of the International Trade and Finance Association. In 1994, I gave my presidential address to 200 or so delegates at the University of Reading. I took a rather similar theme to that I had considered six years ago, but this time more specifically addressed the evolving scholarly interface between mainstream trade and IB theory. Even today, it continues to amaze me that so few trade economists acknowledge the facts – or at least the importance of the facts – that, first, the value of sales of the foreign affiliates of MNEs is more than double that of arm's-length trade; and second, that one-third of all trade is conducted within MNE networks. The interface between trade and FDI still remains a neglected area of study.[16] My own suspicion is that it as much reflects differences in the analytical approach between IB scholars and trade economists, as an unwillingness to widen disciplinary interests. I shall return to this issue in Chapter 12.

****

The thirtieth of September 1992 was a sad date for me – although apart from the fact it was my last day of employment at the University of Reading, it was just like any other day! From 1st October I was to become an Emeritus Professor of the university – a title given to most professors at Reading and other British universities who had spent a reasonable amount of time as a (full) professor.

Ever since I had retired from the headship of the Department, I had relatively little formal contact with the Department. I deemed it best to stay away from departmental meetings to give Mark Casson a completely free hand. But I was always more than ready to give him the benefit of my advice and experience. In fact, I was rather relishing my role as the elder statesman of the Department. In the event, it soon became clear that Mark could manage everything perfectly well without my involvement. Though this was his privilege, I did rather regret that our relationship was a little distant and that he seldom felt it necessary to inform me on any issues of any substance.[17] Even when one of our dearest colleagues, George Yannopoulos, died after a short illness in September, it was ten days before I knew, and then it was almost by accident. Whether Mark thought I knew by other means about George's death, and about several important events which were then occurring in the Department's life, or whether he believed that (being in the US for every other year), I had no further interest in the affairs of the Department, I do not know, but the fact remains that I was a little disappointed that there was not a closer bond between my erstwhile colleague and myself.

If my relationship with the Department of Economics was, perhaps, not as close as I would have liked after I had retired, that between the Vice-Chancellor and myself was non-existent. Up to my retirement Ewan Page did little to endear himself to me. Again, like Mark – but even more so – he played everything strictly by the book. However, my opinion about the quality of a VC rests on how he deals with issues and people over which one has the discretion to be generous and cooperative, or sparing and adversarial. Most of my dealings with the VC suggested he leaned towards the latter stance, which did little to endear himself to his colleagues and, in the long run, probably did not benefit the university either!

I should have known better, but I had rather assumed that if I saved enough money out of my Research Endowment Fund, which was the university's contribution to my ICI Research Professorship, I could employ my then secretary, Melanie Waller, for the final three months of 1992 to complete a book I was writing after I had retired. In the event I had £7000 in the account, so I asked the Personnel Office to extend her appointment (at the cost of £3000) for three months. I was not only frustrated but surprised to learn that the VC had countermanded my instructions, and had refused to authorize any expenditure of the balance in my account once I had retired. Of course it was his privilege to behave in this way, but after more than two decades as the Head of a department, who together with his colleagues had contributed more than most departments to enhancing the reputation of the university, words like petty-minded came easily to my lips. If that was his attitude, I certainly was not going with my begging bowl to him. Mark felt there was little he could do to counteract the VCs ruling, and I respected his decision.

Though this episode left a sour taste in my mouth, it was soon forgotten in the retirement lunch which the Department organized for me, at which I was presented with a lovely gift of a specially commissioned painting of Truro Cathedral and its surroundings. It was so good at that party for Christine and myself to renew friendships with so many colleagues and friends who had been part of my life at Reading University over the past 28 years. The VC was also present, and both he and Mark gave most generous tributes to myself and my work at Reading. For myself I felt very confident that under the strong and innovatory leadership of Mark, the best of the days of the Department were yet to come!

****

NOTES

1. William Shakespeare's fifth age (continued), *As You Like It*, Act II, scene 7.
2. Increased to 90 in the 1990s as a result of the upgrading of colleges of technology in 1991 and 1992.
3. And to give him full credit, Mark Casson, my successor did just this, including the strengthening of IB teaching and research, and recruiting Geoff Jones from LSE, to help build up a strong international business history unit.
4. Westfield is a colonial town which is located a 20-minute train journey from Newark.
5. Although individual Faculty members from these departments did contribute to the work of the Centre for International Business Research (CIBER) when set up in 1996.
6. Again with a limited input from individuals in other departments.
7. Details of which were set out in a 1996 brochure 'Rutgers the State University: Concentration in International Business', PhD in Management Program, Newark Graduate School of Management, Mimeo April.
8. Rutgers University had three campuses at New Brunswick, Newark and Camden (near the border with Pennsylvania).
9. For a brief assessment of my years at Rutgers University see H. Peter Gray, *Extending the Eclectic Paradigm in International Business*, Cheltenham, UK and Northampton, MA, USA, Edward Elgar, 2003, pp. 1–12.
10. Centre for International Business Education and Research. In 1990, the US government began funding a number of specialized research, teaching and outreach centres at US universities. These centres were designed, by way of education, research and interface between academic scholars and the business community, to promote an increased awareness of the challenges and opportunities that could be met by the internationalization of business activities.

11. Although at the time I was combining my work at CIBER with some teaching elsewhere in the university.
12. In a recent survey of the institutions hosting the most prolific authors publishing in the leading IB journals, Rutgers was ranked third and Reading fourth identified by the authors. See S. Xu, G. Yalcinkaya and S.H. Seggie, 'Prolific Authors and Institutions in Leading International Business Journals', *Asia Pacific Journal of Management*, 2008 (forthcoming).
13. Currently (2008) John Cantwell, who succeeded me at Rutgers, is doing a splendid job in rebuilding the PhD programme in IB in the Department of Management and Global Business.
14. 'The Study of International Business: A Plea for an Interdisciplinary Approach', *Journal of International Business Studies*, **20**, Summer, 1989, 411–36.
15. See also my comments in Chapter 12.
16. Though some economists, for example James Markusen and Anthony Venables, have done their best to consider such an interface.
17. One being his most successful initiative on promoting the teaching and research of international business history at Reading.

With Peter Buckley
and Alan Rugman
2000

With Christine at
Chinese Culture
University
Taipei
March 2007

With Philippe Gugler
and Sarianna Lundan
Catania 2007

The Carver!
Rio de Janeiro
2005

In my study
2007

With Christine
2008

Philip
2000

A view from Pendower
2006

Fellows Dinner AIB Meeting
July 2007

11. Spanning spring to autumn: consultancy work

Throughout my academic life, I have always managed to combine my scholarly research and teaching with a variety of consultancy assignments. The only rule I set myself (and indeed my colleagues at Reading) is that whatever I did, it should complement and, if possible, enrich my academic work. Over the past four decades I (or they) have strictly adhered to this principle. *Inter alia*, this is reflected in my (or their) publications. While much of my consultancy work, and particularly that undertaken for the Economists Advisory Group (EAG) and the United Nations (UN) (which I shall describe later in this chapter) was either not published or did not appear under my name, some of it, or a spillover from it, did. Looking through my list of publications since the 1960s I would estimate that a third of my monographs, and a fifth of all my articles and chapters in books, were directly or indirectly the outcome of my consultancy assignments.

I do not have the space, nor do I think it would be of great interest to my readers, to detail fully my career or experiences as a consultant. Suffice it to say, that over the past four decades most of the projects in which I have been involved were commissioned by local authorities, national governments and supranational entities. Not being a product of, or employed by, a business school (my appointment at Rutgers University was an exception) I have never developed close ties with particular business enterprises.[1] Nor are the topics which interest such clients – namely finance, strategic management, marketing, industrial relations, acquisitions and mergers and so on – my main scholarly forte. Rather, any comparative advantage I have evolved over the years has been in the interaction between firms and the economic environment in which they operate; and particularly that affecting or affected by their foreign direct investment (FDI). So my main 'clients' have tended to be national and subnational governments (or their agencies),[2] such as the OECD, the European Commission, several trade associations notably the Committee of Invisible Exports later called the British Invisible Export Council (BIEC), the Japanese Economic and Trade Association (JETRO), the Commonwealth Secretariat, the World Bank and some of the regional banks, for example the Asian Development Bank.

In this chapter, I will confine my attention to two of my extra-university activities which have accounted for about three-quarters of all of my consultancy work since the mid-1960s. The first is my participation as a partner in and later Director and Chairman of, the Economists Advisory Group; and the second is my close association with the United Nations and its various agencies.

****

In April 1965 I attended the annual meeting of the Association of University Teachers in Economics (AUTE) in Swansea. There I met Victor Morgan – at that time Professor of Economics at Swansea University – who asked me if I might be interested in becoming a partner in an economics consultancy group he was about to form. The proposition interested me, not least because it could provide a focus for my consultancy work. I was also impressed by the scholarly calibre of the other economists – Alan Peacock, Denis Lees and Jack Wiseman – who Victor had approached, or was about to approach.

Economists Advisory Group (EAG) was formally constituted in 1966, and was set up to undertake high-quality economic research for clients in both the private and the public sectors. All the partners were university professors; in addition the Group recruited a full-time Managing Director, Malcolm Lamb, who *inter alia* was responsible for marketing, office management, and finance and accounting matters.

EAG held its first meetings at the Liberal Club, near Whitehall in Central London. In 1967 it moved to its own premises in Southampton Street, just off the Strand. At one of our initial gatherings, it was agreed that one (and occasionally two) partners would be responsible for managing projects nearest to own academic interests. Hence Victor took overall responsibility for projects involving macroeconomics and monetary economics; Denis for those involving industrial and labour economics; Alan for those involving public finance; Jack for those involving public utility economics; and myself for those involving international economics.

The consultancy got off to a flying start, and quickly obtained two most interesting assignments. The first was a project commissioned by the Corporation of London on *The Economic Future of the City of London*. Our brief was, first, to present a detailed and up-to-date analysis of the various activities undertaken in the Square Mile and their exact location; and second, to forecast, up to 20 years ahead, the likely changes in the structure of these and the employment they might generate. Although directed by Victor and myself (who also edited the book, detailing the results of our investigations),[3] each of the partners contributed, as did four of the staff of

EAG, and 11 other academic consultants. In fact, as it turned out, this study acted as a template for future projects. A critical idea behind EAG as a consultancy was that it should act as a catalyst, and an opportunity for university teachers and researchers to apply their skills to tackling real-life problems. By 1970, EAG had built up a portfolio of 50 academic economists who it could draw upon when bidding for particular projects. It should, however, be emphasized that in these years there were relatively few privately run economic consultancies in the UK, while even fewer economics departments at universities engaged in such activities. All this was to change in the 1970s and 1980s.

The second major consultancy project of EAG in which I was also involved was for the Committee of Invisible Exports. Its then Director, William Clarke – who was one-time Financial Editor of the *Times* – Victor and I knew quite well. He commissioned EAG to undertake a thorough review of the economic significance of Britain's invisible exports – and particularly those originating in the City of London – for the UK balance of payments, and for the UK economy as a whole. The product of our research was a book which was the first major evaluation of the contribution of tourism, foreign investment, insurance, banking, financial and commodity services, and the arts to the British economy.[4] In addition, for several years afterwards, I and some of my colleagues at Reading University both updated and analysed these data. In particular, we examined the performance of particular service sectors (as invisible earners) relative to that of their counterparts in other countries.[5]

****

In the following two decades, EAG provided regular economic analysis and advice to such organizations as the Advertising Association,[6] the Brewer's Society, the Association of Pharmaceutical Manufacturers, the UNCTC (UN Centre on Transnational Corporations), the UNCTAD (UN Conference on Trade and Development), the Monopolies Commission, the Location of Offices Bureau, the European Commission, several regional investment and development agencies of the UK, the Anglo-German Foundation and the Committee of Enquiry on Small Firms, to name just a few projects in which I was directly involved. Several of these resulted in publications under my own name. My 1986 book *Japanese Participation in British Industry* – the first survey of its kind – was the direct outcome of a project sponsored by the (then) UK Department of Trade and Industry. This project led to several others, commissioned by JETRO (Japan External Trade Organization), the Ministry of International Trade and Industry (MITI), the Institute for Trade and Investment in Tokyo, the Japan

Industrial Policy Research Institute and the Embassy of Japan – all of which, while (hopefully) benefiting the client, advanced my own under-standing of the determinants and impact of inward and outward Japanese FDI, and the strategy of Japanese multinational enterprises (MNEs).

EAG never developed into a major economic consultancy. Perhaps this was because the primary interest of the partners was academically driven. Although the partnership became a limited company in the 1970s and recruited Brian Carsberg, an eminent accounting scholar, and Graham Bannock as new directors,[7] for most of its life, EAG's full-time consultancy staff fluctuated between four and seven. We moved premises several times, and in 1985 the majority shareholding was bought out by John Barber – an ex-Ford finance director who at the time was Chairman of the consultancy and travel group Cox & Kings (C&K). After Graham Bannock left the company and set up his own consultancy, EAG recruited several other senior consultants, including Ian Senior and Jeremy Holmes, both of whom in turn became Managing Director of the company. I took over the chair-manship of EAG, after the resignation of Victor Morgan. I held this position until 2001, although in 1997 EAG was acquired by Beaufort International, a personnel recruitment and management consultancy company.[8]

My overall impression of my 30 years with EAG is that, as a business enterprise, we missed many opportunities to become a leading player in UK economic consultancy. This was particularly the case during our associa-tion with C&K. Partly, I believe, this was due to a variety of personnel difficulties; and partly because EAG was not sufficiently entrepreneurial in obtaining business in the private sector. This, in turn, was due to our inabil-ity to recruit top-level management or organizational strategists. In conse-quence, in 1990, more than 65 per cent of EAG's business was with the public sector or trade associations whose *per diem* fees were only a third to a half of those offered by clients in the private sector.

The one exception – and it was an important one – was the specialized expertise EAG managed to develop into the pricing and product diversification strategies of pharmaceutical firms. Under the leadership of Jeremy Holmes, our Managing Director in the 1990s, EAG built up an envi-able client list of the major UK and Swedish pharmaceutical MNEs; and it was mainly due to the efforts of Jeremy and his team that EAG was able to record a substantial increase in its annual turnover and profits in the latter 1990s. Unfortunately, I was unable to benefit from this turn of events, as by that time the EAG directors, apart from Jeremy, had sold their share-holdings to Beaufort International. In addition, most of the other acade-mic directors, including Alan Peacock and Brian Carsberg, had resigned because of other commitments; and very sadly Jack Wiseman had died.

John Barber also took no interest in the reconstructed EAG. I continued as Chairman of the company (the name was retained) but I had no financial interest in it. I resigned from the chairmanship in 2001, and in 2004 Jeremy Holmes also departed. At that latter date, Beaufort decided to do away with the EAG logo. So after 38 years, Victor Morgan's dreams had ended. But by that time Victor had died; he never witnessed the rather sad end of his brainchild.

****

And so to my association with the UN. This dates back to 1968 when I was asked to prepare a report for UNCTAD on the extent and pattern of UK direct investment in less-developed countries (LDCs). This was followed, six years later, by another request from the same organization to undertake one of the first field surveys into the trade and balance-of-payments effects of the activities of British MNEs in developing countries in 1972.

Indeed, at that time, it was UNCTAD that was the most active of the UN agencies in identifying the unique characteristics of MNEs, and their contribution to economic development.[9] In the 1960s, FDI was generally welcomed as a tool for restructuring and upgrading the indigenous resources and capabilities of recipient countries. Most noteworthily, in 1964 UNCTAD adopted five sets of recommendations with respect to inbound FDI. Two of these are particularly worth reiterating. The first was directed to capital-exporting countries that were urged to 'take all appropriate steps to encourage the flow of private investment to developing countries'.[10] The second was addressed to capital-importing countries, which were encouraged to take 'all appropriate steps to provide favourable conditions for direct private investment including the setting up of investment bureaux and investment advisory services'.[11]

Between the late 1960s and the mid-1970s, however, I was to observe that the 'sweetness and light' of the 1960s had largely disappeared, and a much more critical and aggressive stance by developing countries towards FDI was then emerging. There were several reasons for this. First, the learning experience of several developing countries about the effects of FDI in the 1960s suggested that not only were its beneficial consequences likely to be unevenly spread, but that the large and powerful MNEs – and particularly those in the natural resource-based sectors – were (or were perceived to be) gaining more than their equitable share of the economic rents arising from their foreign activities. Second, there was accumulating evidence that some MNEs were engaging in unacceptable business practices, such as transfer pricing manipulation and export restrictions. Third, some developing countries which had recently gained their political independence saw any attempt by foreign MNEs to dominate their local supply capabilities or markets as a form of economic imperialism, and as a possible threat to their newly found sovereignty. Fourth, on these and other issues (for example to do with employment and training, transfer of technology, research and development and networking with indigenous firms), an increasing body of scholarly work was demonstrating that the goals and strategies of MNEs were not always coincidental with those of the countries host to their affiliates.

At the same time, in 1969, the US Bureau of Intelligence and Research and the Research and Policy Planning Council convened a conference in Washington, DC to discuss some of the implications for US foreign policy which might arise from the growing participation of the US MNEs in the world economy. Participants included academics, businessmen and government officials. The conference recognized the role of outbound FDI both as a modality of cross-border capital and technology transfer, and as a generator of, or substitute for, trade. It accepted the US's responsibility to assist developing countries in their development process. It identified many of the costs and benefits of outbound FDI to the home economy. It acknowledged the various tensions which might arise between home and host governments as a direct result of MNE activity. However, perhaps the key recommendation of the conference was for the establishment of a multilateral mechanism to harmonize national economic regulations and policies towards FDI and MNEs. This, indeed, was the starting point for a bevy of new institutional arrangements initiated by firms, governments and supranational entities in the 1970s and 1980s. These were to range from informal guidelines and codes of conduct directed primarily to MNEs, to binding bilateral and multinational investment agreements between countries.

Yet, the critical lightning rod to the UN's enhanced interest in MNE-related issues in the 1970s was a combination of the Watergate scandal in 1972, and a series of alleged malpractices of a number of large and influential US MNEs. Such allegations were particularly directed to the interference by some US corporations in the political affairs of developing countries. This prompted the setting up of a Senate subcommittee, spearheaded by Frank Church, to investigate the interface between the global objectives and strategies of US MNEs and American foreign policy; and, in the latter part of 1970, more specifically to make a detailed examination of the documents relating to ITT's (International Telegraph and Telephone Corporation) operations in Chile.[12]

It was, indeed, as the direct result of these enquiries, that, backed by several delegations to the UN, including that of the Chilean government, Philippe de Seynes requested the Secretary-General to set up a Group of Eminent Persons (GEP) to advise the Economic and Social Council on the present role of MNEs in economic development and their impact on international relations.

Chapter 9 has already described the deliberations and recommendations of the GEP, and my involvement in it. Among its more important recommendations was the setting up of a permanent UN Commission on MNEs (in future to be called TNCs – transnational corporations) and (supported by a Secretariat), to collect data, undertake research on these activities, and give advice to host (developing) countries of how TNCs might best promote their economic and social goals.

****

In 1974, the Commission, primarily made up of international civil servants, and the Secretariat, mainly staffed by professional economists, lawyers and administrators, began work. Klaus Sahlgren, a Finnish diplomat, was appointed as the first Executive Secretary of the UNCTC; and within six months he had assembled a 30-strong permanent team. For the next two decades, the work of the Commission and the Centre focused on four main tasks. The first was assembling a data bank on the extent, geographical distribution, sectoral characteristics and ownership patterns of TNCs and their affiliates. In this, the Centre was aided by some earlier research undertaken by John Stopford, Klaus Haberich, Bob Pearce, John Cantwell and myself. In the 1970s and early 1980s, and drawing on data published in *Fortune*, Bob Pearce and I had completed a series of statistical exercises detailing the growth and internationalization of the world's leading industrial enterprises.[13] In 1981, Macmillan published a two-volume directory prepared by John Stopford, Klaus Haberich and myself, which profiled each of the 500 largest industrial TNCs in the world;[14] while, later in the decade, John Cantwell and myself completed a statistical exercise of the extent, pattern and ownership of both inward and outward FDI for some 80 countries.[15] Much of this early work was subsequently taken over and extended by the UNCTC (and later the UNCTAD).

Second, the UNCTC undertook and/or commissioned substantive research studies into a variety of TNC activities, and their impact on economic and social development. Throughout the period it was based in New York, the UNCTC produced three quinquennial reviews on this subject, and no less than 55 specialized reports on particular FDI-related issues, for example trade and the balance of payments, technology transfer, transborder data flows, transfer pricing, linkages, negotiating procedures, and so on; and examined the presence and performance of TNCs and their affiliates in several industrial sectors, such as automobiles, pharmaceuticals, petroleum, agricultural machinery, food, beverages and tourism. The UNCTC also played a critical part in the hearings on the role of TNCs in South Africa; in the World Health Organization's (WHO) studies on fostering the sale of tobacco products, and the marketing of breast-milk substitutes; and in a series of training and research programmes on technology transfer and economic development organized by the United Nations Institute for Training and Research (UNITAR).

Third – and this, to my mind, was the UNCTC's most distinctive contribution to our understanding about the interface between the economic strategies of the TNCs and the goals and policies of national regimes in which they were embedded – was the advice it offered to developing-country governments on how best to attract the right kind of inbound FDI, and the appropriate actions they might take to ensure that such investment would upgrade the resources and capabilities within their jurisdiction in the most cost-effective and socially acceptable way. To this end, the UNCTC arranged a series of training sessions for government representatives; and visits and seminars by the staff of the Centre were made to individual developing countries to discuss matters pertinent to their own particular interests.

Fourth, and in pursuance of the recommendation of the GEP and the UN's endorsement of it, the UNCTC almost immediately started work in devising a comprehensive code of conduct for TNCs. It was clear that, at this time, any proposal to extend the work of the General Agreement on Tariffs and Trade (GATT) to embrace guidelines or rules on FDI was likely to be a non-starter; and that any attempt to influence the practices and conduct of MNEs had to be implemented through separately agreed guidelines or codes. However, while such an idea was in keeping with the political ideology and the economic policies of the most national governments in the 1970s and early 1980s – indeed the *OECD Guidelines for Multinational Enterprises* (Paris, OECD) were first adopted in 1986 – some 16 years after discussions on the content and legitimacy of the UN code had started, it was abandoned.[16]

In the first three of these tasks, I was actively involved, as were other academic consultants such as John Stopford and Charles Michelet (each of whom spent a year or so working at the UNCTC), Raymond Vernon, Gerry Helleiner, Oswaldo Sunkel and Sanjaya Lall. Once again I was able to combine my academic and consultancy interests. In particular, two of the research projects I worked on with staff members at the UNCTC – namely the increasing role of TNCs in international tourism, and in the service sector – were at the cutting edge of international business research.[17] In both instances, I was able to apply my OLI framework for understanding the growth, location and form of TNC involvement.[18] As I shall describe later, I was also able to test some concepts and ideas contained in my 1993 book *Multinational Enterprises and the Global Economy* in some training sessions organized by the UNCTC for university lecturers from Asia and the Pacific. And a decade or more later, my own input and new material contained in several of the UNCTAD's *World Investment Reports* helped Sarianna Lundan and I prepare the new and revised edition of the volume which was published by Edward Elgar in May 2008.

****

At this point, however, I must own that in the 1970s and early 1980s I had considerable misgivings about the tenor of the UNCTC's approach to TNC-related topics, as it seemed to me to echo, and sometimes support, the adversarial stance then being taken by so many developing countries towards TNCs. To the extent that the host governments which were most critical of the impact of inbound FDI were also those most likely to engage in market-distorting policies, it was not surprising that TNCs were on to a hiding for nothing. In particular, I felt that the Centre – sometimes guided by the Commission – looked upon itself as the international monitor and regulator of TNC activity; as was most clearly demonstrated by its eagerness to get to work on a Code of Conduct designed to discipline the conduct of TNCs. Many of the regular staff of the UNCTC were from developing countries and, quite understandably, brought their own cultural and ideological predilections with them. In the early days of the UNCTC, a lack of experience of, and professional knowledge about TNCs also led to undisciplined and sometimes biased thinking by both senior and junior personnel, and to a considerable waste of resources in setting up an information system which initially, at least, was ill conceived and poorly executed.

Besides undertaking specific assignments for the UNCTC throughout the 1970s and 1980s, I was regularly asked to provide ad hoc advice on a wide range of issues including those germane to three major quinquennium surveys on the role of TNCs in economic development. I recollect that on practically every occasion I urged the Centre to exercise caution in generalizing about the consequences of inbound TNC activity on such issues as the balance of payments, indigenous technological capacity and human resources development of host countries. So much, I argued, depended on the motives for, and kind of, TNC activity, the strategies pursued by TNCs and their affiliates, the economic, political and cultural characteristics of investing and recipient countries, and the policies pursued by their governments. I also warned of the dangers of attributing to TNCs effects which may have nothing to do with their foreignness or multinationality per se, but to other characteristics that both they and non-MNEs might possess, for example their size and product profiles; and only to evaluate the effects of TNC activity in terms of what might have happened in the absence of such activity. These general principles – which are as valid in 2008 as they were 30 years ago – were difficult for some of the staff at the UNCTC to get to grips with, anxious as they were to come to some clear-cut conclusions about the consequences of inbound and outbound foreign direct investment.

Yet looking back, few of the early documents produced by the UNCTC came to any definitive conclusions. More often than not, however, the Centre put this down to inadequate data or a poorly researched report, and commissioned more ambitious projects on the same questions, which more often than not came up with the same answers. Over its 18-year existence, and in my opinion, the UNCTC reinvented the wheel of TNC activity more than did most other organizations.

****

Since the later 1980s, however, the Centre, and later the Division in Investment Technology and Enterprise Development of the UNCTAD, has become more professional and objective in its research. Partly this reflects a change in personnel, and partly the more positive conciliatory stance of national government representatives who were members of the Commission on TNCs. I have described in some detail elsewhere this change in stance and the reasons for it,[19] but in encapsulated form, the most important of these were in:

1. The renaissance of pro-market policies of several national governments – especially in the US and the UK – in the 1980s and 1990s, the repercussions of the fall of the Berlin Wall, and the emergence of China and India as major players on the world economic stage.
2. The reconfiguration of the development strategies of many developing countries, away from those based on economic autonomy and import substitution policies, to those more efficiency-seeking and outward-looking in their orientation.
3. A variety of major and far-reaching technological advances – including the advent and implementation of new forms of transport and communications technologies.
4. The growing consensus of scholarly research into the potential contribution of globalization and TNC activity to the upgrading of the indigenous resources and capabilities of both investing and recipient countries; and the identification of the kind of actions which national governments and supranational entities need to pursue for these advantages to be fully realized and sustained at minimum cost.

5. As a result of the growing competition between both developed and developing countries for foreign resources, capabilities and markets, and the perceived need of these countries to upgrade their global competitiveness, the 1990s saw an increasing number of fiscal incentives and bilateral investment agreements; a liberalization of performance requirements and other impediments to FDI; and a strengthening of the role and impact of investment promotion agencies.

As a direct result of these developments, I witnessed a marked change in the mindset among developing-country governments towards inbound TNCs. Now they started to see themselves as co-partners with foreign affiliate firms in promoting the dynamic comparative advantage of their resources and capabilities, rather than being reluctantly accepted as a second-best alternative to the activities of locally managed enterprises. Such a change of mindset was especially noticeable among the middle-income developing countries (noticeably in South and East Asia) which, themselves, were becoming significant outward investors. It then spread to the UN itself. From the late 1980s onwards, the focus of the Commission on TNCs was directed to the policies and institutions of host governments which might best attract and sustain the kind of TNC activity most needed by their countries.

The change in the approach to the role of TNCs and development by the UNCTC (and later the UNCTAD) was later reflected in its various research reports; and especially in its annual flagship publication, the *World Investment Report*, which the Centre launched in 1991. Over the past two decades, these annual surveys have been extremely well received by both national governments and TNCs; I think it fair to say that the UNCTAD is now regarded as a renowned – if not the most renowned – centre for research on the impact of TNC-related activities on economic development. In particular, the intellectual calibre of its staff has greatly improved, and many of those now working in Geneva can well hold their own in discussions with both the academic and business communities.

****

In 1992, the UNCTC was disbanded and work on TNCs was transferred to the UNCTAD in Geneva. It is now centred on the Investment Issues Analysis Branch of the Division on Investment, Technology and Enterprise (DITE). Since 1992 I have been Chief Economic Adviser to the Head of that division and Chairperson of the Board of Advisors of UNCTAD's thrice-yearly publication, *Transnational Corporations*. In practice, my involvement has been largely confined to the preparation of the annual publication, the *World Investment Report* (WIR). This report is normally divided into two parts. The first contains a review and analysis of the latest statistical data on the activities of TNCs, and of changes in the national and international policy environment. The second part focuses on a particular contemporary issue in which TNCs play (or could play) an important role. In 2006, for example, the report examined the growth of Third World TNCs; in 2007, the extent and impact of TNC involvement in the extractive industries; and in 2008 their contribution to upgrading the physical infrastructure of developing countries. My own function has been largely that of a 'troubleshooter', advising on the theoretical underpinnings and interpreting the findings of the data assembled. I attend the meetings organized by the DITE, including those held in one of the regional centres of the UN. In 2006, for example, I attended a regional meeting in Johannesburg, and in 2007 one in Santiago, Chile. I read and comment on the drafts of the reports. I like to think that over the years I have made a useful input into their analysis and findings.

****

Finally, I would like to identify two other initiatives of the UN in which I have participated – both of which have enabled me, at one and the same time, to wear my academic and consultancy hats.

The first of these, which was initially an idea of Gustave Feissel and warmly endorsed by myself, was to offer the services of the UNCTC as a broker between experienced researchers and teachers in TNC-related topics, and university Faculty in developing countries teaching Economics, Business and Law courses, wishing to incorporate such topics into their curricula. In January 1983 a meeting was organized by the UNCTC at the UNCTC/ESCAP[20] Regional Centre at Bangkok. Deans of Social Sciences and Law from several Asian and Pacific universities met with a group of senior economists, lawyers and business analysts to discuss the possibility of the UNCTC providing short courses on TNC-related matters which might be attended by Faculty from their universities.

There were two ideas put forward at this meeting. The first was that the UNCTC should prepare a number of syllabi of how TNC-related material might be introduced into existing undergraduate or graduate courses. The second idea was that the Centre, with the help of academic consultants, should itself prepare self-contained syllabuses for three one-year courses, namely those on TNCs and Economic Development, TNCs and Business Policy, and TNCs and Legal Issues which might be taught either at graduate or undergraduate level.

At the end of the meeting, it was decided that to identify better what the interested universities most wanted, a small team from the UNCTC should visit a selection of them in Asia and the Pacific, and there discuss with the heads of the relevant departments how far they might be prepared to incorporate the necessary changes into their degree programmes, and also gauge their willingness to designate one or more of their lecturers to attend a two- or three-week intensive training course which the UNCTC would organize.

To help them and their deans with their decision, detailed course outlines were prepared and circulated in advance of our visits. By this time, Gustave Feissel had left the UNCTC for another part of the UN, and Ellen Seidenstiker had taken his place. It was she that guided Tawfique Nawac, a legal expert, and myself through two quite exhausting tours. Twice round the world in 80 days was, I thought, quite a feat! On the first tour, we visited Thailand, Malaysia, the Philippines and Indonesia. From there I went on to Hawaii and the West Coast of the US, before returning to the UK. The itinerary on my second round the world trip included Sri Lanka, India, Bangladesh, Singapore and Fiji, and then San Francisco, Denver and New York.

The vibrancy of the East Asian economies struck me almost as forcibly as the densely populated, traffic-laden and often pungent cities. Each had (and still has) its own distinctive characteristics – Bangkok for its reputation of being the Amsterdam of the East and for its unique open air markets; Hong Kong for its bustling and impressive harbour, its high-rise buildings, its racing track and its Peak Tramway; Singapore for its incredibly clean and modern subway and its excellent hotels; Jakarta for its noise, its crowded and dreadful roads, but also for its supremely interesting museums of ancient artefacts; Manila for the majesty of its buildings, and the delightful hotel locations along the coast; and Kuala Lumpur for its heritage of British colonialism, its magnificent railway station, its cricket ground right in the centre of the city, and its Islamic culture.

****

At each of the universities it visited, the UN team was welcomed with great courtesy; and I was generally impressed at the quality and dedication of Faculty members to whom we spoke. With almost unreserved enthusiasm, the UNCTC was encouraged to organize a series of training seminars to which the heads of the relevant departments would send one or two of their Faculty. As there was some difference of opinion about the content of the seminars, the Centre decided to offer two groups of workshops. The first was a two-week training seminar during which the first week was devoted to a number of specialist lectures on how TNC-related material might be grafted on to existing economics, business and legal courses; while the second week was intended to focus on a number of TNC-related issues of particular concern to developing countries, such as technology transfer, transfer pricing, and so on, which might be treated from an interdisciplinary perspective. Such a seminar, which I helped to organize and in which I participated, was held for 30 teachers from 12 Asian and Pacific universities in Bangkok in January 1986.

The second, and more ambitious group of workshops comprised a set of three two- to three-week seminars, which set out the possible content of three specialist graduate courses to which earlier reference has been made. I was responsible for the course on TNCs and Economic Development which was held in Kuala Lumpur in January 1988. Sanjaya Lall, Louis Wells and Farok Contractor joined me in teaching a syllabus which I had earlier prepared. The contents of this and the other two syllabi were subsequently published by the UNCTC.[21]

The seminars were generally well received, and several of the participants subsequently introduced specialist courses on TNCs in economic development and/or business strategy. In other cases, teachers revised some of their existing syllabi by grafting on TNC-related material. The idea first put forward by Gustave Feissel five years earlier was now beginning to bear fruit. I had hoped that the Asian experiment would have been repeated in Africa, Latin America and Central and Eastern Europe. And, although a couple of years later, I presented a shortened version of my Kuala Lumpur course in Harare for lecturers from various African universities, neither those from Latin America nor from the erstwhile Communist countries seemed interested in the UNCTC making similar arrangements for them.

****

My other quasi-academic accomplishment at the UNCTC was with the full and enthusiastic backing of Karl Sauvant, in the early 1990s. It was to launch a series of state-of-the-art publications on the economic, strategic, organizational and legal role of transnational corporations in the contemporary world economy. The idea was to produce a 20-volume compendium, which incorporated some of the most influential published contributions on a range of issues, embracing the determinants, impact and policy implications of the activities of TNCs. Each of these volumes was to be edited by a distinguished scholar in the field, and I was to be General Editor of the series. A twenty-first volume was also planned, which would contain each of the Editor's introductions to the 20 volumes, and their list of contents.

In the event, the publisher of these volumes – Routledge – decided to market all 20 as a complete set; and issued each in five sets of four volumes over a 15-month period in 1993–94. Prior to signing the contract with the

UNCTC, Routledge had already secured an order of several hundred copies of the complete set from Japanese organizations and libraries. From all accounts, these and other buyers, particularly universities from developing countries, have found the UNCTC library a most useful source to some 312 seminal contributions on TNC-related matters, which were originally written between 1960 and 1989.

****

From its inception, I believed that one of the main tasks of the UNCTC was to collect and disseminate statistical and other information about TNCs and their activities. During the first few years of the Centre's existence, it made several attempts to assemble a directory of statistics and international direct investment, and to compile profiles on the world's leading TNCs, but these were generally unsuccessful. Indeed, it was the failure of the UNCTC to provide this critical service to the scholarly community that persuaded John Cantwell and myself to produce our own directory. Funded with a relatively small grant from the Institute of Research on Multinationals (IRM) of Geneva, a private research foundation, John and I put together a compendium of statistics on the stocks and flows of inward and outward direct investment for some 80 countries; on their industrial and geographical distribution; and on their relative significance to the economies of both home and host countries. The 850-page directory was the first of its kind, and we were pleased that we had prepared it. But we were disinclined to repeat this very time-consuming exercise, and I made arrangements with the UNCTC to take over the responsibility for updating and extending it. John and I continued to be associated with the venture as consultant editors, and after two years of preparation and at the cost of more than three times that of the original directory, the UNCTC published the first of five regional volumes, covering Asia and the Pacific, in September 1992.[22] At last, I felt the Centre had begun to fulfil its role as a primary source of statistical data, in addition to that as a leading research institution and as a foremost provider of consultancy services on TNC-related issues to the governments of developing countries.

****

As already recounted, most of the earlier UNCTC work on TNCs was transferred from New York to Geneva in 1992. Since that date, my advisory role has been mainly confined to the contents and analytical underpinnings of the *World Investment Report* (WIR). This is the flagship publication of the Division of Investment and Technology at the UNCTAD.

The WIR was very much the brainchild of Karl Sauvant, and he and Peter Hansen, the last Director of the UNCTC, issued the first edition in 1991 from New York. Thereafter, Karl became the energetic driving force behind its publication at the UNCTAD; and, for most of the years before his retirement, led a team of a score or more of in-house researchers, and (usually) up to 100 academic and other specialists, in the preparation of the reports. In 2005, Anne Miroux took over the responsibility for the WIR, and currently has a first-rate in-house team working for her.

There are many other TNC-related areas in which the UNCTAD has made, and is making, an important contribution. However, the only one in which I have been directly involved is as Chairperson of the Board of Editors of the thrice-yearly journal *Transnational Corporations*. It is the intention of that journal that each of the articles should examine some aspect or other of the interaction between the activities of TNCs, and the economic and social environments in which they operate. The publication is quite unique in its objectives and contents, and to my mind provides a valuable complement to the more business-focused periodicals such as the *Journal of International Business Studies* and *International Business Review*. Though *Transnational Corporations* is likely to continue to be a UN-sponsored journal, at the time of writing (July 2008), plans are under way to collaborate with a commercial publisher to promote its production and marketing.

****

The year 2008 is then my forty-first year of being associated with the UN. New challenges continue to open up. I am now involved in a major exercise initiated by the United Nations Industrial Development Organization (UNIDO) on the role of inward FDI in enhancing indigenous technical and managerial capabilities in 30 or so sub-Saharan countries. But looking back to the late 1960s, and acknowledging the dramatic and far-reaching changes which have taken place in the global economy since then, I would be the first to recognize that not only has the work of the various UN agencies benefited my own research and scholarly endeavours, but it has also helped forge closer links and understanding between those agencies and the wider academic community. This, I believe, is particularly the case in respect of the policies pursued by national governments and supranational entities towards TNCs and their affiliates.

As to the future, I believe it should be incumbent on the UN – perhaps more than any other international organization – to focus more attention on examining the institutions and belief systems underpinning and influencing the actions of TNCs and governments. Moreover, it needs to do so in a global economy in which change, volatility and uncertainty are endemic features;

and one in which the character and content of the human environment is playing an increasingly important role in fashioning economic success and societal transformation. The UN's Global Compact[23], and the work of the World Commission on the Social Dimension by the International Labor Office (ILO)[24] are useful starting points, but a more coordinated value-based approach to TNCs and globalization needs to embrace every aspect of the work of the UN. The social, cultural and economic aspects of TNC-related activities are too intertwined to be treated independently of each other. A holistic institutional approach is needed. In particular, informal (bottom-up) and formal (top-down) incentive structures and enforcement mechanisms directed towards TNCs and their affiliates need to be coordinated and jointly monitored. Centralized modern governance needs to be integrated with more decentralized modes. It is here, again, where a sustained dialogue and exchange of views between the UN and its various agencies, and academic scholars is likely to offer high dividends.

A more detailed and comprehensive review of the interface between the various UN agencies over the past 40 years is contained in a recently authored volume by Tagi Sagafi-Nejad entitled *The UN and Transnational Corporations: From Code of Conduct to Global Compact*, Bloomington, Indiana University Press (2008). I have had the privilege of advising and working with Tagi on this project, which was one of a series of studies master-minded by Richard Jolly, Louis Emmerij and Thomas Weiss on the intellectual history of the United Nations. The title of the volume is very appropriate, as it examines the evolving, and mainly centrist stance of the UNCTC, and later UNCTAD, on the impact of TNC activity on economic development and international relations; and of how, in the early 2000s, it is taking a more pro-active and consensual stance in its policy recommendations both to national governments and supranational agencies.

****

NOTES

1. Exceptions include various pieces of work for Shell, IBM, Unilever and ICI.
2. In the case of the UK, for example, the Treasury, the Board of Trade (later Department of Trade and Industry, DTI); the National Economic Development Office (NEDO); The Ministry of Economic Development (now the Department of International Development (DFID)) and the Welsh Office.
3. *An Economic Study of the City of London*, London, Allen & Unwin 1971, (reprinted by Routledge (Routledge Library Edition), London and New York, 2003.
4. W.M. Clarke (ed.), *Britain's Invisible Exports*, London Committee on Invisible Exports, 1968.
5. For example J.H. Dunning and D. Robertson (1972), *World Invisible Trade*, London, Committee on Invisible Exports.

6. See particularly Brian Chiplin and Brian Sturgess (who were consultants to EAG), *Economics of Advertising*, London, Holt Rinehart & Winston, 1981.
7. Graham Bannock was appointed Managing Director in place of Malcolm Lamb.
8. Which was looking to extend its business into economic consultancy.
9. Though in some more specialized areas ILO, UNIDO and UNITAR were also involved.
10. UNCTAD, *Proceedings of the United Nations Conference on Trade and Development, Volume 1 Final Act and Report*, Geneva, UN, 1964, p. 49.
11. UNCTAD *op cit*, pp. 49–50.
12. For further details see Chapter 3 of Tagi-Sagafi-Nejad in collaboration with John H. Dunning, *The UN and Transnational Corporations: From Code of Conduct to Global Compact*, Bloomington, IN, Indiana University Press.
13. See for example *The World's Largest Industrial Enterprises 1962–82*, Farnham, Gower Press, 1985.
14. *The World Directory of Multinational Enterprise*, London, Macmillan, 1981 (two volumes).
15. *IRM Directory of Statistics on International Investment and Prediction*, London and New York, 1987. This work was financed by a grant from the Institute for Research and Information (IRM) on MNEs, a private organization then located in Geneva.
16. Not only because of the intractable difficulties surrounding the implementation of parts of the code, but also because globalization was bringing out a very different assessment by most national governments to the contributions of TNCs to economic development.
17. I particularly enjoyed working on the tourism project with my good friend, Hans Fredrik Samuelsson, as it gave me the opportunity, over a period of six months, to visit some of the most stunning holiday resorts, and stay in some of the most luxurious hotels in the world.
18. (With M. McQueen.) 'The Eclectic Paradigm and the International Hotel Industry', *Managerial and Decision Economics*, **2**, 1981, 197–210; 'Multinational Corporations in the International Hotel Industry', *Annuals of Tourism Research*, **9**, 1982, 69–90; and 'Multinationals and the Growth of Services: Some Conceptual and Theoretical Issues', *Service Industries Journal*, **9**, 1989, 5–39.
19. J.H. Dunning, 'The United Nations and Transnational Corporations: A Personal Assessment', in L. Cuyvers and F. de Beule (eds), *Transnational Corporations and Economic Development: From Internationalization to Globalization*, Basingstoke, Palgrave Macmillan 2005, 11–37.
20. Economic and Social Commission for Asia and Pacific.
21. *University Curriculum on Transnational Corporations* (Volume 1 *Economic Development*, Volume 2 *International Business* and Volume 3 *International Law*), New York, United Nations, 1991.
22. The other four volumes embraced the OECD countries, Central and Eastern Europe, Latin America, and Africa and the Middle East.
23. The Global Compact is an instrument originally devised by Kofi Annan, the then Secretary General of the UN, in 1999, to promote responsible global capitalism, and to best ensure the basic human needs of the world's poorest countries. Initiated at the annual meeting of the *World Economic Forum* in Geneva, the original purpose of the compact was for multinational enterprises, national governments and representatives of civil society to voluntarily accept, and adhere to, nine behavioural principles (including the protection of human rights, the upholding of collective bargaining, the effective abolition of child labour, and the encouragement of environmentally friendly technology). In June 2004, an additional principle – that businesses should work against all forms of corruption – was added. Further details of the Global Compact are set out in Tagi Segafi-Nejad, in collaboration with John H. Dunning, *The UN and Transnational Corporations: From Code of Conduct to Global Compact*, Bloomington, Indiana University Press (2008).
24. The report of which was published in 2004 under the title *A Fair Globalization: Creating Opportunities For All*, Geneva, ILO.

Part IV: 2008

Autumn–winter

12. Towards the final season and second childhood[1]

From time to time in my sixties and seventies I thought about what I would like to do when my time came to retire from academic life. I did not anticipate continuing with my research or teaching much beyond the early 1990s, but rather expected to do something to which I could apply my Christian beliefs. Much earlier in the 1950s and early 1960s, I had enjoyed lay preaching, but, as I have already recounted, I ruled this option out after the events of the subsequent decade.

Again, serendipity entered the picture. As I have already mentioned in Chapter 10, in 1998 I was invited to give a talk on the Christian response to global capitalism at the annual meetings of the European International Business Academy (EIBA) in Jerusalem.[2] This, along with parallel presentations by Jewish and Islamic speakers, stimulated a great deal of interest among my friends and colleagues, and after careful thought, and with a growing realization that moral and ethical issues were now increasingly entering the domain of globalization, I redirected much of my scholarly attention in the early 2000s towards identifying the ways and means by which global capitalism could be made both more economically inclusive and socially acceptable.

One of the results of this work was the publication of my edited volume *Making Globalization Good*, subtitled *The Moral Challenges of Global Capitalism*, in 2003 by Oxford University Press. To finance the project, I secured generous grants from the Templeton and Carnegie Bosch Foundations. My aim was to gain the insights of distinguished scholars, religious leaders, businessmen and statesmen on (what they perceived to be) the essential moral and ethical attributes of a sustainable global market-based system.[3] In this, I believe I was successful. I certainly learned a lot about the different views expressed, but at the end of the day, I was comforted to discover that there was a substantial commonality among the contributors as to what they thought needed to be done if global capitalism was to be an efficient, fair and sustainable economic system for both the creation and utilization of scarce human and physical resources.

The volume was launched at three half-day conferences in London and New York in 2003, and in New Delhi early in 2004. But, in spite of a sensitive introduction to the volume by the Prince of Wales, the press coverage was disappointing; and although subsequent reviews of the book have been favourable, they have not been as many as I would have wished. In short, the impact of my efforts has been much less than I had hoped for; and this in spite of the almost daily indicators of corruption, corporate malfeasance, and differences among belief systems on the content of the 'good' society. It would seem that moral issues do not rate high on the agenda for action of most people.[4] In this respect, I compare the present attitudes to the ethical imperatives of capitalism to those towards climate change 20–30 years ago. And like the latter, I fear that by the time it is recognized that there are endemic moral challenges to the contemporary global market system which must be tackled, it will be too late!

I continue to address this issue in my writings and lecturing. For example in 2000, I contributed a paper on 'The Moral Response to Capitalism: Can We Learn from the Victorians?' to a symposium organized by Julian Birkinshaw and his colleagues at the London Business School in honour of John Stopford.[5] I also observe that, almost every day, in the popular media, and in gatherings ranging from the World Economic Forum to the United Nations, and in interfaith dialogues, the issue of religion in business is aired. In January 2008, for example, there was a report that the Chief Rabbi of Israel had proposed a UN Commission of Spiritual Leaders to examine, and possibly coordinate, an active religious participation in, and response to global economic, political and cultural events.[6]

Why such initiatives and the huge array of monographs and papers dissecting, and warning about, the erosion of many (but not all) of our traditional moral values and social norms, and the tension and clashes this is causing among the extreme wings of the leading traditional religions of the world, are apparently having so little effect, I do not know. I fear there is a strong 'burying heads in the sand' phenomenon, with the current generation assigning first priority to freedom of behaviour as their fundamental right, irrespective of its consequence to others.[7] Yet history suggests that this kind of libertarianism, or sensate society, has usually been halted or reversed by some dramatic exogenous event or events, rather than by a gradual and voluntary improvement of individual and societal ethical mores.[8]

****

Elsewhere I have documented some of the events of my professional life and expressed views on the recent history and likely prospects of international business research, viewed through my own particular lens.[9] A short professional autobiography of mine was published in 2002 when I was 75.[10]

At its conclusion I suggested that I might wind down some of my commitments and travel arrangements. In fact, between 2003 and the end of 2007, I travelled abroad more, and published more monographs and papers, than at any other corresponding five years of my scholarly career.

In 1993, when I gave the Geary lecture in Dublin, I was reminded by my Chairman that Robert Geary, the founder of the Irish Economic and Social Research Institute, wrote and published a larger number of books and papers after he retired at 65, than before. If you count separately the two editions of *Multinational Enterprises and the Global Economy*, I think, since 1992, I have matched this achievement – at least in terms of number of words!

But much more important is that since the mid-1990s, the focus of my research has changed. While I have continued to work closely with the UNCTAD, the UNIDO, the World Investment Promotion Agency (WIPA) and the national investment promotion agencies of China and Korea, an increasing proportion of my scholarly attention is devoted to two topics, namely: (1) the moral imperatives of global capitalism, and corporate social responsibility; and (2) the role and content of micro and macro institutions in influencing both the determinants and effects of international business (IB) activity.

I have outlined my interest, and some of my publications, on the first topic, elsewhere in this chapter. As to the second, under the strong influence of Douglass North[11] and several IB scholars in the early 1990s, Sarianna Lundan and I have summarized some of our views on the interface between institutions and MNEs in the second edition of *Multinational Enterprises and the Global Economy*. Indeed, apart from updating the data, and extending the analysis and empirical content contained in the first edition, I would regard our explicit incorporation of country (national) and firm (corporate) specific institutions into mainstream IB research as one of the most valuable scholarly responses to the globalization of the world economy over the past 20 years.[12] The essential point here is that this event has led not only to a much closer economic interdependence between the wealth-creating activities of firms and nations, but also between that of widely differing cultural and belief systems. And it is in this latter domain that it is much less easy, let alone desirable, to exploit the benefits of economic integration. Moreover, it is only by reconfiguring corporate and/or national institutions that the social and cultural consequences of such integration can be made more inclusive and creditable. In this connection, many IB and other writers have stressed the increasing importance of relational capital[13] as a critical competitive advantage of firms and countries in the global economy. And it is at this juncture that my own interests in the moral imperatives of global capitalism and that of institutions intersect. I hope to continue working in the area of institutions, and the evolutionary theory of economic change, and of how each interacts on a whole variety of IB topics.

****

Since the mid-1970s, Christine and I have been regular visitors to Cornwall. For many years we regularly rented a National Trust holiday cottage. Then, in 1999, came an opportunity to acquire an apartment in a small, recently converted hotel, originally built in the 1930s. Pendower Court is situated above a beautiful beach in South Cornwall, 'twixt St Mawes and Mevagissey. The area is known as the Roseland, and near to it are some wonderful attractions such as the Eden Project, the Maritime Museum at Falmouth and the Lost Gardens of Heligan. However, to Christine and myself it is the spectacular coastline, magnificent walks, stunning beaches, delightful small ports and harbours, enchanting creeks, beautiful gardens and the multiple delights of the most western county in Great Britain that we so dearly love. Just 15 miles away is Truro, the busy, but delightful and intimate city of Cornwall, with its magnificent three-spire cathedral built in the late nineteenth and early twentieth centuries. To the north of the county, there is the charming and thriving fishing port of Padstow, the lovely, but often challenging, waters of the Camel Estuary, and its surrounding beaches and coastal walks. On the west side of the estuary and directly opposite Padstow lies Rock – a sailing resort often frequented by the more affluent younger generation including Princes William and Harry. A little further down the north coast is Newquay, the surfing capital of Europe, and St Ives – an artist's paradise, and now well renowned for its modern art gallery, the Tate St Ives.

Nowhere in Cornwall – from Looe in the east to Land's End in the west of the county – is more than an hour's drive from Pendower Court. At Penzance – the western terminus of the First Great Western Railway – it is possible to take a boat or a helicopter trip to the idyllic Isles of Scilly, which comprise the most westerly landmass of Great Britain. Christine and I have visited three of these islands – St Mary's, Tresco and St Martin's, each with its own distinctive character. We had delightful weather while we were there in the spring of 2004, but the Scillies can be pounded by the most vicious storms. Indeed, over the last three centuries there have been more shipwrecks within a short distance of the Scillies' three lighthouses than anywhere else along the British coastline.

The gentle and undulating coastline of south Cornwall contrasts with the towering cliffs, swirling seas, and the relics of old tin mines on the north coast, 600 of which were active in the nineteenth century.[14] Cornwall also has a thriving fishing and farming industry, and Cornish clotted cream is well renowned throughout the world. However, nowadays the tourist industry is the largest employer in Cornwall, an emerging feature of which is the growth of cruiseline activity in both Falmouth and Fowey. The county also has its own university (with its headquarters in Penryn just outside Falmouth); and several of its churches reflect the richness of its Celtic history and of the early Christian religion in the UK.

In such a delightful setting, I have spent about three months each year since 1999. It has been in my study at Pendower Court, with its uninterrupted view of the sea, that I have done a great deal of my recent thinking and writing. Most of my contribution and editorial work on *Making Globalization Good* was undertaken in Cornwall; as was my reading of the revised drafts of the second edition of *Multinational Enterprises and the Global Economy*. I find the coastal scenery of the Roseland Peninsula inspiring and unspoilt. I am attracted by the deep-rooted values and the homespun leisure pursuits of the Cornish people, who are so engagingly proud of their country. I am also fascinated by the myths and folklore surrounding the history of Cornwall. Did King Arthur hold his court with the Knights of the Round Table in Tintagel in the ninth century? Possibly, but no one knows for sure. Is it fact or fiction that an evil giant, Cornelian, was slain on the pathway steps leading to his own castle at St Michael's Mount (near Penzance) by a lad called Jack? And what about Daphne du Maurier's story of Jamaica Inn as a headquarters of the nineteenth-century smuggling industry? Is the Beast (reputed to be a large cat) of Bodmin Moor real or imaginary?

****

The tragedy of Philip's brain damage – almost certainly caused by a lack of oxygen to his brain at the time of his birth – has always been at the back of my mind; and in the last few years, it has come increasingly to the fore. How best, I have wondered, and continued to wonder, might I help to support research into the causes of brain-damaged babies; how might these be avoided; and how, once identified, might they be mitigated or remedied? It soon became apparent that the only way I could become personally involved was through identifying the charities and foundations working in this area, publicizing the results of recent research as to what needs to be done, and by donating some money towards further research and its more positive findings.

But exactly what is the state of knowledge on this issue 50 years after Philip was born? Is the likelihood of babies being born with damaged brains, or damage caused during the time of birth, greater or less in 2008 than it was? And what about mitigating or reversing brain damage?

My first port of call was Mencap (formerly the National Society for Mentally Handicapped Children). I soon discovered two things. First, there were many different – and often interrelated – causes of both prenatal and immediately post-natal brain damage; the symptoms of which (as happened in the case of Philip) might frequently take several months to show themselves. Second, the medical profession's ability to diagnose prenatal brain damage (or potential damage), and the capabilities of the nursing staff to deal with problems of delivery at birth, have considerably improved since the 1950s, although many of the underlying causes and possible treatments of brain damage still remain unresolved. But the focus of Mencap is primarily directed to identifying ways in which the lives of babies, children and adults who have suffered from one form of brain damage or another can be made more comfortable and meaningful. So my search for information and advice had to turn elsewhere.

Shortly after my meeting with Lord Brian Rix, the President of Mencap, David Congdon, its fund-raising manager, telephoned me to tell me about research into brain-damaged babies then being undertaken by a Dr Hussyan at Imperial College, London. When I tried to contact him, I found he had moved to the US to work on a related problem for a US pharmaceutical company, Merck. Further correspondence and telephoning led me to contact a senior paediatrician researching at the college, Professor David Edwards. In December 2007, I motored to see him and Dr Deanne Taylor, a lecturer in Neuroimmunology. Professor Edwards updated me on progress (and lack of progress) in this area of medicine. He confirmed that by a variety of screening devices, it was now possible to identify certain types of prenatal brain damage; and also, if discovered at time of birth, to mitigate or even eliminate some of the effects of oxygen starvation. However, he reiterated the observation made by Lord Rix and others that some kinds of infant brain damage did not display themselves until several months after birth, and that, by that time, it was extremely difficult to repair the damaged cells.

Since only 3 in 1000 infants are normally brain damaged at either the prenatal stage or at birth, Professor Edwards indicated that this area of medicine at Imperial College did not receive large sums of governmental or private funding. But he was of the opinion that his own department was at the cutting edge of world research; and that several new avenues of investigations, such as stem cell implantation, were currently being actively explored. In the short run, however, the early diagnosis of prenatal brain damage, and combating at least some kinds of any brain damage caused at the time of birth, was his first priority.

As a follow-up to our meeting, Professor Edwards recommended I approach a UK foundation, Action Medical Research (AMR), which frequently funded research by Imperial College and other organizations into brain-damaged babies. He also informed me that this funding was

sometimes provided by an individual or a charity that specified the particular medical problem they wanted investigated. It was suggested that this
might be an avenue for taking further my idea for more financed research
into the areas of particular concern to me.

In March 2008, Rear Admiral (Rtd) Simon Moore, the Chief Executive
of Action Medical Research (AMR) visited Christine and myself and
brought us up to date with the charity's work. Research on brain-damaged
babies is an important part of AMR's funding remit, named – I thought
quite appropriately – Touching Tiny Lives. One of the most recent projects
they are helping to finance is that by Professor John Wyatt of Edinburgh
University and a team of researchers to develop a water-cooled cap for
newly born babies deprived of oxygen at birth. Earlier experimental studies
in northern Scandinavia and Russia had demonstrated that cooling the
brain at this time slows down its chemical reactions to any oxygen loss, and
gives the brain cells' natural repair mechanism a chance to work.

Christine and I were most impressed by the professionalism of AMR,
and in the months and years ahead we intend to seek ways and means
by which we might do what we can to publicize support for this very
worthwhile charity.

****

The first five months of my eightieth birthday year were among the busiest
travelling periods of my life. For the UNCTAD I took flights to Geneva
and Santiago (Chile); for the UNIDO I presented a paper at a high-level
conference on foreign direct investment in sub-Saharan Africa at Addis
Ababa (Ethiopia). I spent a week at Rutgers University in meetings with the
PhD students. I gave talks in Bucharest (Romania), Laredo (Texas),
Atlanta (Georgia), and at the UK chapter of the AIB in London. I received
honorary doctorates from the Chinese Culture University in Taipei
(Taiwan) and the University of Lund (Sweden). I participated in a conference in Geneva organized by the Institute of Development in Oxford in
honour of Sanjaya Lall. I spent a couple of days relaxing in Miami, and in
Eleuthera (one of the Islands of the Bahamas). In between these trips, I
managed two visits of 14 days each to the Roseland, putting some final
touches to *Multinational Enterprises and the Global Economy*.[15]

This spate of travelling (apart from my visit to Lund in June 2007) came to
an end in late April when I attended a conference on Forty Years of
International Business at the University of Reading. With the exception of
Geoff Jones, all the stalwarts of the Reading School – Peter Buckley, Mark
Casson, Alan Rugman, Bob Pearce, John Cantwell and Rajneesh Narula,
and latterly Klaus Meyer – were there, together with many of the past

students such as Jeremy Clegg and Nigel Driffield, both of whom had undertaken doctoral studies at the university. The conference concluded with a birthday party for myself, organized by Rajneesh, at which Danny van den Bulcke presented a series of slides depicting stages of my professional, and not so professional, life! I was also handed a book with the birthday greetings of a large number of my friends and colleagues, which I shall treasure for the rest of my life. It was a most enjoyable and memorable party, which reminded me both of the unique and enormous contribution those present had made to IB scholarship over the previous 30 years or more and, no less important to me at any rate, their influence on my own intellectual development.

My actual birthday is on 26th June but I knew that, in 2007, I would be attending the annual meetings of the AIB in Indianapolis. This meant that Christine and I had to organize my birthday celebrations earlier. I had made up my mind that I wanted to arrange a lunch party for my immediate family, friends and closest colleagues at the Phyllis Court Club in Henley; and this took place on 16th June. It was a splendid affair, and helped bring together several of my friends and colleagues who had not seen each other for several years. Earlier, in May, Christine had arranged a party at our home for 30 of our family, on both her and my own sides. We were fortunate with the weather, and again I think a good time was had by all.

My fourth birthday party was part of the Fellows of the AIB dinner at Indianapolis. This was a complete surprise to me. Not only was another birthday cake provided, but all the female Fellows (I think about 12 in all) touchingly serenaded me. Incidentally, and this is not intended to be the least patronizing, I am really delighted that women are playing such an important role in AIB affairs. As I write (May 2008) Stephanie Lenway is President of the Academy, Lorraine Eden is Editor of JIBS and Eleanor Westney is Dean Elect of the Fellows. Each brings her own particular branch of charm, elegance and expertise to the offices she holds. Klaus Macharzina on behalf of the Fellows of EIBA also presented me with a gift. I was extremely moved – and I much appreciated the kindness and the good wishes of all those present.

The second half of 2007 was a much quieter period in my life. Christine and I took a holiday in the Bernese Oberland in early September, and a short cruise to Belgium, Northern France and the Channel Islands later that month. Earlier in July, I had spent a couple of weeks in Cornwall, and revisited a draft of the first part of this volume of reminiscences which I had written during my visits to Rutgers University in the mid-1990s. Apart from attending a meeting at the UNCTAD in Geneva to discuss the outline of the WIR for 2008, I made no overseas visits until December when I attended the annual meeting of the EIBA in Catania, Sicily. Little known to me, this provided another occasion for a birthday celebration – this time as part of the gala banquet which took place in the splendid fourteenth-century Palace of Bellini. A special birthday cake, topped with wild strawberries and eight candles, along with a gift was presented to me; and a small orchestra, which had entertained the 300 people present, throughout the dinner struck up 'Happy Birthday to You'. Earlier, Danny had recounted some of the highlights of my career. Apparently, although I had not realized it at the time, the seventh year of each decade of my professional life had been especially marked by scholarly achievement and recognition.[16]

Although remaining intellectually active, I began to lose some of my earlier taste for long-distance travelling in the second half of 2007. Fortunately Sarianna Lundan came to my rescue, and she, on our behalf, presented two of our co-authored papers – one at Columbia University in New York in October, and the other at St Petersburg University in Russia in December. Taking 2007 as a whole, I edited two books and wrote eight papers, five of which were jointly with other scholars.

In December 2007 I went for a series of medical tests as I was experiencing some atrial fibrillation and an unusual degree of tiredness. All showed there was nothing seriously wrong with me, but in each case the consultants I saw suggested that I stopped behaving like a 40-year-old in a body of a man twice that age. I took note, as did Christine who accompanied me at the time. But, as of 1st January 2008, my diary was already uncomfortably full – at least for the first six months of the year!

****

However, later in that month, things dramatically changed. On yet another visit to my heart specialist Dr John Bell, on 9th January, he discovered (or at least thought) that my liver was somewhat enlarged. He immediately arranged for a CT scan of the abdomen, which I had a week later. Later on that same day, 16th January, Christine and I saw Dr Bell, who informed us sympathetically, but in no uncertain terms, that I had metastatic liver disease – which, in my case, consisted of a cluster of cancers covering one-third of the liver, the origin of which was uncertain. On the following Monday, 21st January, my consultant oncologist Dr Gildersleve confirmed the diagnosis, but before deciding on any treatment, he advised that I should have a biopsy of the liver which was fixed for 31st January.

The biopsy confirmed the positioning and type of cancer, and its origin – the pancreas. After some days of hard thinking, Christine and I decided to opt for chemotherapy, even though the chances of success were only 15 per cent. The first of three cycles of treatment began in early February, and all went well until the end of the second week when a blood test revealed that my immune system was being adversely affected by the chemo. Dr

Gildersleve immediately stopped the treatment, and I then had two weeks of reasonably good health. On 13th March I began a second three-week cycle, but it was not until the end of the third cycle at the end of April that we would know how effective the treatment had been. In the meantime, Christine and I had been overwhelmed by a large numbers of letters, emails, faxes and gifts from friends and colleagues, all expressing love and concern about our situation. These have done much to help us to take as positive an attitude as possible to what has happened.

Although otherwise reasonably fit, but easily tired, I then set about cancelling most of my travel plans for February through to May, though I decided not to inform most of my friends and colleagues about my condition until my oncologist could give me an accurate prognosis together with possible treatments. On 8th May I saw Dr Gildersleve again. While a variety of blood tests had revealed a marked improvement in my liver function, there were no signs of a reduction in the cancerous tumours. However it was decided that we should continue with the chemotherapy at least for the following three weeks.

****

Needless to say, when Christine and I were first told about the cancer, we were in a stage of shock. However, this did not stop us from thinking about the future and the possible worst-case scenario. I decided the first thing which needed to be done was drastically to reduce the copious volume of my business and personal papers that I had accumulated over the past 40–50 years. These included multiple copies of some 300 articles of mine dating back to 1952. I decided to keep a file of just one copy of most of these, apart from those which I thought were among my most influential. Much of the material for *Multinational Enterprises and the Global Economy* I also boxed into 30 storage containers, while I initiated separate files covering copies of published and unpublished papers on my more recent areas of research, including the moral and ethical issues of global capitalism, institutions, locational competitiveness, and foreign direct investment in sub-Saharan Africa. These I hoped would later find a welcome and congenial home, some thoughts about which I will touch upon in the next section of this chapter.

****

What would I like to think were the most enduring and satisfying memories of my long career? I have enjoyed so many – such as being the recipient of six Honorary Doctorates, an Honorary Professorship, two Festschrifts and several different kinds of awards, details of which are set out in an Appendix to the volume. But of these highlights, two in particular stand out. In 2008 the Reading University Business School and the Henley Management College merged. As a result, the Henley Business School of the University of Reading will be the fourth-largest school of its kind in Europe. A critical part of the new entities' research and teaching will be in the domain of IB, and I was honoured when I received a letter from the Vice-Chancellor in February 2008 informing me that the Centre for International Business would be named the John H. Dunning Centre for International Business. I was particularly pleased as it acknowledges the hard work I and my colleagues had put in over the 1960s, 1970s and 1980s, to help make Reading a world-renowned centre on this subject. I am also currently (May 2008) in discussion with the Business School for my library of books and papers to be donated to the Centre.

The second thing which has given me tremendous pleasure is the time spent with my graduate students, and of later witnessing how successful most of them have been in their careers. Space does not permit me to name each of the 50 or so graduate students for whom I have been responsible, but I cannot fail to mention Terry Coram, who worked closely with me on my project on UK MNEs in North America at Southampton University; Jeremy Clegg and John Cantwell, two of my more distinguished PhD students at Reading University; and Sumit Kundu, Rajneesh Narula and Sarianna Lundan, three of my first Rutgers graduates, each of whom now has a professorship at a well-renowned university, and publishes regularly in the leading international business journals. It is the success of these students, each of whom I have been privileged to have under my care for three to four years, that has given me the most satisfaction in my scholarly career.

****

What of my failures and disappointments? Yes, there have been several over my career, and it would have been surprising if there had not been. But I will recount just three of these. The first has been my inability to persuade my colleagues in economics and other related subjects at both Reading and Rutgers to appreciate fully the relevance of international business research to an understanding of their own lines of scholarly research, but perhaps more importantly, to acknowledge the uniqueness of IB as a subject area (which I shall have more to say about later in this chapter). However, let me be the first to admit that there are exceptions to this rather sweeping statement. These include James Markusen in international economics, Paul Streeten and Sanjaya Lall in economic development, Mira Wilkins and Geoff Jones in business history, Peter Dickens and Nigel Thrift in geography, and Michael Porter and Sumantra Ghoshal in management. Each of these individuals and several others in the domain of IB have been important bridge-builders between the different disciplines comprising this field of study, and between it and other related scholarly endeavours.

Second, I have been disappointed that my writings on the moral imperatives of globalizing capitalism have not been more widely noticed. I had thought that, with such an illustrious group of contributors, *Making Globalization Good* would have sparked off much more debate and interest than it did; and for it to give me more enthusiasm to pursue a new book on this topic. But, although I have several files of notes and references, and a few first drafts of the chapters to this book, which would link my interest in globalization and institutions with those of the challenges of different faith systems, I have not taken this project any further.

Third – and this is more of a niggle than anything else – I have been disappointed that so many of my letters, faxes and emails, requesting information and advice about my work (and even in the case of Rutgers about my budget!), not to mention complimentary copies of my papers and books sent to scholars, political leaders and businessmen, have not been acknowledged. I do not know if this is a cultural phenomenon, but I find I get the fewest acknowledgements from US and Japanese colleagues. My IB colleagues are a noticeable exception. To my mind, this lack of response borders on the discourteous. For my part, I have always tried to find time to reply to all correspondence that lands on my desk, or in Jill Turner's email, even though its contents may not be exactly what was wished for!

****

Taking, next, a wider perspective of the seasons of my life, what single word would I use to sum up my contemporary feeling towards my earthly journey? The answer is 'Gratitude':

- Gratitude for a warm and loving family life. Gratitude to my parents for their selfless devotion to me and providing a moral compass to my life. In particular, gratitude to my former wife Ida, for the sacrifices she made early in our marriage so that I could pursue an academic career; and to Christine who, over the past 40 years, has been such a devoted, supportive and caring wife, and has shared with me so many memorable moments and experiences.
- Gratitude for my health and strength until the late 1990s; the only times I had earlier been admitted to hospital was for two hernia operations in 1975 and 1990.
- Gratitude for the joy, intellectual challenges and fulfilment most of

my academic and consultancy career have given me; and for the friendship, inspiration, scholarly insights and cooperation of so many of my friends, colleagues and past students.

- Gratitude for so many opportunities to travel and experience the cultures of so many different parts of the planet; and to meet such interesting people – each with his or her own unique perspective on life. In particular, I recall several memorable holidays spent with Christine. From a 'big five' African game safari in the Kruger National Park, South Africa to whale watching off the coast of the Hawaiian island of Maui; from the breathtaking majesty of the glaciers in the Alaskan fjords, to the serene calm of the Swiss and Italian lakes; from the awe inspiring and evocative grandeur of the Taj Mahal in India to one of the seven wonders of the world – the Great Wall of China; all these, and many other delightful and momentous experiences, will live with us for ever.

- Gratitude to God – my God – first, for allowing me to live with my life in the way in which I have lived it; second, for the insights I have been given into the teachings and exhortations of the great religious leaders, philosophers and mystics of past years,[17] and uniquely those of Jesus Christ; and third, for enabling me to draw upon their spiritual heritages.

****

Finally, what of my professional legacy? How best would I like to be remembered? I shall just offer two thoughts. First, I would like to think I have been at the forefront of advances in international business and research, and that, throughout the last 40 years, have used a consistent and (I think) useful analytical tool in which to ground my work. From *American Investment in the British Manufacturing Industry* in 1958, to my discussion of the impact of Britain's accession to the European Common Market in 1973, on the ownership (O) advantages of UK firms and the locational (L) advantages of a Continental European base, to the birth of the eclectic (OLI) paradigm in 1976, to the first airing of the investment development path in 1979, to my work on service MNEs in the early 1980s, to my study of the determinants and impact of Japanese FDI in the UK in 1986, to my focus on asset-seeking and competence-enhancing FDI in the 1990s, and to my (and Sarianna's) explicit incorporations of institutions into the OLI framework – in each of these developments, I believe that I have been ahead, or near ahead, of the curve.

Second, and very briefly, I would like to be remembered for stressing the need for my colleagues to take an interdisciplinary approach to IB. While I would not go as far as Gert Hostede in writing *The Business of International Business is Culture*,[18] I think that he, and Jack Behrman and Robert Grosse in their 1990 book *International Business and Governments: Issues and Institutions*,[19] are right when they argue that the more companies cross over distinctive economic systems, political and legal boundaries, and social and ideological regimes, the more interdisciplinary our perspectives to understanding the full ramifications need to become. And, as I have already stated, such an interdisciplinary approach embraces not only the traditional subject areas of IB but also those of psychology, geography, history, law – to mention just a few. Indeed, the true and unique contribution of IB, as a body of knowledge, is to identify, meld and build upon these disciplinary inputs to make the totality of its intellectual knowledge more than the sum of the individual parts. From my 1988 Presidential address to the AIB meetings in San Diego to a couple of my most recent published contributions,[20] I have tried to give a sense of how worthwhile and challenging I regard our unique task as IB scholars to be; and none of us should ever forget it.

I have always striven to be courteous, tolerant and understanding towards my friends, colleagues and acquaintances. I sometimes think that in their efforts to put their own views forward academics are sometimes unnecessarily critical of each other, particularly in their comments on papers delivered at conferences, or when reviewing submissions to journals. Even when I agree that constructive criticism is necessary, I have always tried to recognize that there may be various ways of viewing and tackling a particular problem, and that each should be treated with respect and understanding.

In short, then, I would like to think I have conducted my scholarly endeavours as a forward-looking, interdisciplinary and gentlemanly individual; and it is these qualities that are my legacy to all who have been so much part of each of the seasons of my life over the past half-century or more.

****

POSTSCRIPT

Since completing this volume in May 2008, I have received two further recognitions of both my own scholarship and, no less important, of the growing significance of international business as a unique body of knowledge.

The first recognition – perhaps the most prestigious of my most recent accolades – was the award of an OBE in the Queen's Birthday Honours List for 2008. Late in May, I received the following letter from the Ceremonial Officer at the Cabinet Office of the Prime Minister:

Dear Sir,

The Prime Minister has asked me to inform you, in strict confidence, that, having accepted the advice of the Cabinet Secretary and the expert Honours Committees, he proposes, on the occasion of the forthcoming list of Birthday Honours, to submit your name to The Queen with a recommendation that Her Majesty may be graciously pleased to approve that you be appointed an Officer of the Order of the British Empire in recognition of your 'services to international business scholarship'. If you agree that your name should go forward and The Queen accepts the Prime Minister's advice, the announcement will be made in the Birthday Honours List (on June 14th, 2008).

I am, Sir,

Your obedient Servant,

Denis Brennan

For those readers unfamiliar with the honours system, which I think is unique to the UK, every six months – in January and June – men and women, who are UK citizens, are 'appointed' to various ceremonial orders which were initially set up to recognize valiant and distinguished services given to the British Crown. In the Order of the British Empire, to which I have been appointed, these range from a Knighthood or Damehood (KBE or DBE), which honour is normally conferred on 30 or so top business executives, statesmen and (in recent years) world-class entertainers and sports personalities, to a Member of the British Empire (MBE) which is awarded to over 2000 individuals each year, primarily in recognition of their voluntary services to the community. The OBE is one of the highest honours which any academic scholar might achieve, so needless to say I was absolutely delighted for myself and my discipline to be acknowledged in this way. I am sure it will give a major boost both to the reputation and influence of the Academy of International Business, and encourage its members to 'stand tall', and be proud of the distinctive contributions our field of study is making to an understanding of the determinants and effects of the global spread of business activities.

For the moment, however, and as I write (10th July), I am savouring my letter from the Cabinet Office. So is Christine, who over the next few months (before this volume is published) will have to decide what new hat she is going to wear when she attends the investiture at Buckingham Palace late in 2008![21]

Then, secondly, on July 8th I received a letter from the Vice Chancellor of the University of Reading, informing me that I was to be awarded an Honorary Degree of Doctor of Letters at a congregation to be held in December 2008. I particularly appreciated this recognition by my own

University, both in respect of my scholarly and administrative endeavours over a period of 28 years, and of the world-wide acclaim of the work of the Reading School of international economists[22] to international business teaching and research. I am confident that, as a result of the merger between Henley Management College and the Reading University Business School in August 2008, the University, and particularly the School of Management within a newly created Faculty – The Henley Business School – that the best and most influential days of its contribution to IB scholarship are yet to come.

NOTES

1. William Shakespeare's seventh age of man, *As You Like It*, Act II, scene 7.
2. Published as Chapter 2 in my volume *Global Capitalism at Bay*, London and New York, Routledge, 2002.
3. While recognizing that there was no single or uniform capitalist system but, rather, through the integration of economies each with their own brand of capitalism.
4. Although occasionally something – for example, the coming to light of corruption of certain governments or unethical behaviour by a large corporation – brings people's attention to the subject, it is usually quickly forgotten. At the same time, there are various initiatives, for example by UN agencies, and groups of interested parties, to draw the attention of specific issues (for example fair trade) of consumers and producers.
5. The papers presented at the conference were published in *The Future of the Multinational Company* edited by Julian Birkinshaw, Sumantra Ghoshal, Constantinos Markides, John Stopford and George Yip, Chichester, John Wiley, 2003, pp. 14–33.
6. This in spite of the intense concern among individuals and societies about such issues as 'making poverty history', promoting human rights, and eliminating or reducing diseases and illness throughout the world.
7. As well expressed by Anne Glyn Jones in her book *Holding up a Mirror*, Bowling Green, OH Imprint Academic, 1996.
8. A proposal not so different to the one I set out in *Making Globalization Good*.
9. 'The Study of International Business: A Plea for a More Interdisciplinary Approach', *Journal of International Business Studies*, 1989, **20** (3), 411–36. 'New Directions in International Business Research', in J. Boddewyn (ed.), *The Evolution of International Business Scholarship. AIB Fellows in the First 50 Years and Beyond*, New York, Elsevier, JAI Press, 2008, pp. 247–258.
10. John H. Dunning (2002) 'Perspectives on international business research: a professional autobiography fifty years researching and teaching international business', *Journal of International Business Studies*, **33** (4), 817–35, December.
11. Notably his books *Institutions, Institutional Change and Economic Performance*, Cambridge, Cambridge University Press, 1990 and *Understanding the Process of Economic Change*, Princeton, NJ, Princeton University Press, 2005.
12. Sarianna and I have contributed several papers and chapters in books on this topic since the mid-1990s.
13. See my own chapter in *Making Globalization Good* and the work of Tom Donaldson.
14. And in the mid-2000s, because of the escalating world price of tin, at least one of the derelict mines has been reopened.
15. Which was eventually dispatched to Edward Elgar in May 2007, and was published in May 2008.
16. Four of my six Doctorates had been awarded in these years.

17. As brilliantly described in *A History of God* by Karen Armstrong, London, Vintage Books, 1999.
18. *International Business Review*, **3** (1), 1994, 1–14.
19. Columbia, South Carolina University Press.
20. 'A New *Zeitgeist* for International Business Activity and Scholarship', *European Journal of International Management*, **1** (4), 2007, 278–301, and 'Space, Location and Distance in IB Activities: A Changing Scenario', in J.H. Dunning and P. Gugler (eds), *Foreign Direct Investment, Location and Competitiveness*, Amsterdam and London, Elsevier, 2008, pp. 83–110.
21. Late in July, I received the Royal Warrant of Appointment to my OBE, which is reproduced at the end of this volume.
22. The members of which include Peter Buckley, John Cantwell, Jeremy Clegg, Mark Casson, Tony Corley, Geoff Jones, Rajneesh Narula, Bob Pearce and Alan Rugman.

Appendix: Short biography of the author's professional achievements

Professor John Dunning has been researching into the economics of international direct investment and the multinational enterprise since the 1950s. He has authored, co-authored, or edited 50 books on this subject, and on industrial and regional economics. Among his most recent publications are a two volume compendium of his more influential contributions to international business over the past 30 years (Edward Elgar, 2002), an edited volume on *Making Globalization Good* (Oxford University Press, 2003) and a jointly authored monograph (with Rajneesh Narula) *Multinationals and Industrial Competitiveness*, Edward Elgar (2004). In May 2008 Edward Elgar also published a revised and updated edition to his seminal and widely acclaimed treatise *Multinational Enterprises and the Global Economy* (jointly authored with Sarianna Lundan). He has recently collaborated with Professor Tagi Sagafi-Nejad on a study of the UN's role in our understanding of MNEs and economic development. It is expected that a volume containing the results of this study will be published by Indiana University Press in October 2008. Professor Dunning is further working on a new book of his essays scheduled for publication in late 2009.

Professor Dunning is Emeritus Professor of International Business at the University of Reading, UK and State of New Jersey Emeritus Professor of International Business at Rutgers University, New Jersey, USA. In addition, he has been Visiting Professor at several universities in North America, Europe and Asia. Professor Dunning is currently Chief Economic Adviser to the Director of the Division on Investment, Technology and Enterprise Development of UNCTAD in Geneva, and Senior Consultant to the Federation of Investment Promotion Agencies of China. In December 2007, he was appointed by UNIDO as Chairperson of a high level advisory group overseeing the preparation and conduct of a Euro 5 million project on the contribution of inward foreign direct investment in 25 sub-Saharan African countries. He is also past Chairman of a London based economics and management consultancy, *Economists Advisory Group Ltd.*

Professor Dunning has honorary doctorates from the University of Uppsala in Sweden (1975), the Autonomous University of Madrid in Spain (1990), the University of Antwerp in Belgium (1997), the Chinese Culture University in Taiwan (2007), the University of Lund in Sweden (2007) and the University of Reading (2008). He is also honorary Professor of International Business at the University of International Business and Economics at Beijing. He is past President of the International Trade and Finance Association, and of the Academy of International Business. A festschrift, edited by Peter Buckley and Mark Casson was published in his honour in 1992; and, in 2003, a second festschrift, embracing his work at Rutgers University, and edited by H. Peter Gray, was published. Also in 2003, a volume edited by John Cantwell and Rajneesh Narula entitled *International Business and the Eclectic Paradigm* was devoted to his theoretical contributions to international business. In August 2002, Professor Dunning was honoured as Distinguished Scholar in International Management at the Academy of Management's annual meeting at Denver. In December 2004, he was presented with a Lifetime Achievement Award at the annual meeting of the European Academy of International Business in Ljubljana, Slovenia.

Over the period 1996–2007 Professor Dunning was one of the three most cited scholars in the world (and first in Europe) for his writings on globalization and international business. He has twice received a winning award for the most influential article published in the *Journal of International Business Studies*; the second of which was presented to him at the AIB meetings in July 2008.

On August 1st, 2008 the Reading University Business School and Henley Management College merged. To underline the heritage and strength of the Reading Business School in International Business, the Centre of that name is to be renamed *The John H. Dunning Centre for International Business*.

Professor Dunning is Chairman of the Board of Editorial Advisors of the UNCTAD journal *Transnational Corporations*, and serves on several other editorial and advisory boards. He and his wife Christine have homes at Henley on Thames in Oxfordshire, and in Roseland, Cornwall.

In the Queen's Birthday Honours list for 2008, Professor Dunning was appointed as an Officer of the British Empire (OBE).

Elizabeth the Second, *by the Grace of God of the United Kingdom of Great Britain and Northern Ireland and of Her other Realms and Territories Queen, Head of the Commonwealth, Defender of the Faith and Sovereign of the Most Excellent Order of the British Empire to Our trusty and well beloved John Harry Dunning Esquire*

Greeting

Whereas *We have thought fit to nominate and appoint you to be an Ordinary Officer of the Civil Division of Our said Most Excellent Order of the British Empire*

We do *by these presents grant unto you the Dignity of an Ordinary Officer of Our said Order and hereby authorise you to have hold and enjoy the said Dignity and Rank of an Ordinary Officer of Our aforesaid Order together with all and singular the privileges thereunto belonging or appertaining.*

Given *at Our Court at Saint James's under Our Sign Manual and the Seal of Our said Order this Fourteenth day of June 2008 in the Fifty-seventh year of Our Reign.*

By the Sovereign's Command.

Grand Master

Grant of the Dignity of an Ordinary Officer of the Civil Division of the Order of the British Empire to Professor John Harry Dunning

Copy of Royal Warrant of Appointment of the author's OBE

Index

Most biographical entries start with a chronological sequence, followed by thematic terms.